£25.00

2

FOUNDATIONS OF
ILLOCUTIONARY LOGIC

FOUNDATIONS OF ILLOCUTIONARY LOGIC

JOHN R. SEARLE
and
DANIEL VANDERVEKEN

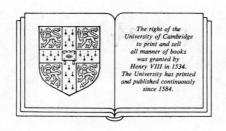

The right of the
University of Cambridge
to print and sell
all manner of books
was granted by
Henry VIII in 1534.
The University has printed
and published continuously
since 1584.

CAMBRIDGE UNIVERSITY PRESS

Cambridge

London   New York   New Rochelle
Melbourne   Sydney

Published by the Press Syndicate of the University of Cambridge
The Pitt Building, Trumpington Street, Cambridge CB2 1RP
32 East 57th Street, New York, NY 10022, USA
10 Stamford Road, Oakleigh, Melbourne 3166, Australia

© Cambridge University Press 1985

First published 1985

Printed in Great Britain at the University Press, Cambridge

Library of Congress catalogue card number: 84–4948

British Library Cataloguing in Publication Data
Searle, John R.
Foundations of illocutionary logic.
1. Speech acts (Linguistics)
I. Title   II. Vanderveken, Daniel
149'.943   P95.55
ISBN 0 521 26324 7

NP

CONTENTS

Contents

Contents

PREFACE

In the past two decades the study of speech acts has become a thriving branch of the philosophy of language and linguistics. However, advances in the theory of speech acts have had little or nothing to do with contemporaneous advances in philosophical logic, and there have been few attempts to present formalized accounts of the logic of speech acts. True, there have been systematic logical studies of particular types of speech acts such as directives, but to our knowledge there has been no attempt to present a formalized logic of a general theory of speech acts. The aim of this book is to fill that gap by constructing a precise formalized theory of illocutionary acts using the resources of modern logic.

In presenting this account we attempt to answer such questions as the following: What is an illocutionary force? Can the set of all illocutionary forces be defined recursively from a few primitives, and if so, how? What are the conditions of success of elementary illocutionary acts which consist of an illocutionary force with a propositional content, such as statements, orders, promises, requests? How can the conditions of success of the complex illocutionary acts such as conditional speech acts and acts of illocutionary denegation be defined from the conditions of success of their constituent parts? What is the relation between illocutionary force and the meaning of sentences? What is the logical form of performative sentences?

The first chapters are introductory. Each of the fundamental notions, definitions or axioms is explained progressively from chapter to chapter. Chapter 1 presents a general introduction to the theory of speech acts. Chapters 2 and 3 discuss the nature of the components of illocutionary forces and the logical structure of the set of all illocutionary forces. Chapter 4 is concerned with the conditions of success of illocutionary acts and Chapter 5 gives further explanations of the components of illocutionary force. Chapter 6 is the central chapter of the book in the sense that it presents a systematic and complete exposition of the logical theory. All definitions and independent axioms and postulates of the logical theory are explicitly stated in that chapter. Chapters 7 and 8 enumerate a series of philosophically or linguistically significant laws concerning illocutionary forces, speech acts and propositions that follow deductively from the axioms. Finally, in Chapter 9 there are semantic definitions of over a hundred English performative or illocutionary verbs.

ACKNOWLEDGEMENTS

We are grateful to Msgr H. Van Camp, the Fonds National Belge de la Recherche Scientifique, the Commission for Educational Exchange between Belgium and USA, the Francqui Foundation, the NATO Scientific Committee, the US National Science Foundation, the Humanities Institute of the University of California at Berkeley, the Fonds Institutionnel de Recherche and the Décanat des Etudes Avancées et de la Recherche of the Université du Québec à Trois-Rivières, the Fonds FCAC pour l'Aide et le Soutien à la Recherche du Québec and the Social Sciences and Humanities Research Council of Canada for grants that enabled us to work on this book and related topics. We have benefited enormously from discussions with students, colleagues, and friends and we are especially grateful to Prof. I. Bellert, Prof. G. G. Granger, F. Récanati, the referee of Cambridge University Press, and members of the Research Group on Analytic Philosophy of the Université du Québec. Most of all we wish to thank Helene Vermote and Dagmar Searle for constant help and encouragement.

Some of the formal material in this book has already been presented in earlier papers by D. Vanderveken and the authors are grateful to the following publishers for permission to use this material here: "Illocutionary logic and self-defeating speech acts", in J. R. Searle et al. (eds.), Speech Act Theory and Pragmatics (Reidel, 1980), and "What is an illocutionary force?", in M. Dascal (ed.), Dialogue: An Interdisciplinary Study (forthcoming).

Chapter 1

INTRODUCTION TO THE THEORY OF SPEECH ACTS[1]

1. ILLOCUTIONARY ACTS AND ILLOCUTIONARY LOGIC.

The minimal units of human communication are speech acts of a type called *illocutionary acts*.[2] Some examples of these are statements, questions, commands, promises, and apologies. Whenever a speaker utters a sentence in an appropriate context with certain intentions, he performs one or more illocutionary acts. In general an illocutionary act consists of an illocutionary force F and a propositional content P. For example, the two utterances "You will leave the room" and "Leave the room!" have the same propositional content, namely that you will leave the room; but characteristically the first of these has the illocutionary force of a prediction and the second has the illocutionary force of an order. Similarly, the two utterances "Are you going to the movies?" and "When will you see John?" both characteristically have the illocutionary force of questions but have different propositional contents. Illocutionary logic is the logical theory of illocutionary acts. Its main objective is to formalize the logical properties of illocutionary forces. Illocutionary forces are realized in the syntax of actual natural languages in a variety of ways, e.g. mood, punctuation, word-order, intonation contour, and stress, among others; and it is a task for empirical linguistics to study such devices as they function in actual languages. The task of illocutionary logic, on the other hand, is to study the entire range of possible illocutionary forces however these may be realized in particular natural languages. In principle it studies all possible illocutionary forces of utterances in any possible language, and not merely the actual realization of these possibilities in actual speech acts in actual

1 The theory which follows is based on and is a development of the theory expressed in J. R. Searle, *Speech Acts* (Cambridge University Press, 1969), and *Expression and Meaning* (Cambridge University Press, 1979).
2 The term is due to J. L. Austin, *How to Do Things with Words* (Oxford: Clarendon Press, 1962).

I

languages. Just as propositional logic studies the properties of all truth functions (e.g. conjunction, material implication, negation) without worrying about the various ways that these are realized in the syntax of English ("and", "but", and "moreover", to mention just a few for conjunction), so illocutionary logic studies the properties of illocutionary forces (e.g. assertion, conjecture, promise) without worrying about the various ways that these are realized in the syntax of English ("assert", "state", "claim", and the indicative mood, to mention just a few for assertion) and without worrying whether these features translate into other languages. No matter whether and how an illocutionary act is performed, it has a certain logical form which determines its conditions of success and relates it to other speech acts. We will try to characterize that form independently of the various forms of expression that may exist in actual natural languages for the expression of the act. However, though the results of our investigation are in general independent of empirical linguistic facts, the method of the investigation will require us to pay close attention to the facts of natural languages, and the results should help us to analyze actual performative verbs and other illocutionary forces indicating devices of natural languages. In Chapter 9 we will apply our results to the analysis of English illocutionary verbs.

Any element of a natural language which can be literally used to indicate that an utterance of a sentence containing that element has a certain illocutionary force or range of illocutionary forces we will call an *illocutionary force indicating device*. Some examples of illocutionary force indicating devices are word order and mood as in: (1) "Will you leave the room?", (2) "You, leave the room!", (3) "You will leave the room", (4) "If only you would leave the room!" In each of these examples, there is some syntactical feature which, given the rest of the sentence and a certain context of utterance, expresses an illocutionary force F, and some syntactical feature p which, given the rest of the sentence and a context of utterance, expresses a propositional content P. From the point of view of the theory of speech acts, then, the general form of such simple sentences, which express elementary illocutionary acts of form $F(P)$, is $f(p)$. We will call these *elementary sentences*.

A special class of elementary sentences are the *performative sentences*. These consist of a performative verb used in the first person present tense of the indicative mood with an appropriate complement clause. In uttering a performative sentence a speaker performs the illocutionary act with the illocutionary force named by the performative verb by way of representing himself as performing that act. Some examples of performative sentences (with the performative verbs italicized) are: (5) "I *promise* that I will come tomorrow", (6) "I *apologize* for what I have done", (7) "I *order* you to report to the commanding officer", (8) "I *admit* that I committed the crime." There has been a great deal of philosophical controversy concerning the proper analysis of performative sentences. The two most widely held views are: First, that the performative element in the sentence functions simply as an illocutionary force indicating device on all fours with other devices, such as word order. On this view an utterance of a sentence such as (5) consists simply in the making of a promise. Secondly, that all utterances of performative sentences are statements, and thus for example in utterances of (5), a speaker makes a promise only by way of making a true statement to the effect that he promises. On the first view, performative utterances such as (5) do not have truth values; on the second view they do. In this book we will try a third approach, according to which performative utterances are *declarations* whose propositional content is that the speaker performs the illocutionary act named by the performative verb. On this account, the illocutionary force of a performative sentence is always that of a declaration, and then, derivatively, the utterance has the additional force named by the performative verb. Since the defining trait of a declaration[3] is that it actually brings about the state of affairs represented by its propositional content, and since the propositional content of a performative utterance is that the speaker performs a certain sort of illocutionary act, the successful declaration that a speaker performs that act will always constitute its performance.

Not all illocutionary acts are of the simple $F(P)$ form. More complex cases we will call *complex illocutionary acts* and the sentences used to express them *complex sentences*. Complex sentences are composed of simple sentences using connectives that we will call *illocutionary connectives*. For example, the connectives of conjunction ("and", "but") enable speakers to conjoin different illocutionary

3 See J. R. Searle, 'A taxonomy of illocutionary acts', in *Expression and Meaning*, pp. 1–29.

acts in one utterance. In general, the utterance of a sentence which is the conjunction of two sentences constitutes the performance of the two illocutionary acts expressed by the two sentences. Thus in a certain context by uttering (9) "I will go to his house, but will he be there?", a speaker both makes an assertion and asks a question. This conjunction of two illocutionary acts constitutes the performance of a complex illocutionary act whose logical form is $(F_1(P_1)$ & $F_2(P_2))$. The illocutionary connective of conjunction is "success functional" in the sense that the successful performance of a complex illocutionary act of form $(F_1(P_1)$ & $F_2(P_2))$ is a function of the successful performances of its constituents. Not every pair of sentences will grammatically admit every illocutionary connective. For example, the following conjunction is syntactically ill formed in English: (10) "When did John come and I order you to leave the room?"

Another type of complex illocutionary act involves the negation of the illocutionary force, and we will call these acts of *illocutionary denegation*. It is essential to distinguish between acts of illocutionary denegation and illocutionary acts with a negative propositional content, between, for example, (11) "I do not promise to come" and (12) "I promise not to come." The utterance of (11) is typically an act of illocutionary denegation and it is of form $\neg F(P)$. The utterance of (12) by contrast is an illocutionary act with a negative propositional content and it is of the form $F(\sim P)$. We can say generally that an act of illocutionary denegation is one whose aim is to make it explicit that the speaker does not perform a certain illocutionary act.

The fact that illocutionary denegation is not success functional is shown by the fact that the non-performance of an illocutionary act is not the same as the performance of its illocutionary denegation; for example, from the fact that I did not make a promise, it does not follow that I declined or refused to make a promise. And the usual asymmetry between the first person present and other occurrences of performative verbs reveals the same phenomenon. A person's silence may be sufficient for somebody to say truly of him (13) "He did not promise." But a person's silence is not the same as the overt act of saying (14) "I do not promise." Most acts of illocutionary denegation are performed in English by way of negating a performative verb as in (11) but some, very few,

4

verbs are explicit performatives for illocutionary denegation. "Permit" is the denegation of both "forbid" and "prohibit"; "refuse" is frequently used as the denegation of "accept" and "disclaim" as the denegation of "claim".

The conditionals "if" and "if . . . then" are also used as illocutionary connectives. A conditional speech act is a speech act which is performed on a certain condition; its characteristic forms of expression therefore are sentences of the form "If p then $f(q)$" and "If $p, f(q)$". Some examples are: (15) "If he comes, stay with me!", (16) "If it rains, I promise you I'll take my umbrella." It is essential to distinguish between a conditional speech act and a speech act whose propositional content is a conditional. In a conditional speech act expressed by a sentence of the form "If p then $f(q)$" the speech act expressed by "$f(q)$" is performed on condition p. Syntactically the "if" clause modifies the illocutionary force indicating device. This form is quite distinct from that of the speech act performed by an utterance of a sentence of the form "f(if p then q)" whose propositional content is conditional, for in this case an illocutionary act of force F is categorically performed. Thus, for example, in a bet on a conditional of the form (17) "I bet you five dollars that if a presidential candidate gets a majority of the electoral votes he will win" one either wins or loses five dollars depending on the truth or falsity of the conditional proposition (provided all the presuppositions hold). On the other hand, in a conditional bet of the form (18) "If Carter is the next Democratic candidate, I bet you five dollars that the Republicans will win", there is a winner or a loser only if Carter is the next Democratic candidate. The logical form of (18) is $P \rightarrow F(Q)$. This conditional is not truth-functional, for from the fact that Carter does not run for the presidency, it does not follow that every speaker performs a conditional bet of the form (18). Part of the task of illocutionary logic is to analyze illocutionary denegation and illocutionary conditionals.

In carrying out the general project of illocutionary logic some of the main questions we will attempt to answer are: (1) What are the components of illocutionary force and what are the necessary and sufficient conditions for the successful performance of elementary illocutionary acts? How can the conditions of success of complex illocutionary acts be defined in terms of the conditions of success of their constituent parts? (2) What is the logical structure of the set of all illocutionary forces? Is there a recursive definition of this set, i.e. can all illocutionary forces be obtained from a few primitive forces by applying certain operations and, if so, how? (3) What are the logical relations between the various types of illocutions? In particular, under which conditions does the successful performance of one illocutionary act commit the speaker to another illocutionary act?

A theory of the foundations of illocutionary logic capable of answering these questions should be able to characterize a set of logical laws governing illocutionary forces. Thus, for example, there are laws of distribution of illocutionary forces with respect to truth-functions, e.g. if a speaker succeeds in asserting a conjunction of two propositions (P and Q) then he succeeds both in asserting P and in asserting Q. Furthermore, such a theory should explain the relations between illocutionary forces and intensionality, modalities, time, presuppositions, and indexicality. It should also explain the reasons why the utterances of certain sentences of natural language constitute self-defeating illocutionary acts. Self-defeating illocutionary acts have self-contradictory conditions of success and are thus odd semantically.[4] Some examples of sentences expressing self-defeating illocutions are: (19) "I promise you not to keep this promise", (20) "I assert that I do not make any assertion", (21) "Disobey this order!"

A theory of illocutionary logic of the sort we are describing is essentially a theory of illocutionary commitment as determined by illocutionary force. The single most important question it must answer is simply this: Given that a speaker in a certain context of utterance performs a successful illocutionary act of a certain form, what other illocutions does the performance of that act commit him to? To take the simplest sort of example, a speaker who warns a hearer that he is in danger is committed to the assertion that he is in danger. A speaker who denies a proposition P is committed to the denegation of an assertion that P. And, as is obvious from even these examples, we will need to distinguish between the overt performance of an illocutionary act and an illocutionary commit-

---

4 For further discussion of self-defeating illocutionary acts, see D. Vanderveken: 'Illocutionary logic and self-defeating speech acts', in Searle *et al.* (eds.), *Speech-Act Theory and Pragmatics* (Dordrecht, Netherlands: D. Reidel, 1980).

ment. The overt performance of one illocutionary act may involve the speaker in a commitment to another illocution, even though that commitment does not involve a commitment to an overt performance of that illocution. Thus, for example, if I order you to leave the room I am committed to granting you permission to leave the room even though I have not performed an overt act of granting you permission and have not committed myself to performing any such overt act. Among other things, a logical theory of illocutionary acts will enable us to construct a formal semantics for the illocutionary force indicating devices of natural language.

Illocutionary logic is part of the over-all project of logic, linguistics, and the philosophy of language for at least the following two reasons:

1. *Illocutionary force is a component of meaning.*
Part of the meaning of an elementary sentence is that its literal utterance in a given context constitutes the performance or attempted performance of an illocutionary act of a particular illocutionary force. Thus, for example, it is part of the meaning of the English sentence, (22) "Is it raining?", that its successful literal and serious utterance constitutes the asking of a question as to whether it is raining. Every complete sentence, even a one-word sentence, has some indicator of illocutionary force; therefore, no semantical theory of language is complete without an illocutionary component. A materially adequate semantics of a natural language must recursively assign illocutionary acts (elementary or complex) to each sentence for each possible context of utterance. It is not sufficient for it simply to assign propositions or truth conditions to sentences. In order to assign illocutionary acts to sentences an illocutionary logic would need first to provide a semantic analysis of illocutionary verbs and other illocutionary force indicating devices found in actual natural languages. In the sense that it provides an analysis of the illocutionary aspects of sentence meaning, illocutionary logic is part of a theory of meaning.[5]

---

5 For further discussion, see D. Vanderveken, 'Pragmatique, sémantique et force illocutoire', *Philosophica*, vol. 27, no. I, 1981.

2. *An adequate illocutionary logic is essential to an adequate universal grammar (in Montague's sense of "universal grammar").*[6]
Since illocutionary forces and propositions are two components of the meanings of elementary sentences, the ideal language of a universal grammar must contain logical constants and operators capable of generating names for all possible illocutionary forces of utterances. Any sentence in any natural language should be translatable into sentences of the ideal language of universal grammar, and those sentences must reflect the illocutionary potentiality of the natural language sentences. Up to the present time universal grammar has been mostly concerned with propositions, but it also needs to include an account of illocutionary forces, and therefore it goes beyond the boundaries of intensional logic as traditionally conceived.

II. ILLOCUTIONARY ACTS AND OTHER TYPES OF SPEECH ACTS.

In order to prepare the way for a formalization of the theory of illocutionary acts we need first to clarify the relations between an illocutionary act and certain types of speech acts, specifically utterance acts, propositional acts, indirect speech acts, perlocutionary acts and conversations.

Just as the sentences used to perform elementary speech acts have the form $f(p)$, where f is the indicator of illocutionary force and p expresses the propositional content, so we can say that the illocutionary act itself has the logical form $F(P)$, where the capital F stands for the illocutionary force, and P for the propositional content. The distinction between illocutionary force and propositional content, as was suggested by our earlier remarks, is motivated by the fact that their identity conditions are different: the same propositional content can occur with different illocutionary forces and the same force can occur with different propositional contents. The character of the whole illocutionary act is entirely determined by the nature of its illocutionary force and propositional content. This distinction also motivates the introduction of another speech act notion, that of the propositional act.

6 See R. Montague, 'Universal grammar', *Theoria*, vol. 36, 1970.

In the performance of an illocutionary act the speaker performs the subsidiary act of expressing the propositional content and this act we will call the *propositional act*. A propositional act is an abstraction from the total illocutionary act in the sense that the speaker cannot simply express a proposition and do nothing more. The performance of the propositional act always occurs as part of the performance of the total illocutionary act. Syntactically this fact is reflected in natural languages by the fact that "that" clauses, the characteristic form of isolating the propositional content, cannot stand alone; they do not make complete sentences. One can say "I promise that I will leave the room", but one cannot say simply "That I will leave the room".

Some, but not many, types of illocutionary forces permit a content that does not consist of an entire proposition but only a reference, as in an utterance of "Hurrah for the Raiders!" Such an utterance does not have the form $F(P)$ but rather $F(u)$ where u is some entity of the universe of discourse. And some permit an utterance consisting only of an illocutionary force and no propositional content, e.g. "Hurrah", "Ouch", and "Damn". These utterances simply have the form F. With these very few sorts of exception, all illocutionary acts have a propositional content and hence (with such exceptions) all performances of illocutionary acts are performances of propositional acts.

Illocutionary acts are performed by the utterance of expressions, and this fact motivates the introduction of yet another speech act notion, that of the *utterance act*: an utterance act consists simply in the utterance of an expression. One can perform the same illocutionary act in the performance of two different utterance acts, as, for example, when one says either "It's raining" in English or "Il pleut" in French; or even in the same language, when, for example, one uses synonymous sentences, as one may say either "John loves Mary" or "Mary is loved by John" to perform the same illocutionary act. Furthermore, an utterance act can be performed without performing an illocutionary act, as, for example, when one simply mouths words without saying anything. And finally, the same utterance act type can occur in the performance of different illocutionary acts. For example, if Bill says "I am hungry" and John says "I am hungry", in the two token utterances the same utterance act type is performed but two different illocutionary acts

9

are performed, since the reference and hence the proposition is different in the two cases.

This account of the general form of the illocutionary act and the relation of its performance to that of propositional and utterance acts can be summarized as follows. In the utterance of a sentence of the form $f(p)$ the speaker performs an utterance act. If the utterance is in certain ways appropriate he will have expressed the proposition that P (which proposition is a function of the meaning of p), and he will thereby have performed a propositional act. If certain further conditions are satisfied he will have expressed that proposition with the illocutionary force F (which force is a function of the meaning of f) and he will thereby have expressed an illocutionary act of the form $F(P)$. Furthermore, if the conditions of success of that act obtain, he will thereby have successfully performed that act.

Often speakers perform one illocutionary act implicitly by way of performing another illocutionary act explicitly. The explicitly performed act is used to convey another speech act; and the speaker relies on background knowledge and mental capacities that he shares with the hearer in order to achieve understanding. So, for example, if someone on the street says to you, "Do you know the way to the Palace Hotel?", it would be in most contexts inappropriate to respond simply "yes" or "no", because the speaker is doing more than just *asking a question* about your knowledge: he is *requesting* that you tell him the way to the hotel. Similarly, if a man says to you, "Sir, you are standing on my foot", the chances are he is doing more than describing your location: he is requesting you to get off his foot. In these cases two speech acts are involved: the non-literal primary speech act ("Tell me the way to the Palace Hotel!", "Get off my foot!") is performed indirectly by way of performing a literal secondary speech act ("Do you know the way to the Palace Hotel?"; "Sir, you are standing on my foot"). Such implicit acts are called *indirect speech acts*.[7] The speaker may convey indirectly a different illocutionary force or propositional content from what is directly expressed; hence in one

---

7 J. R. Searle, 'Indirect speech acts', in *Expression and Meaning*, pp. 30–57; and H. P. Grice, 'Logic and conversation', in P. Cole and J. L. Morgan (eds.). *Syntax and Semantics*, vol. 3, *Speech Acts* (New York: Academic Press, 1975).

utterance act he may perform one or more non-literal indirect illocutionary acts.

Just as indirect speech acts are quite pervasive in real life, so in real life illocutionary acts seldom occur alone but rather occur as parts of conversations or larger stretches of discourse. Traditional linguistics tends to construe a speaker's linguistic competence as a matter of his ability to produce and understand sentences; and traditional speech act theory tends to construe each illocutionary act as an isolated unit. But we will not get an adequate account of linguistic competence or of speech acts until we can describe the speaker's ability to produce and understand utterances (i.e. to perform and understand illocutionary acts) in *ordered speech act sequences* that constitute arguments, discussions, buying and selling, exchanging letters, making jokes, etc. For terminological convenience we will call these ordered sequences simply *conversations*. The key to understanding the structure of conversations is to see that each illocutionary act creates the possibility of a finite and usually quite limited set of appropriate illocutionary acts as replies. Sometimes the appropriate illocutionary act reply is very tightly constrained by the act that precedes it, as in question and answer sequences; and sometimes it is more open, as in casual conversations that move from one topic to another. But the principle remains that just as a move in a game creates and restricts the range of appropriate countermoves so each illocutionary act in a conversation creates and constrains the range of appropriate illocutionary responses.

When an illocutionary act is successfully and nondefectively performed there will always be an effect produced in the hearer, the effect of understanding the utterance. But in addition to the illocutionary effect of understanding, utterances normally produce, and are often intended to produce, further effects on the feelings, attitudes, and subsequent behavior of the hearers. These effects are called *perlocutionary effects*,[8] and the acts of producing them are called *perlocutionary acts*. For example, by making a statement (illocutionary) a speaker may convince or persuade (perlocutionary) his audience, by making a promise (illocutionary) he may reassure or create expectations (perlocutionary) in his audience. Perlocutionary effects may be achieved intentionally, as,

8 Following Austin, *How to Do Things with Words.*

for example, when one gets one's hearer to do something by asking him to do it, or unintentionally, as when one annoys or exasperates one's audience without intending to do so.

Perlocutionary acts, unlike illocutionary acts, are not essentially linguistic, for it is possible to achieve perlocutionary effects without performing any speech act at all. Since illocutionary acts have to do with understanding they are conventionalizable. It is in general possible to have a linguistic convention that determines that such and such an utterance counts as the performance of an illocutionary act. But since perlocutionary acts have to do with subsequent effects, this is not possible for them. There could not be any convention to the effect that such and such an utterance counts as convincing you, or persuading you, or annoying you, or exasperating you, or amusing you. And that is why none of these perlocutionary verbs has a performative use. There could not, for example, be a performative expression "I hereby persuade you", because there is no way that a conventional performance can guarantee that you are persuaded, whereas there are performative expressions of the form "I hereby state" or "I hereby inform you", because there can be conventions whereby such and such counts as a statement or counts as informing you. It is essential to keep this distinction clear in what follows, for we will be investigating speech acts proper – that is, illocutionary acts. Perlocutionary acts will figure only incidentally in our discussions.

III. THE SEVEN COMPONENTS OF ILLOCUTIONARY FORCE.

The study of illocutionary logic is mainly the study of the illocutionary forces of utterances. We therefore need to analyze the notion of illocutionary force into its component elements. On our analysis there are seven interrelated components of illocutionary force, and in this section we will provide an informal explanation and definition of these seven components and of the ways in which they are interrelated. The formalization will be presented in subsequent chapters.

One way to understand the notion of an illocutionary act is in terms of the notion of the conditions of its successful and nondefective performance. Illocutionary acts, like all human acts, can succeed or fail. An act of excommunication, for example, can be successful only if the speaker has the institutional power to excommunicate someone by his utterance. Otherwise, it is a complete failure. Just as any adequate talk of propositions involves the pair of concepts truth and falsity, so any adequate talk of speech acts (and of acts in general) involves the pair of concepts success and failure. And even when they succeed, illocutionary acts are subject to various faults and defects, such as insincerity or failure of presuppositions. We therefore have the following three possibilities: a speech act may be unsuccessful, it may be successful but defective, and it may be successful and nondefective. For example, if one of us now attempts to excommunicate the other by saying "I hereby excommunicate you" the speech act will be totally unsuccessful. The various conditions necessary for such an utterance to be a successful excommunication do not obtain. But if one of us now makes a statement for which he has hopelessly insufficient evidence or warrant, he might succeed in making the statement; however, it would be defective, because of his lack of evidence. In such a case the speech act is successful but defective. Austin's distinction between "felicitous" and "infelicitous" speech acts fails to distinguish between those speech acts which are successful but defective and those which are not even successful, and for this reason we do not use his terminology, but instead use the terminology of *Speech Acts.*[9] In the ideal case a speech act is both successful and nondefective, and for each illocutionary force the components of that illocutionary force serve to determine under what conditions that type of speech act is both *successful* and *nondefective*, at least as far as its illocutionary force is concerned. In this section we will present the seven components in a way which will make clear how they determine the conditions of successful and nondefective performance of illocutions.

1) *Illocutionary point.*

Each type of illocution has a point or purpose which is internal to its being an act of that type. The point of statements and descriptions is to tell people how things are, the point of promises and vows is to commit the speaker to doing something, the point of

9 Searle, *Speech Acts* (1969).

orders and commands is to try to get people to do things, and so on. Each of these points or purposes we will call the *illocutionary point* of the corresponding act. By saying that the illocutionary point is internal to the type of illocutionary act, we mean simply that a successful performance of an act of that type necessarily achieves that purpose and it achieves it in virtue of being an act of that type. It could not be a successful act of that type if it did not achieve that purpose. In real life a person may have all sorts of other purposes and aims; e.g. in making a promise, he may want to reassure his hearer, keep the conversation going, or try to appear to be clever, and none of these is part of the essence of promising. But when he makes a promise he necessarily commits himself to doing something. Other aims are up to him, none of them is internal to the fact that the utterance is a promise; but if he successfully performs the act of making a promise then he necessarily commits himself to doing something, because that is the illocutionary point of the illocutionary act of promising.

In general we can say that the illocutionary point of a type of illocutionary act is that purpose which is essential to its being an act of that type. This has the consequence that if the act is successful the point is achieved. Some characteristic illocutionary points are the following: The illocutionary point of a promise to do act A is to commit the speaker to doing A. The illocutionary point of an apology for having done act A is to express the speaker's sorrow or regret for having done A. The illocutionary point of issuing a declaration that P (e.g. a declaration of war) is to bring about the state of affairs that P represents.

Illocutionary point is only one component of illocutionary force, but it is by far the most important component. That it is not the only component is shown by the fact that different illocutionary forces can have the same illocutionary point, as in the pairs assertion/testimony, order/request and promise/vow. In each pair both illocutionary forces have the same point but differ in other respects. The other elements of illocutionary force are further specifications and modifications of the illocutionary point or they are consequences of the illocutionary point, but the basic component of illocutionary force is illocutionary point.

In the performance of an act of form $F(P)$ the illocutionary point is distinct from the propositional content, but it is achieved only as part of a total speech act in which the propositional content is expressed with the illocutionary point. We will say therefore that the *illocutionary point is achieved on the propositional content*. A speaker can be committed to an illocutionary point that he does not explicitly achieve. Thus, for example, if he promises to carry out a future course of action he is committed to the illocutionary point of the assertion that he will carry out that course of action, even though he may not have explicitly *asserted* that he will do it.

2) *Degree of strength of the illocutionary point.*

Different illocutionary acts often achieve the same illocutionary point with different degrees of strength. For example, if I *request* someone to do something my attempt to get him to do it is less strong than if I *insist* that he do it. If I *suggest* that something is the case the degree of strength of my representation that it is the case is less than if I *solemnly swear* that it is the case. If I *express regret* for having done something my utterance has a lesser degree of strength than if I *humbly apologize* for having done it. For each type of illocutionary force *F* whose illocutionary point requires that it be achieved with a certain degree of strength, we will call that degree of strength the *characteristic degree of strength* of illocutionary point of *F*. There are different sources of different degrees of strength. For example, both pleading and ordering are stronger than requesting, but the greater strength of pleading derives from the intensity of the desire expressed, while the greater strength of ordering derives from the fact that the speaker uses a position of power or authority that he has over the hearer.

3) *Mode of achievement.*

Some, but not all, illocutionary acts require a special way or special set of conditions under which their illocutionary point has to be achieved in the performance of the speech act. For example, a speaker who issues a command from a position of authority does more than someone who makes a request. Both utterances have the same illocutionary point, but the command achieves that illocutionary point by way of invoking the position of authority of the speaker. In order that the utterance be a successful command the speaker must not only be in a position of authority; he must be using or invoking his authority in issuing the utterance. Analogously a person who makes a statement in his capacity as a witness in a court trial does not merely make a statement, but he *testifies*, and his status as a witness is what makes his utterance count as testimony. These features which distinguish respectively commanding and testifying from requesting and asserting we will call *modes of achievement* of their illocutionary points. When an illocutionary force *F* requires a special mode of achievement of its point we will call that mode the *characteristic mode of achievement* of illocutionary point of *F*. Sometimes degree of strength and mode of achievement are interdependent. For example, the characteristic mode of achievement of a command will give it a greater characteristic degree of strength of illocutionary point than that of a request.

4) *Propositional content conditions.*

We have seen that the form of most illocutionary acts is $F(P)$. In many cases the type of force *F* will impose certain conditions on what can be in the propositional content *P*. For example, if a speaker makes a promise, the content of the promise must be that the speaker will perform some future course of action. One cannot promise that someone else will do something (though one can promise to *see to it* that he does it) and one cannot promise to have done something in the past. Similarly if a speaker apologizes for something it must be for something that he has done or is otherwise responsible for. A speaker cannot successfully apologize for the law of *modus ponens* or the elliptical orbit of the planets, for example. Such conditions on the propositional content which are imposed by the illocutionary force we will call *propositional content conditions*. These conditions obviously have syntactic consequences: sentences such as "I order you to have eaten beans last week" are linguistically odd.

5) *Preparatory conditions.*

For most types of illocutionary acts, the act can be both successful and nondefective only if certain other conditions obtain. For ~ample, a promise might be successfully made and so have achieved its illocutionary point but it would still be defective if the thing the speaker promised to do was not in the hearer's interest and the hearer did not want him to do it. In making a promise the speaker presupposes that he can do the promised act and that it is in the hearer's interest to do it. Similarly if a speaker apologizes he presupposes that the thing he apologizes for is bad or reprehensible. Such conditions which are necessary for the successful and nondefective performance of an illocutionary act we call *preparatory conditions*. In the performance of a speech act the speaker *presupposes* the satisfaction of all the preparatory conditions. But this does not imply that preparatory conditions are psychological states of the speaker, rather they are certain sorts of states of affairs that have to obtain in order that the act be successful and non-defective. Speakers and hearers internalize the rules that determine preparatory conditions and thus the rules are reflected in the psychology of speakers/hearers. But the states of affairs specified by the rules need not themselves be psychological.

Preparatory conditions determine a class of presuppositions peculiar to illocutionary force. But there is another class of pre-suppositions peculiar to propositional content. To take some famous examples, the assertion that the King of France is bald presupposes that there exists a King of France; and the question whether you have stopped beating your wife presupposes both that you have a wife and that you have been beating her. Regardless of which of the various philosophical accounts one accepts of these sorts of presuppositions, one needs to distinguish them from those that derive from illocutionary forces. The same propositional presuppositions can occur with different illocutionary forces, as, for example, one can both ask whether and one can assert that Jones has stopped beating his wife.

As we noted earlier a speech act can be successfully, though defectively, performed when certain preparatory conditions are unsatisfied. Even in such cases, the presupposition of the preparatory conditions is internal to the performance of the illocutionary act, as is shown by the fact that it is paradoxical to perform the act and deny that one of the preparatory conditions is satisfied. One cannot, for example, consistently make a promise while denying that one is able to do the act promised.

Many preparatory conditions are determined by illocutionary

point. For example, all acts whose point is to get the hearer to do something – orders, requests, commands, etc. – have as a preparatory condition that the hearer is able to do the act directed. But some preparatory conditions are peculiar to certain illocutionary forces. For example, a promise differs from a threat in that the act promised must be for the hearer's benefit. Preparatory conditions and mode of achievement are connected in that normally certain preparatory conditions must obtain in order that an illocutionary act can be performed with its characteristic mode of achievement. For example, a speaker must satisfy the preparatory condition of being in a position of authority before he can nondefectively issue an utterance with the mode of achievement of a command.

6) *Sincerity conditions.*

Whenever one performs an illocutionary act with a propositional content one expresses a certain psychological state with that same content. Thus when one makes a statement one expresses a belief, when one makes a promise one expresses an intention, when one issues a command one expresses a desire or want. The propositional content of the illocutionary act is in general identical with the propositional content of the expressed psychological state.

It is always possible to express a psychological state that one does not have, and that is how sincerity and insincerity in speech acts are distinguished. An insincere speech act is one in which the speaker performs a speech act and thereby expresses a psychological state even though he does not have that state. Thus an insincere statement (a lie) is one where the speaker does not believe what he says, an insincere apology is one where the speaker does not have the sorrow he expresses, an insincere promise is one where the speaker does not in fact intend to do the things he promises to do. An insincere speech act is defective but not necessarily unsuccessful. A lie, for example, can be a successful ~~assertion. Nevertheless, successful performances of illocutionary~~ necessarily involve the expression of the psychological state ~~by the sincerity conditions of that type of act.~~ that the expression of the psychological state is internal

18

to the performance of the illocution is shown by the fact that it is paradoxical to perform an illocution and to deny simultaneously that one has the corresponding psychological state. Thus, one cannot say "I promise to come but I do not intend to come", "I order you to leave but I don't want you to leave", "I apologize but I am not sorry", etc. And this incidentally explains Moore's paradox that one cannot say consistently "It is raining but I don't believe that it is raining" even though the proposition that it is raining is consistent with the proposition that I do not believe that it is raining. The reason for this is that when one performs the speech act one necessarily expresses the sincerity condition, and thus to conjoin the performance of the speech act with the denial of the sincerity condition would be to express and to deny the presence of one and the same psychological state.

Just as the performance of an illocution can commit the speaker to an illocution that he has not performed, so the expression of a psychological state in the performance of an illocution can commit him to having a state he has not expressed. Thus, for example, a speaker who expresses a belief that P and a belief that if P then Q is committed to having the belief that Q. The expression of a state commits the speaker to having that state; and one can be committed to having a state without actually having it.

The verb "express", by the way, is notoriously ambiguous. In one sense a speaker is said to express propositions and in another to express his feelings and attitudes such as fear, belief, or desire. In this discussion of the sincerity conditions of speech acts we are using it in this second sense, which should not be confused with the first. Both senses of "express" are used throughout this book and we believe the contexts will make it clear in each case which sense is intended.

7) *Degree of strength of the sincerity conditions.*

Just as the same illocutionary point can be achieved with different degrees of strength, so the same psychological state can be expressed with different degrees of strength. The speaker who makes a request expresses the desire that the hearer do the act requested; but if he *begs*, *beseeches*, or *implores*, he expresses a stronger desire than if he merely requests. Often, but not always, the degree of strength of the sincerity conditions and the degree of strength of the illocutionary point vary directly, as in the above examples. But an order, for example, has a greater degree of strength of its illocutionary point than a request, even though it need not have a greater degree of strength of its expressed psychological state. The greater degree of strength of the illocutionary point of ordering derives from the mode of achievement. The person who gives an order must invoke his position of power or authority over the hearer in issuing the order.

In cases where illocutionary force requires that the psychological state be expressed with a degree of strength, we will call that degree of strength *the characteristic degree of strength* of the sincerity condition.

IV. DEFINITIONS OF ILLOCUTIONARY FORCE AND RELATED NOTIONS.[10]

1) *Definition of the notion of illocutionary force.*

Our discussion so far of the components of illocutionary force enables us to define the notion of illocutionary force as follows: An illocutionary force is uniquely determined once its illocutionary point, its preparatory conditions, the mode of achievement of its illocutionary point, the degree of strength of its illocutionary point, its propositional content conditions, its sincerity conditions, and the degree of strength of its sincerity conditions are specified. So two illocutionary forces F_1 and F_2 are identical when they are the same with respect to these seven features. To illustrate these points, here are a few examples of illocutionary forces that differ in (at least) one aspect from the illocutionary force of assertion. The illocutionary force of the testimony of a witness differs from assertion in that a speaker who testifies acts in his status as a witness when he represents a state of affairs as actual. (This is a special mode of achievement that is specific to testimony.) The illocutionary force of a conjecture differs from assertion in that the speaker who conjectures commits himself to the truth of the propositional content with a weaker degree of strength than the degree of commitment to truth of an assertion. The illocutionary

10 These definitions are in Vanderveken, 'Illocutionary logic and self-defeating speech acts'.

force of a prediction differs from assertion in that it has a special condition on the propositional content. The propositional content of a prediction must be future with respect to the time of the utterance. The illocutionary force of reminding (that *P*) differs from assertion only in that it has the additional preparatory condition that the hearer once knew and might have forgotten the truth of the propositional content. The illocutionary force of complaining differs from assertion in that it has the additional sincerity condition that the speaker is dissatisfied with the state of affairs represented by the propositional content.

2) *Definition of a successful and nondefective performance of an elementary illocutionary act.*

Whether or not an utterance has a certain force is a matter of the illocutionary intentions of the speaker, but whether or not an illocutionary act with that force is successfully and nondefectively performed involves a good deal more than just his intentions; it involves a set of further conditions which must be satisfied. Prominent among these conditions are those that have to do with achieving what Austin called "illocutionary uptake".[11] The conditions for correctly understanding an utterance normally involve such diverse things as that the hearer must be awake, must share a common language with the speaker, must be paying attention, etc. Since these conditions for understanding are of little theoretical interest in a theory of speech acts, we will simply henceforth assume that they are satisfied when the utterance is made; and we will concentrate on the speaker and on how his utterance satisfies the other conditions on successful and nondefective performance.

The seven features of illocutionary force that we have specified reduce to four different types of necessary and sufficient conditions for the successful and nondefective performance of an elementary illocution. Assuming that all the conditions necessary and sufficient for hearer understanding are satisfied when the utterance is made, an illocutionary act of the form $F(P)$ is successfully and nondefectively performed in a context of utterance iff:

(1) The speaker succeeds in achieving in that context the illo-

---

11 *How to Do Things with Words.*

cutionary point of F on the proposition P with the required characteristic mode of achievement and degree of strength of illocutionary point of F.

(2) He expresses the proposition P, and that proposition satisfies the propositional content conditions imposed by F.

(3) The preparatory conditions of the illocution and the propositional presuppositions obtain in the world of the utterance, and the speaker presupposes that they obtain.

(4) He expresses and possesses the psychological state determined by F with the characteristic degree of strength of the sincerity conditions of F.

For example, in the performance of a particular utterance act, a speaker succeeds in issuing a nondefective command to the hearer iff:

(1) The point of his utterance is to attempt to get the hearer to do an act A (illocutionary point). This attempt is made by invoking his position of authority over the hearer (mode of achievement), and with a strong degree of strength of illocutionary point (degree of strength).

(2) He expresses the proposition that the hearer will perform a future act A (propositional content condition).

(3) He presupposes both that he is in a position of authority over the hearer with regard to A and that the hearer is able to do A. He also presupposes all of the propositional presuppositions if there are any. And all his presuppositions, both illocutionary and propositional, in fact obtain (preparatory conditions and propositional presuppositions).

(4) He expresses and actually has a desire that the hearer do A (sincerity condition) with a medium degree of strength (degree of strength).

As we remarked earlier, a speech act can be *successful* though *defective*. A speaker might actually succeed in making a statement or a promise even though he made a mess of it in various ways. He might, for example, not have enough evidence for his statement or his promise might be insincere. An ideal speech act is one which is both successful and nondefective. Nondefectiveness implies success, but not conversely. In our view there are only two ways that an act can be successfully performed though still be defective. First, some of the preparatory conditions might not obtain and yet the act might still be performed. This possibility holds only for some, but not all, preparatory conditions. Second, the sincerity conditions might not obtain, i.e. the act can be successfully performed even though it be insincere.

3) *Definition of illocutionary commitment.*

The idea behind the notion of illocutionary commitment is simply this: sometimes by performing one illocutionary act a speaker can be committed to another illocution. This occurs both in cases where the performance of one act by a speaker is *eo ipso* a performance of the other and in cases where the performance of the one is not a performance of the other and does not involve the speaker in a commitment to its explicit performance. For example, if a speaker issues an order to a hearer to do act A he is committed to granting him permission to do A. Why? Because when he issues the order he satisfies certain conditions on issuing the permission. There is no way he can consistently issue the order and deny the permission. And the kind of consistency involved is not the consistency of sets of truth conditions of propositions, but illocutionary consistency or compatibility of conditions of success. In many cases illocutionary commitments are trivially obvious. For example, a report commits the speaker to an assertion because a report just is a species of assertion, an assertion about the past or the present. A report differs from an assertion in general only by having a special propositional content condition. Similarly, a speech act of reminding a hearer that P commits the speaker to the assertion that P because reminding that P is a species of assertion that P made with the preparatory condition the hearer once knew and might have forgotten that P. Thus reminding differs from assertion only by having a special additional preparatory condition. In such cases, which we will call *strong* illocutionary commitments, an illocutionary act $F_1(P)$ commits the speaker to an illocutionary act $F_2(Q)$ because it is not possible to perform $F_1(P)$ in a context of utterance without also performing $F_2(Q)$.

But there are also cases, which we will call *weak* illocutionary commitments, where the speaker is committed to an illocutionary act $F(P)$ by way of performing certain illocutionary acts $F_1(P_1)$, ..., $F_n(P_n)$ although he does not perform $F(P)$ and is not committed to its performance. Thus a speaker can be committed to an illocution without explicitly achieving the illocutionary point of that illocution, and similarly he can be committed to an illocution without explicitly expressing the propositional content or without expressing the psychological state mentioned in the sincerity conditions. For example, if he asserts that all men are mortal and that Socrates is a man, he is committed to the assertion that Socrates is mortal; even though he has not explicitly represented as actual the state of affairs that Socrates is mortal, nor expressed the proposition representing that state of affairs, nor expressed a belief in the existence of that state of affairs.

As a general definition we can say that *an illocutionary act of the form $F_1(P_1)$ commits the speaker to an illocutionary act $F_2(P_2)$* iff in the successful performance of $F_1(P_1)$:

(1) The speaker achieves (strong) or is committed (weak) to the illocutionary point of F_2 on P_2 with the required mode of achievement and degree of strength of F_2.

(2) He is committed to all of the preparatory conditions of $F_2(P_2)$ and to the propositional presuppositions.

(3) He commits himself to having the psychological state specified by the sincerity conditions of $F_2(P_2)$ with the required degree of strength.

(4) P_2 satisfies the propositional content of F_2 with respect to the context of utterance.

Both strong and weak illocutionary commitments satisfy this definition. Thus, for example, a speaker who asserts that all men are mortal and that Socrates is mortal is committed to the illocutionary point of the assertion that Socrates is mortal and similarly he is committed to having the belief that Socrates is a man. A report commits the speaker to an assertion because a report is simply an assertion about the past or the present. Giving testimony commits the speaker to an assertion because to testify is simply to assert in one's status as a witness. A complaint about P commits the speaker to an assertion that P because to complain that

P just is to assert that P while expressing dissatisfaction with the state of affairs represented by the proportional content. A *speaker is committed to an illocution* $F(P)$ in a context of utterance iff he successfully performs in that context a speech act which commits him to $F(P)$. Thus, for example, a speaker who successfully testifies, reports, or complains that P is committed to an assertion that P.

4) *Definition of a literal performance.*

A speaker performs *literally* an illocutionary act $F(P)$ in a context of utterance when he performs $F(P)$ in that context by uttering a sentence which expresses literally that force and content in that context. Thus, for example, a speaker who requests someone to leave the room by uttering in an appropriate context the sentence "Please leave the room" performs a literal request. Many speech acts are not performed literally but rather are performed by way of metaphor, irony, hints, insinuation, etc. Two classes of speech acts which are not expressed literally in an utterance are of special interest to us: First, there are speech acts $F_1(P)$ performed by way of performing a stronger illocutionary act $F_2(Q)$. In such cases the conditions of success of $F_1(P)$ are conditions of success of $F_2(Q)$, and $F_2(Q)$ strongly commits the speaker to $F_1(P)$. For example, begging commits the speaker to requesting. Second, as we noted earlier, there are *indirect* speech acts $F_1(P)$ performed by way of performing another illocutionary act $F_2(Q)$ that does not commit the speaker to them. In such cases, all the conditions of success of $F_2(Q)$ are satisfied, but the speaker conveys $F_2(Q)$ by relying on features of the context as well as on understanding of the rules of speech acts and of the principles of conversation to enable the hearer to recognize the intention to convey $F_2(Q)$ in the utterance of a sentence that literally expresses $F_1(P)$.[12]

5) *Definitions of illocutionary compatibility.*

Attempts to perform several illocutionary acts in the same context can break down because of various sorts of inconsistency. For example, if a speaker attempts to perform an illocutionary act and

12 For further discussion see Searle, 'Indirect speech acts', and D. Vanderveken, 'What is an illocutionary force?', in M. Dascal (ed.), *Dialogue: An Interdisciplinary Study* (Amsterdam: Benjamins, forthcoming).

its denegation (if he says for example "Please leave the room!" and "I am not asking you to leave the room") his speech act will be unsuccessful because of illocutionary inconsistency. The denegation of an illocutionary act is incompatible with that act because the aim of an act of illocutionary denegation of form $\neg F(P)$ is to make it explicit that the speaker does not perform $F(P)$. We will say that a set of illocutionary acts is *simultaneously performable* iff it is possible for a speaker to perform simultaneously all illocutionary acts belonging to it in the same context of utterance. Two illocutionary acts are *relatively incompatible* iff any set of illocutionary acts that contains both of them is not simultaneously performable. Otherwise they are relatively compatible.

Two possible contexts of utterance are *relatively compatible* when the union of the two sets of illocutionary acts that are performed in them is simultaneously performable, i.e. when it is possible to perform simultaneously in the context of an utterance all illocutionary acts that are performed in them. If two contexts of utterance are relatively compatible, no illocutionary act performed in one is incompatible with any illocutionary act performed in the other.

Chapter 2

BASIC NOTIONS OF
A CALCULUS OF SPEECH ACTS

So far we have presented a simple version of the theory of illocutionary acts according to which most elementary illocutionary acts consist of a propositional content expressed with a certain illocutionary force, and according to which an illocutionary force can be divided into seven components. The main aim of this chapter is to define in set-theoretical terms the formal nature of illocutionary forces and their components and to give an explication of the concepts of those components. To prepare the way for this, we will begin by stating some general properties of the set of contexts of utterance and of the set of propositions.

I. DEFINITION OF THE SET OF POSSIBLE
CONTEXTS OF UTTERANCE.

We will call the context in which an illocutionary act is performed by an utterance *the context of utterance*. We need this notion primarily because the same sentence can be uttered in different contexts to perform different illocutionary acts. For example, in one context an utterance of the sentence "I will come back in five minutes" might be a prediction; in another, it might be a promise. Furthermore, since the sentence is indexical the propositional content will also vary from context to context – because different speakers and different times would be referred to in different contexts. Context is, therefore, one of the determinants of the illocutionary act performed by an utterance. For the purposes of formalization a context of utterance consists of five distinguishable elements and sets of elements: a speaker, a hearer, a time, a place, and those various other features of the speaker, hearer, time, and place that are relevant to the performance of the speech acts. Especially important features are the psychological states – intentions, desires, beliefs, etc. – of the speaker and hearer.

These various other features we will call the *world of the utterance*, and we use this jargon of "worlds" because it will enable us later to talk of "possible worlds", which are just ways things might have been in addition to the "actual world", which is just the way things are. These five aspects enable us to say everything we need to say about contexts of utterance. Possible worlds are needed in illocutionary logic for at least two reasons. First, the determination of the exact nature of the illocutionary force of an utterance requires certain information about the speaker, hearer, and the objects of reference in the world of utterance which can be conveniently explained using the notion of a possible world. For example, given the same speaker, hearer, and time and place of utterance, an utterance of the sentence "Leave the room!" might be an order (in a world of utterance in which the speaker is in a position of authority over the hearer, and he invokes his authority in the utterance) and yet in another world of utterance (where the speaker is not in authority) it might be merely a request. Moreover, an attempt to issue an order may be successful in one world of utterance and unsuccessful in another world, depending on different relations between the speaker and the hearer in the two worlds. Furthermore, knowledge of the various features of a world of utterance enables hearers to disambiguate the illocutionary forces of an utterance. For example, in a typical dinnertable situation, the hearer would know that an utterance of the sentence "Can you reach the salt?" is really more than just a question about his salt-reaching abilities, but is primarily a request to him to pass the salt. Secondly, the propositional content can be conveniently explained using the notion of possible worlds, because a proposition can be identified by the conditions under which it is true (or false) in any given possible world.

Let I_1, I_2, I_3, I_4 be the four sets (non-empty of course) which contain respectively all possible speakers, hearers, times and places of utterance, and let W be the set of all possible worlds in which sentences and other expressions could be uttered: we will call these *possible worlds of utterance*. Then the set I of all possible contexts of utterance is a proper subset of the Cartesian product of these five sets. $I \subset I_1 \times I_2 \times I_3 \times I_4 \times W$. Each context of utterance $i \in I$ has five constituents, which we will call the *coordinates* of the context: the speaker, a_i, the hearer, b_i, the time, t_i, the location, l_i, and the world, w_i. Thus $i \underset{\text{def}}{=} \langle a_i, b_i, t_i, l_i, w_i \rangle$. If we want to discuss a context of utterance which differs at most from a context $i \in I$ by the fact that it takes place in a world of utterance $w \neq w_i$, we shall often write $i[w/w_i]$ as an abbreviation for $\langle a_i, b_i, t_i, l_i, w \rangle$.

The set I has the following formal structure. There is a reflexive and symmetric binary relation $\geqslant$ of compatibility between possible contexts of utterance. If i and $j \in I$, "$i \geqslant j$" means that there is a possible context of utterance in which all illocutionary acts performed in i and all performed in j are simultaneously performed. Thus, a speaker could perform all these acts in another context. We need the relation of compatibility in illocutionary logic in order to define the conditions of success of complex illocutionary acts. There is also a linear ordering $\leqslant$ on the set I_3 of the temporal coordinates of the contexts of I. If t_1, $t_2 \in I_3$, "$t_1 \leqslant t_2$" means that t_1 is a moment of time which is either anterior to or simultaneous with the moment t_2. Temporal anteriority and posteriority are defined in the usual way as follows:

$$t_1 < t_2 \ (t_1 \text{ is anterior to } t_2) \underset{\text{def}}{=} t_1 \leqslant t_2 \text{ and } t_1 \neq t_2;$$

$$t_1 > t_2 \ (t_1 \text{ is posterior to } t_2) \underset{\text{def}}{=} t_2 < t_1$$

(A linear ordering $\leqslant$ on a set is a binary relation which is total and (1) reflexive; (2) anti-symmetrical: if $t_1 \leqslant t_2$ and $t_2 \leqslant t_1$ then $t_1 = t_2$; and (3) transitive.)

We take the notion of a possible world as a primitive notion of illocutionary logic. (The situation, incidentally, is the same in modal logic where this notion is also undefined.) The set W of all possible worlds contains a designated element w_0, which is the actual world. We can think of a possible world as a world in which the objects of the actual world (the actual objects) have different properties and/or as a world which has objects different from the actual ones. The actual objects could have been different from the way they are, and objects which do not exist could have existed. Moreover, there are several mutually inconsistent alternative possible courses of events for the future of this world. To these possible future courses of events correspond different possible worlds that, as is commonly said in modal logic, are "accessible" from the actual one. As a consequence of this, the set W of illocutionary logic is provided with a binary relation of accessibility R. A possible world w' is *accessible* from a world w (symbolically: $w R w'$) when all the laws of nature which hold in w also hold in w', i.e. when no state of affairs of w' violates any physical law of w. Accessibility is reflexive: every world is accessible from itself. Physical or causal possibility must be distinguished from logical or universal possibility. A state of affairs is *universally possible* when there is at least one possible world where it exists. On the other hand, a state of affairs is *physically possible* in a world w when there is at least one possible world that is accessible from w in which that state of affairs exists. By definition, all states of affairs that are physically possible in a world are universally possible; but the converse does not hold, for relatively inconsistent laws of nature might hold in different worlds. We need the notion of physical possibility in illocutionary logic because the abilities of the speaker and the hearer often enter in the preparatory conditions of the illocutionary act.

Though we need the notion of possible worlds, the amount of information that is needed about the world of utterance for determining the illocutionary force of the utterance and whether an elementary illocutionary act of a given form is successfully performed in a context of use is rather small. We need to know only which illocutionary points the speaker intends to achieve and succeeds in achieving in that world, with which modes of achievement and degrees of strength, which propositional acts are performed, which presuppositions are made, and which psychological states are expressed and with what degree of strength in that world.

Associated with each possible world $w \in W$, there is a set $U(w)$ which contains all the objects which belong to that world. This set of individuals $U(w)$ is called the *domain of w*. The domain of the real world $U(w_0)$ consists in all the *actual objects*. Since in general objects persist in time, each set $U(w)$ is indexed by the set I_3 of times of utterance.

For each moment of time $t \in I_3$, there is a set $U_t(w) \subseteq U(w)$ containing all objects of w that exist at that time. By definition $U(w) = \bigcup_{t \in I_3} U_t(w)$. Each individual object that belongs to the domain of one world exists at some moment of time in that world.

The union $\hat{U} = \bigcup_{w \in W} U(w)$ of the domains of all possible worlds is the *universe of discourse* in illocutionary logic. It is the set which contains all past, present and future individuals whose existence is possible. By definition the speaker and the hearer of a possible context of utterance whose world of utterance is w, belong to the domain $U(w)$ of that world. And this is just another way of saying that an individual who is a possible speaker or hearer in a world of utterance is an object in that world. Consequently, $I_1 \cup I_2 \subset \hat{U}$. The set of all possible speakers and hearers of a natural language is included in the universe of discourse. The fact that for all $i \in I$, $\{a_i, b_i\} \subset U_{t_i}(w_i)$ explains why I is a proper subset of the Cartesian product $I_1 \times I_2 \times I_3 \times I_4 \times W$. A quintuple $\langle a, b, t, l, w \rangle$ belongs to I only if the speaker a and the hearer b exist at moment of time t in w, and a is located at place l at that time in that world.

II. SOME FORMAL PROPERTIES OF THE SET OF ALL PROPOSITIONS.

In this section and the next we will state some formal properties of the two sets Prop of propositions and Φ of illocutionary forces. We will continue to use $F, F_1, F_2, \ldots, F', F'_1, F'_2, \ldots$, as variables for illocutionary forces and $P, P_1, P_2, \ldots, P', P'_1, P'_2, \ldots$, $Q, Q_1, Q_2, \ldots, Q', Q'_1, Q'_2, \ldots$, as variables for propositions. Illocutionary acts of form $F(P)$ consist in an illocutionary force $F \in \Phi$ and a proposition $P \in \text{Prop}$. Thus two illocutionary acts $F_1(P), F_2(Q)$ are identical when both $F_1 = F_2$ and $P = Q$.

The general characterization of the logical form of propositions is the main task of intensional logic, but for our purposes we can leave the notion of a proposition as an undefined primitive.[1] However, we do need to make explicit some features of propositions for the purposes of illocutionary logic.

First, each proposition represents a state of affairs and has a truth value. Understanding a proposition consists in knowing its truth conditions, i.e. in knowing what states of affairs must obtain

---

1 For further discussion of the task of intensional logic, see D. Vanderveken, 'Some philosophical remarks on the theory of types in intensional logic', *Erkenntnis*, vol. 17, no. 1 (1982), pp. 85–112.

in order that it be true. A proposition P is *true in a world w* when the state of affairs that it represents exists in that world. Just as we speak of the proposition (that) P so we will also speak of the state of affairs that P, represented by P. A proposition is timeless in the sense that it cannot be true at one time and false at another time: if it is true it is always true; if false, always false. Therefore a proposition P divides the set W of all possible worlds in two distinct complementary subsets: i.e. the set of possible worlds $W_1 \subseteq W$ in which it is true and the set of possible worlds $W_2 \subseteq W$ in which it is false. A proposition, P, *is true*, *simpliciter*, when it is true in the actual world w_0. We will use the set $2 = \{1, 0\}$ to represent alternatively the set of truth values, 1 for truth and 0 for falsehood and the set of success values, 1 for success and 0 for failure. In case all propositions Q belonging to a set $\Gamma \subseteq$ Prop are true in a world w, we will often write $\Gamma/w/$. Thus $\Gamma/w/$ iff for all $Q \in \Gamma$, Q is true in w.

Certain propositions presuppose the truth of other propositions. Consider, for example, the familiar example: "The present King of France is bald." The proposition expressed by an utterance of that sentence presupposes the existence in the world of the utterance of one and only one king of France. We will use the symbols "$\sigma(P)$" to name the set of all propositions that are presuppositions of a proposition P. All propositions strictly imply their presuppositions, i.e. if a proposition P is true in a world w, then all its presuppositions must be true in that world. Thus, $\{w/P$ is true in $w\} \subseteq \{w/\sigma(P)/w/\}$. For convenience we will treat presuppositions in such a way that if a presupposition is false, the proposition which presupposes it is also false. From a formal point of view this treatment has the consequence that all propositions are either true or false, and this permits us to use classic bivalent propositional logic where the law of excluded middle applies to truth and falsity. Thus to each proposition $P \in$ Prop corresponds a unique (total) function from possible worlds into truth values. For each world $w \in W$, P is either true or false in w.

A second important feature of propositions for our study is that propositions are the contents of illocutionary acts, i.e. they are the contents of assertions, orders, promises, declarations, etc. A speaker who performs an illocutionary act with a propositional content thereby expresses a proposition.

Corresponding to these two features of propositions, there are two conditions for the identity of propositions in illocutionary logic.

1. *The condition of strict equivalence.*
$P = Q$ entails that for all $w \in W$, P is true in w iff Q is true in w. Identical propositions have identical truth values in the same worlds.

2. *The condition of illocutionary interchangeability.*
$P = Q$ only if, for all $F \in \Phi$, illocutionary acts $F(P)$ and $F(Q)$ have the same conditions of successful performance.

Notice that since strictly equivalent propositions do not always satisfy the criterion of illocutionary interchangeability, propositions in a theory of speech acts cannot be identified as they are in modal logic with functions from possible worlds into truth values. It is simply not the case, for example, that the assertion that two plus two equals four is the same assertion as that all triangles have three sides, since though both are assertions of necessary truths, the propositional content is different in the two cases and on our account of propositions we recognize that difference. On our account, two propositions which are both necessarily true can still be different propositions: For all w, $P(w) = Q(w)$ does not entail $P = Q$.

The last feature of propositions relevant to our study is that the set of all propositions is closed under a certain number of operations that correspond to (but are not identical with) the rules of formation generating complex sentences in natural languages. The set Prop contains elementary propositions and all other propositions are obtained from the elementary ones by reiterating the application of the operations under which Prop is closed. Part of the task of intensional logic is to characterize the logical form of elementary propositions and the formal properties of all operations that generate complex propositions. By definition, to each possible world w corresponds a unique set $\hat{w}$ of elementary propositions that are true in that world. Thus $w_1 = w_2$ iff $\hat{w}_1 = \hat{w}_2$. Many, though not all, elementary propositions are time-marked in the sense that they are true iff certain individual objects have certain attributes at a certain moment of time $t \in I_3$. Because the time indication is inside the proposition, its truth value is timeless.

We will now specify some of the operations on propositions which are important for a logical study of illocutionary acts.

If P and Q are propositions, t is a moment of time, and u is an individual belonging to the universe of discourse, then $\sim P$, $(P \rightarrow Q)$, $\Box P$, and $\Diamond P$ are new complex propositions that are functions of P and Q (if Q occurs within them). The truth conditions of these new propositions are defined in the usual way as follows:

(i) *The operation of truth-functional negation* $\sim$.
Proposition $\sim P$ is true in a world w iff P is false in that world.

(ii) *The operation of material implication* $\rightarrow$.
Proposition $(P \rightarrow Q)$ is true in a world w iff P is false in w or Q is true in w.

(iii) *The operation of universal necessity* $\Box$.
Proposition $\Box P$ is true in a world w iff P is true in all possible worlds $w' \in W$.

(iv) *The operation of physical possibility* $\Diamond$.[2]
$\Diamond P$ is true in a world w iff P is true in at least one world w' accessible from w.

(v) *The notions of action and of reasons.*
Finally there are two new notions we need to introduce into

---

2 We shall make use hereafter of the following conventional abbreviations:

$$(P \,\&\, Q) \underset{\text{def}}{=} \sim (P \rightarrow \sim Q)$$

$$(P \vee Q) \underset{\text{def}}{=} \sim (\sim P \,\&\, \sim Q)$$

$$(P \leftrightarrow Q) \underset{\text{def}}{=} (P \rightarrow Q) \,\&\, (Q \rightarrow P); \quad (P \dashv Q) \underset{\text{def}}{=} \Box (P \rightarrow Q)$$

$$(P \dashv\!\vdash Q) \underset{\text{def}}{=} (P \dashv Q) \,\&\, (Q \dashv P)$$

$\Diamond P$ ('it is universally possible that P') $\underset{\text{def}}{=} \sim \Box \sim P$.

$\boxdot P$ ('it is physically necessary that P') $\underset{\text{def}}{=} \sim \Diamond \sim P$.

According to these definitions, & is the operation of conjunction, $\vee$ is the operation of disjunction, $\leftrightarrow$ is the operation of material equivalence, and $\dashv$ and $\dashv\!\vdash$ are the operations of strict implication and strict equivalence.

illocutionary logic, the notion of an *action* and the notion of a *reason*, whether "theoretical" or "practical". In performing an action, an agent intentionally brings about a state of affairs represented by a proposition; in having a reason, an agent has a "justification" (whether adequate or inadequate) either for an action (practical reason) or for supposing that a proposition is true (theoretical reason). We need both of these notions in illocutionary logic because speech acts are themselves acts and they concern other acts and also because a speech act can both create reasons and be subject to the demand for reasons, i.e. for justifications. We express these two notions as follows. For each individual u and proposition P, there are two complex propositions δutP and ρutP with the following truth conditions:

δutP is true in a world w iff u at time t in w does something which makes it the case that P is true in w, and ρutP is true in a world w iff either u at time t in w has (theoretical) reasons for supposing that P is true in w or (practical) reasons for making it the case that P is true in w.

(vi) *Operations corresponding to certain psychological states: propositional attitudes.*

Certain psychological states with propositional contents such as beliefs, desires, intentions, regrets, etc., the so-called propositional attitudes, are important for illocutionary logic because such states play an essential role in the performance of speech acts. These psychological states are of the form $m(P)$ where m is a type of psychological state and P is a propositional content. In addition to the above-mentioned operations on propositions we will therefore introduce another set of operations that correspond to types of psychological states with propositions as contents. If M is the set of all types of such psychological states, there corresponds to each type $m \in M$ and each proposition P, for each individual u and moment of time t, a new proposition $mutP$ that is true in a world w iff u at time t in w has the psychological state of type m with the propositional content P. Because of the central role of belief, intention, and desire we will introduce three special constants, "Bel", "Int", and "Des", naming respectively the types of belief, intention, and desire or want. Thus, in our notation BelutP is the proposition that person u at time t believes that P; IntutP is the proposition that u at time t intends that P and DesutP is the proposition that u at time t desires or wants that P. It is the task of a logic of propositional attitudes to define formally the truth conditions of these propositions.

Since to each pair of the form $m(P)$ corresponds a propositional attitude of type m with propositional content P, the Cartesian product $M \times$ Prop will represent the set of all psychological states with propositional contents. Some psychological states commit the speaker to others, e.g. a belief that P and a belief that $(P \rightarrow Q)$ commit the speaker to a belief that Q. In case it is not possible for a speaker to express all psychological states of a set Γ without being committed to having all psychological states of another set Δ, we will often write for short: $\Gamma \rhd \Delta$. The strongest cases of propositional attitude commitments are cases where it is not possible for the speaker to possess all psychological states Γ without also necessarily possessing all psychological states Δ, e.g. if a speaker a desires that P and Q he also desires P. In such cases of strong propositional attitude commitments, we will write $\Gamma \rhd \Delta$.

III. SOME FORMAL PROPERTIES OF ILLOCUTIONARY FORCES.

Illocutionary logic requires a materially and formally adequate definition of the components of illocutionary force. Before introducing this definition, we will first introduce a few symbolic conventions. Each performative or illocutionary verb f of a natural language names a certain illocutionary force or type of speech act. We will name that illocutionary force or type of speech act by writing f within the symbols $\| \ \|$. Thus, for example, " $\| predict \|$ " will be the name of the illocutionary force of prediction and " $\| report \|$ " the name of the illocutionary force of reports.

As we argued in Chapter 1, an illocutionary force can be divided into seven components: namely an illocutionary point, a mode of achievement of this illocutionary point, the degree of strength of the illocutionary point, propositional content conditions, preparatory conditions, sincerity conditions, and the degree of strength of the sincerity conditions. We will now define in set theoretical terms the formal nature of these various components of illocutionary force and in so doing we will give an explication, in Carnap's sense,[3] of these concepts.

1) *Illocutionary point.*[4]

The notion of illocutionary point is the fundamental undefined primitive notion of illocutionary logic. In the last chapter we gave an informal explanation of the notion by saying that the point of a type of illocutionary act is the purpose which is internal to its being an act of that type. Thus, for example, the point of a statement is to say how things are, the point of an order is to try to get somebody to do something, the point of an apology is to express remorse for some act of the speaker. We believe a formal definition of this notion could be given within a theory of intentionality, but as such a theory goes beyond the scope of this book, we will here simply list the various illocutionary points of possible utterances and thus define the notion in extension.

There are five and only five illocutionary points:[5]

(1) The *assertive* point is to say how things are. More cumbersomely but more accurately: in utterances with the assertive point the speaker presents a proposition as representing an actual state of affairs in the world of utterance.

(2) The *commissive* point is to commit the speaker to doing something. Again, more cumbersomely but more accurately: in utterances with the commissive point the speaker commits himself to carrying out the course of action represented by the propositional content.

(3) The *directive* point is to try to get other people to do things: in utterances with the directive point the speaker attempts to get the hearer to carry out the course of action represented by the propositional content.

(4) The *declarative* point is to change the world by saying so: in utterances with the declarative point the speaker brings about the state of affairs represented by the propositional content solely in virtue of his successful performance of the speech act.

3 See R. Carnap, *Meaning and Necessity* (University of Chicago Press, 1947).
4 We use the formalization of illocutionary forces that is developed in Vanderveken, 'What is an illocutionary force?'
5 Searle, 'A taxonomy of illocutionary acts'.

(5) The *expressive* point is to express feelings and attitudes. In utterances with the expressive point the speaker expresses some psychological attitude about the state of affairs represented by the propositional content.

Different illocutionary points have different conditions of achievement. As a consequence of this, each illocutionary point can be identified with the unique relation Π on $I \times$ Prop that determines the conditions of achievement of that illocutionary point. $i\Pi P$ holds iff the speaker a_i in the context of utterance i succeeds in achieving that illocutionary point on propositional content P. If Π represents the conditions of achievement of the illocutionary point of an illocutionary force F, we will often write hereafter $\Pi = \Pi_F$. Thus $i\Pi_F P$ holds iff the speaker a_i in the context of utterance i succeeds in achieving the illocutionary point of illocutionary force F on propositional content P. In illocutionary logic the illocutionary points are thus represented by the relations that determine their conditions of achievement.

The conditions of achievement of the assertive, commissive, directive, declarative, and expressive illocutionary points are defined respectively by the following relations Π_1, Π_2, Π_3, Π_4, and Π_5 on $I \times$ Prop:

a) The assertive illocutionary point Π_1.
A speaker a_i *succeeds in achieving the assertive illocutionary point on a proposition P* in a context i (for short: $i\Pi_1 P$) iff in that context he represents the state of affairs that P as actual in the world of utterance w_i. We will call the illocutionary forces with the assertive point *assertive illocutionary forces* and the performatives or illocutionary verbs which name an assertive illocutionary force *assertives*. Some English assertives are: "assert", "claim", "argue", "assure", "predict", "report", "inform", "admit", "remind", "testify", "confess", "conjecture", "guess", "state", "hypothesize", "swear", and "insist".

b) The commissive illocutionary point Π_2.
A speaker a_i *succeeds in achieving the commissive illocutionary point on a proposition P* in a context i (for short: $i\Pi_2 P$) iff in that context he

commits himself to carrying out the future course of action represented by P. We will call the illocutionary forces with the commissive point *commissive forces* and the performatives or illocutionary verbs that name a commissive illocutionary force *commissives*. Some English commissives are: "commit", "promise", "threaten", "accept", "pledge", "vow", "consent", "covenant", and "guarantee".

c) *The directive illocutionary point* Π_3.

A speaker a_i *succeeds in achieving the directive illocutionary point on a proposition P in a context i* (for short: $i\Pi_3P$) iff in that context in an utterance he makes an attempt to get the hearer b_i to carry out the future course of action represented by P. We will call the illocutionary forces with the directive point *directive illocutionary forces* and the performatives or illocutionary verbs that name a directive illocutionary force *directives*. Some English directives are: "request", "ask", "order", "command", "solicit", "incite", "invite", "beg", "suggest", "advise", "recommend", "supplicate", "entreat", and "pray".

d) *The declarative illocutionary point* Π_4.

A speaker a_i *succeeds in achieving the declarative illocutionary point on a proposition P in a context i* (for short: $i\Pi_4P$) iff in that context he brings about by his utterance in the world of utterance w_i the state of affairs that P. We will call the illocutionary forces with the declarative point *declarative illocutionary forces* and the performatives or illocutionary verbs which name a declarative illocutionary force *declaratives*. Some English declaratives are: "declare", "approve", "endorse", "excommunicate", "name", "christen", "resign", "abbreviate", and "bless".

e) *The expressive illocutionary point* Π_5.

Finally, a speaker a_i *achieves the expressive illocutionary point* Π_5 *on a proposition P in a context i* (for short: $i\Pi_5P$) iff in that context in an utterance he expresses his feelings (or attitudes) about the state of affairs represented by P. We will call the illocutionary forces with the expressive point *expressive illocutionary forces* and the performatives or illocutionary verbs that name expressive illocutionary forces *expressives*. Thus "apologize" is an expressive since the illocutionary point of an apology for the state of affairs that P is to express to the hearer the speaker's sorrow or remorse for that state of affairs. Some other English expressive verbs are: "congratulate", "thank", "compliment", "deplore", "condole", and "welcome".

This classification of illocutionary points is materially adequate in the sense that there is no need to appeal to other points in order to define explicitly all the illocutionary forces that are realized syntactically or named in English. In Chapter 9 we give some support to this claim by analyzing a large number of English illocutionary verbs using these notions. We give also a philosophical justification of this classification in Chapter 3 by showing that the five different types of illocutionary point exhaust the different possible "directions of fit" between the propositional content of an illocution and the world of utterance. Furthermore in Chapters 5 and 6 we give various definitions and axioms that serve to explain further the notion of illocutionary point.

2) *The mode of achievement of the illocutionary point.*

Most illocutionary points can be achieved in various ways that alter the illocutionary force of the utterance. Certain illocutionary forces have a special mode of achievement of their point. Thus, for example, a speaker who issues an order achieves the directive illocutionary point by invoking a position of authority or power over the hearer. A speaker who begs the hearer to do something achieves the same directive illocutionary point in a humble way.

Formally, a mode of achievement of an illocutionary point Π is determined in illocutionary logic by a function $\mu(\Pi)$ from $I \times \text{Prop}$ into truth values that gives the truth value 1 for a pair (i, P) iff the speaker a_i in the context i succeeds in achieving or being committed to the illocutionary point Π on proposition P in that particular mode. Thus, by definition, $\mu(\Pi)(i, P) = 1$ only if a_i is committed to Π on P in i. If μ is the characteristic mode of achievement of an illocutionary force F, we will often write $\mu = \text{mode}(F)$. Thus, $\text{mode}(F)(i, P) = 1$ iff a_i in i achieves or is committed to illocutionary point Π_F on proposition P in the mode required by F. For example, $\text{mode}(\|\text{order}\|)(i, P) = 1$ iff the speaker a_i in the context i achieves the directive illocutionary point on P by invoking his position of authority or power over the hearer b_i. Mode $(\|\text{testify}\|)(i, P) = 1$ iff a_i achieves or is committed in the context i to the assertive illocutionary point on P in his capacity as a witness. A mode of achievement of illocutionary point that restricts the conditions of achievement of or commitment to that point we will call *a special mode of achievement*. For example, the mode of achievement of an order is special. If F has no special characteristic mode of achievement of its illocutionary point, as is the case for an assertion, we will often write, for short, mode $(F) = \Pi_F$, where mode (F) adds nothing.

3) *The degree of strength of the illocutionary point.*

Most illocutionary points can be achieved with greater or lesser degrees of strength, e.g. suggesting that the hearer leave the room is weaker than ordering him to leave the room; swearing that it is raining is stronger than merely stating that it is raining. In illocutionary logic we can represent such facts by assigning greater or lesser integers to the different strengths with which an illocutionary point can be achieved in the performance of an illocutionary act. For each illocutionary force F, let degree (F) be the integer that represents the characteristic degree of strength with which the illocutionary point Π_F is achieved in the performance of an act of force F. By definition, for any two illocutionary forces F_1, F_2 with the same illocutionary point $(\Pi_{F_1} = \Pi_{F_2})$, degree $(F_1) <$ degree (F_2) iff the illocutionary point Π_{F_1} is achieved with a greater degree of strength in the case of a successful performance of an illocution of force F_2 than in the case of a successful performance of an illocution of force F_1. Thus, for example, degree $(\|\text{order}\|) >$ degree $(\|\text{request}\|)$; i.e. a speaker who issues an order makes a stronger attempt to get the hearer to do something than a speaker who simply makes a request. Similarly degree $(\|\text{assert}\|) >$ degree $(\|\text{conjecture}\|)$; i.e. the degree of strength of an assertion is stronger than that of a conjecture.

The selection of the base point of the sequence of degrees of strength of greater and lesser strengths is more or less arbitrary. The important thing is to get the relations of greater and lesser strength correctly ordered, and thus the set Z of integers can be used to mark the relation of greater and lesser. Direct comparisons of greater and lesser degrees of strength of course only make sense within the same illocutionary point. One illocutionary point, the declarative point Π_4, is always achieved with the same degree of strength and consequently all illocutionary forces with that point have the same degree of strength. All other illocutionary points can be achieved with different degrees of strength.

We will write "$i\Pi^k P$" as short for "the speaker a_i in the context i achieves illocutionary point Π on P with degree of strength k". In each context of utterance where an illocutionary point is achieved, there is some possible speech act that achieves it with a maximal degree of strength. Thus if $i\Pi P$ then, for some $k \in Z$, $i\Pi^k P$ and, for all $n > k$, it is not the case that $i\Pi^n P$. We use the infinite set Z of integers to measure the degrees of strength with which illocutionary points are achieved because there is no theoretical finite lower or upper limit on the strength of most illocutionary points. Of course if $\Pi = \Pi_4$ then for only one $k \in Z$, $\Pi_4^k \neq \varnothing$ since, as we just noted, the declarative illocutionary point is always achieved with the same degree of strength.

The transitivity of degrees of strength of illocutionary point is stated by the following postulate:

If $i\Pi^{k+1} P$ and $\Pi \neq \Pi_4$ then $i\Pi^k P$.

To achieve the illocutionary point of an illocution with a certain degree of strength is to achieve it with all smaller degrees of strength. For example, if one insists that someone do something one has already achieved the directive illocutionary point with the degree of strength of requesting that he do it or suggesting that he do it.

The mode of achievement of an illocutionary force and its degree of strength of illocutionary point are often logically related. Certain modes of achievement, such as, for example, the mode of achievement of a testimony, require the degree of strength of illocutionary point to be high (i.e. $\geqslant 1$). A speaker who achieves the assertive illocutionary point in his status as a witness speaking under oath commits himself strongly to the truth of the propositional content. Since each possible mode of achievement requires a certain minimal degree of strength with which the illocutionary point must be achieved if it is to be achieved in that mode, there will be a greatest integer k indicating that minimal degree of strength. This greatest degree of strength with which a certain illocutionary point must be achieved if it is to be achieved in a possible mode μ we will write $|\mu|$. The degree of strength of illocutionary point of an illocutionary force degree (F) is always equal to or greater than the degree of strength $|\text{mode }(F)|$ determined by its mode of achievement.

4) *Propositional content conditions.*

As we remarked in the last chapter, some illocutionary forces place restrictions on propositional contents. We call these the propositional content conditions of these illocutionary forces. Formally, a propositional content condition is determined by a function θ from I into $\mathscr{P}(\text{Prop})$ that associates with each possible context of utterance a set of propositions having a certain feature. Thus, for example, the function θ_{fut} that associates with each context of utterance i the set of all propositions that are future with respect to the moment of time t_i determines a propositional content condition. In case a function θ from I into $\mathscr{P}(\text{Prop})$ gives as value, for each context i, the set of all propositions which satisfy the propositional content conditions of an illocutionary force F with respect to that context, we will write $\theta = \text{Prop}_F$. Thus, for example, $\theta_{fut} = \text{Prop}_{\|\text{predict}\|}$ since θ_{fut} determines the propositional content conditions of a prediction. Since a proposition P may be future with respect to a moment t_i and past with respect to a moment t_j for different t_i, t_j such that $t_i < t_j$, $\text{Prop}_{\|\text{predict}\|}(i) \neq \text{Prop}_{\|\text{predict}\|}(j)$ for certain $i, j \in I$. The same proposition could be the content of a prediction in one context but not in another context. In case F has no propositional content conditions, $\text{Prop}_F(i) = \text{Prop}$. Thus, for example, $\text{Prop}_{\|\text{assert}\|}(i) = \text{Prop}$. Any proposition P can be the content of an assertion in an appropriate context of utterance. Such forces have *empty* propositional content conditions.

5) *Preparatory conditions.*

The preparatory conditions of an illocutionary force F are defined by specifying for each context of utterance i and proposition P, which states of affairs the speaker a_i must presuppose to obtain in the world of the utterance w_i if he performs the illocution $F(P)$ in

43

i. To presuppose that a state of affairs obtains is tantamount to presupposing that the proposition that represents that state of affairs is true. Formally, a preparatory condition is then determined in illocutionary logic by a function $\Sigma \in (\mathscr{P}(\mathrm{Prop}))^{I \times \mathrm{Prop}}$ from possible contexts of utterance and propositions into sets of propositions having a certain feature. Thus, for example, the function Σ that associates with each pair $\langle i, P \rangle$ the singleton $\{\Diamond P\}$ determines a common preparatory condition of the illocutionary forces of commands, orders, and requests. A preparatory condition for the issuance of a command, an order, or a request that P in a context of utterance i, is that it is physically possible that P, i.e. that the hearer is capable of carrying out the future course of action represented by P. A speaker who presupposes certain propositions can be committed to presupposing other propositions. For example if a speaker presupposes that the hearer is responsible for a state of affairs, then he also presupposes that that state of affairs exists. We will use hereafter "$[\Gamma]$" as a name for the set of all propositions that a speaker necessarily presupposes in a context of utterance if he presupposes all propositions Γ in that context. Moreover, we will say that a preparatory condition Σ_1 is *the closure of* a preparatory condition Σ_2 iff $\Sigma_1(i, P) = [\Sigma_2(i, P)]$. By definition any illocutionary force F with a preparatory condition also has the closure of that condition. In case a function Σ from $I \times \mathrm{Prop}$ into $\mathscr{P}(\mathrm{Prop})$ determines the preparatory conditions of a force F, we shall hereafter write $\Sigma = \Sigma_F$. Thus, for example, $\Sigma_{\|\mathbf{assert}\|}$ is that function such that $\Sigma_{\|\mathbf{assert}\|}(i, P) = [\{\rho a_i t_i P\}]$. The preparatory conditions for an assertion that P in a context of utterance i are that the speaker a_i has at moment t_i in w_i reasons or evidence for the truth of P.

6) *Sincerity conditions.*

The sincerity conditions of an illocutionary force F are defined by specifying for each context of utterance i and proposition P which psychological states the speaker a_i expresses in the performance of $F(P)$ in i. Formally, a sincerity condition is then determined in illocutionary logic by a function $\Psi \in (\mathscr{P}(M \times \mathrm{Prop}))^{I \times \mathrm{Prop}}$ from contexts of utterance and propositions into sets of psychological states of certain types. Thus, for example, the function Ψ that associates with each pair (i, P) the set $\{\text{Bel}(P)\}$ determines a common sincerity condition of assertions, testimonies, and conjectures. A speaker who asserts, testifies, or conjectures that P, expresses in varying degrees of strength a belief that P. When the psychological states expressed by a speaker in a context of utterance strongly commit him to other psychological states, that speaker also expresses these states in that context. Thus, for example, a speaker who expresses a regret for a state of affairs also expresses a belief in the existence of that state of affairs because he cannot have that regret without having that belief. We will use hereafter "$[\Gamma]$" as a name for the set of all psychological states to which the psychological states Γ strongly commit the speaker. Moreover, we will say that a sincerity condition Ψ_1 is *the closure of* a sincerity condition Ψ_2 iff $\Psi_1(i, P) = [\Psi_2(i, P)]$. By definition, any illocutionary force F with a sincerity condition also has the closure of that condition. When a function $\Psi \in (\mathscr{P}(M \times \text{Prop}))^{I\text{Prop}}$ determines the sincerity conditions of a force F, we shall write hereafter $\Psi = \Psi_F$. Thus, for example, $\Psi_{\|\text{commit}\|}(i, P) = \Psi_{\|\text{promise}\|}(i, P) = [\{(\text{Int } P)\}]$. A speaker who commits himself to doing something or promises that he will do it is sincere iff he intends to do it. $\Psi_{\|\text{direct}\|}(i, P) = [\{\text{Des}(P)\}]$. A speaker who directs a hearer to do something is sincere iff he wants or desires him to do it.

7) *The degree of strength of the sincerity conditions.*

Psychological states are expressed in speech acts with greater or lesser strength depending on the illocutionary force. Thus, for example, a speaker who solemnly vows to do something expresses a stronger intention than a speaker who simply commits himself to doing it. The characteristic degree of strength of the sincerity conditions of an illocutionary force F, $\eta(F)$, can be represented as the degree of strength of its illocutionary point by an integer $k \in Z$. For most illocutionary forces F, their degree of strength of illocutionary point and of sincerity conditions are identical. Thus for example $\eta(\|\text{assert}\|) = \text{degree} \, (\|\text{assert}\|)$, and $\eta(\|\text{commit}\|) = \text{degree} \, (\|\text{commit}\|)$.

The degree of strength of illocutionary point derives from two sources, the degree of strength of the sincerity conditions and the degree of strength conferred by the mode of achievement. So the degree of strength of an illocutionary point degree (F) will be identical with the degree of strength of the sincerity condition $\eta(F)$ except when the mode of achievement mode (F) determines a degree of illocutionary point |mode (F)| superior to $\eta(F)$. Thus, for example, in the case of testimony, degree $(\|\text{testify}\|) > \eta$ $(\|\text{testify}\|)$ because the mode of achievement of testifying increases the strength of the assertive illocutionary point without necessarily increasing the strength of the expressed belief. As a consequence of this, for each illocutionary force F, degree $(F) \geqslant \eta(F)$. The degree of strength with which the psychological state of an illocutionary act is expressed cannot be superior to the degree of strength of its illocutionary point. It may be the case that degree $(F) > \eta(F)$, as for example in the case of orders. This is because to increase the degree of strength of the psychological state is not the only way to increase the degree of strength of the illocutionary point.

IV. DEFINITION OF AN ILLOCUTIONARY FORCE.

The set-theoretical definitions of the illocutionary point Π_F, the mode of achievement of illocutionary point mode (F), the degree of strength of illocutionary point degree (F), the propositional content conditions Prop_F, the preparatory conditions Σ_F, the sincerity conditions Ψ_F, and the degree of strength of sincerity conditions $\eta(F)$ of an illocutionary force F permit us to *identify* set-theoretically that illocutionary force. *Each illocutionary force $F \in \Phi$ is a septuple consisting of these seven elements.* Thus, two illocutionary forces F_1, F_2 are identical when $\Pi_{F_1} = \Pi_{F_2}$, mode $(F_1) = $ mode (F_2), degree $(F_1) = $ degree (F_2), $\text{Prop}_{F_1} = \text{Prop}_{F_2}$, $\Sigma_{F_1} = \Sigma_{F_2}$, $\Psi_{F_1} = \Psi_{F_2}$ and $\eta(F_1) = \eta(F_2)$.

By definition an illocutionary point Π_F is a relation on $I \times \text{Prop}$, a mode of achievement mode (F) is a function from $I \times \text{Prop}$ into truth values, degrees of strength degree (F) and $\eta(F)$ are integers, propositional content conditions Prop_F are a function from I into $\mathscr{P}(\text{Prop})$, preparatory conditions Σ_F are a function from $I \times \text{Prop}$ into $\mathscr{P}(\text{Prop})$, and sincerity conditions Ψ_F are a function from $I \times \text{Prop}$ into $\mathscr{P}(M \times \text{Prop})$. As a consequence of these definitions the set of all illocutionary forces is a subset of the set $\mathscr{P}(I \times \text{Prop})$

$\times\ 2^{I\times\text{Prop}}\ \times\ Z\ \times\ (\mathscr{P}(\text{Prop}))^{I}\ \times\ (\mathscr{P}(\text{Prop}))^{(I\times\text{Prop})}\ \times\ (\mathscr{P}(M\ \times$ $\text{Prop}))^{(I\times\text{Prop})}\ \times\ Z$. In defining the set of illocutionary forces Φ, we do not need any entities except those belonging to I, Prop, Z, and M.

Of course not any relation on $I\times$ Prop determines an illocutionary point, not any function from $I\times$ Prop into 2, from I into $\mathscr{P}(\text{Prop})$, from $I\times$ Prop into $\mathscr{P}(\text{Prop})$ or from $I\times$ Prop into $\mathscr{P}(M\times\text{Prop})$ determines a mode of achievement of illocutionary point, a propositional content, a preparatory, or a sincerity condition. Thus, for example, there are only five relations on $I\times$ Prop that determine the conditions of achievement of illocutionary points. Moreover the only functions from $I\times$ Prop into 2 that determine a mode of achievement of an illocutionary force are functions μ such that $\left\{(i,P)/\mu(i,P)=1\right\}\neq\varnothing$ because each mode of achievement of an illocutionary force is a *possible* mode of achievement of its point. The set of all illocutionary forces is thus *a small proper subset* of the set $\mathscr{P}(I\times\text{Prop})\times 2^{I\times\text{Prop}}\times$ $Z\times(\mathscr{P}(\text{Prop}))^{I}\times(\mathscr{P}(\text{Prop}))^{I\times\text{Prop}}\times(\mathscr{P}(M\times\text{Prop}))^{I\times\text{Prop}}\times Z$.

Furthermore, not any arbitrary septuple consisting of elements of these seven types is an illocutionary force, because there are logical relations between the various components of a possible illocutionary force which restrict the possible combinations of the elements. For example, the mode of achievement mode (F) of an illocutionary force F must be a mode of achievement of its illocutionary point Π_F, and requires a degree of strength of illocutionary point, degree (F), of a certain value; degree (F) must be the maximum of $\eta(F)$ and $|\text{mode }(F)|$. Also, certain illocutionary points Π require certain propositional content conditions $\theta\in\mathscr{P}(\text{Prop})^{I}$, certain preparatory conditions $\Sigma\in\mathscr{P}(\text{Prop})^{I\times\text{Prop}}$ and certain sincerity conditions $\Psi\in\mathscr{P}(M\times\text{Prop})^{I\times\text{Prop}}$, i.e. whenever $i\Pi_F P$ it must be the case that $\text{Prop}_F(i)\subseteq\theta(i)$, $\Sigma(i,P)\subseteq\Sigma_F(i,P)$ and $\Psi(i,P)\subseteq\Psi_F(i,P)$. For example, all illocutionary forces with the directive illocutionary point must have a propositional content that represents a future course of action of the hearer, the preparatory condition that the hearer is capable of carrying out that future course of action, and the sincerity condition that the speaker wants or desires the hearer to carry out that action. Similarly certain modes of achievement μ and certain sincerity conditions Ψ determine certain preparatory conditions Σ because it is not possible to achieve a point in mode μ or to express the sincerity conditions Ψ without presupposing these preparatory conditions. Thus for example an illocutionary force with the mode of achievement of a command must have the preparatory condition that the speaker is in a position of authority over the hearer. An illocutionary force with the sincerity condition that the speaker is dissatisfied with the existence of the state of affairs represented by the propositional content must have the preparatory condition that this state of affairs is bad. A septuple can be a possible illocutionary force only in cases where such logical relations as these between components are preserved.

Chapter 3

THE LOGICAL STRUCTURE OF THE SET OF ILLOCUTIONARY FORCES

Ordinary languages such as English or French have a vast vocabulary of verbs, nouns, and modifiers for specifying illocutionary forces. The size and variety of this vocabulary often make it difficult to perceive the underlying logical structure of the phenomena it is used to describe. One of the aims of a formalization such as we are attempting in this book is to lay bare the logical flesh and skeleton beneath the clothing of the surface vocabulary. Among the advantages of such a project are the increases in theoretical insight and precision to be gained from the formalization; the chief risk is in the distortion of the phenomena to fit the theory. Some degree of idealization is essential but it is important to our project that the idealization should not distort the logico-linguistic facts.

In the last chapter we defined illocutionary force as consisting of seven features. On this account the set Φ of all illocutionary forces is a subset of the set $\mathscr{P}(I \times \text{Prop}) \times 2^{I \times \text{Prop}} \times Z \times (\mathscr{P}(\text{Prop}))^{I} \times (\mathscr{P}(\text{Prop}))^{I \times \text{Prop}} \times (\mathscr{P}(M \times \text{Prop}))^{I \times \text{Prop}} \times Z$. In this chapter we will use this apparatus to generate formally the set of all illocutionary forces, and we will attempt to do that in a way that shows how this set can be defined recursively from a few primitive forces.

I. THE HYPOTHESIS OF CONSTRUCTIBILITY.

The hypothesis that such a recursive definition is possible – let us call it the hypothesis of constructibility – seems intuitively plausible when one reflects on the following three sets of considerations.

First. Sometimes one can form new illocutionary forces out of old ones by adding propositional content, preparatory, or sincerity conditions. For example, the illocutionary force of a report that P has one more propositional content condition than the illocutionary force of an assertion that P, namely P must be about a past or present state of affairs with respect to the time of the utterance.

49

The illocutionary force of an act of reminding that P has one more preparatory condition than the illocutionary force of asserting that P, namely that the hearer once knew and might have forgotten that P. Propositional content, preparatory, and sincerity conditions of an illocutionary force that are not common to all illocutionary forces with the same point we will call *special* conditions of that force. Conditions of an illocutionary force F that are common to all forces with the same point as F we will call *general* conditions of that force. Thus, for example, all illocutionary forces which have the commissive point have the general propositional content condition that their propositional content must represent a future course of action of the speaker, the general preparatory condition that the speaker is capable of carrying out that future course of action, and the general sincerity condition that the speaker intends to carry out that action. All general propositional content, general preparatory, and general sincerity conditions of an illocutionary force are determined by its illocutionary point. The sense in which they are determined is simply that one cannot achieve that illocutionary point without presupposing these preparatory conditions, without expressing these sincerity conditions, and without expressing a proposition satisfying those propositional content conditions.

Second. We can take certain typical degrees of strength of illocutionary points and of sincerity conditions of illocutionary forces as the measure (or standard) for comparing the degrees of strength of all other illocutionary forces with the same illocutionary points and the same sincerity conditions. For example, we can treat the characteristic degree of strength of commitment to truth and the characteristic degree of strength of belief of the illocutionary force of assertion as the standard for comparing other forces with the same point. Thus other illocutionary forces with the assertive point mark either the same, less, or greater degrees of strength of commitment to truth and degrees of strength of belief. We will call a characteristic degree of strength of illocutionary point of an illocutionary force F a *medium or null degree of strength* if it is in the middle of the scale of degrees of strength with which the illocutionary point F can be achieved according to our system of comparison. Similarly the characteristic degree of strength of the sincerity conditions of an illocutionary force F is *medium or null* if it is in the middle of the scale of the degrees of strength with which the psychological state specified by the sincerity conditions can be expressed. Since we can represent degrees of strength by integers, we will call the medium degree of strength zero. Thus the primitive illocutionary forces have zero degree of strength and all other forces have a degree of strength that is either zero or can be obtained by adding or subtracting from zero.

Third. Certain forces have a special mode of achievement of their illocutionary point that is not common to all illocutionary forces with that point. For example, the illocutionary force of commands is such that the speaker who issues a command achieves the illocutionary point of attempting to get the hearer to do something in virtue of his position of authority over him. Other illocutionary forces with the same illocutionary point, such as, for example, requesting and asking, do not have that mode of achievement.

These three sets of considerations suggest that we can now formulate the hypothesis of constructibility in a more precise form as follows: First, there is a finite number of illocutionary points and for each illocutionary point there is a primitive illocutionary force which has that point, which has no special mode of achievement, null degrees of strength, and only the general propositional content, preparatory, and sincerity conditions that are determined by its point. Secondly, all other illocutionary forces are obtainable from the few primitive illocutionary forces by applying operations affecting the mode of achievement, the degrees of strength, the propositional content conditions, the preparatory conditions, or the sincerity conditions of these primitive illocutionary forces.

If this hypothesis is true, the set of all illocutionary forces is definable recursively from a few primitive forces. In this chapter we will formulate a formal definition of the set of all illocutionary forces which is in accordance with the hypothesis of constructibility. We will first define the five illocutionary points and second the various operations on illocutionary forces.

II. THE FIVE ILLOCUTIONARY POINTS.

In spite of frequent philosophical protestations to the contrary, there is a rather limited number of things one can do with language.

One can, for example, declare war, apologize for one's bad behavior, or assert that the roof is leaking; but one cannot fry an egg, patch a roof leak, or split an atom with words alone. What are the boundaries on possible speech acts? We have claimed that as far as illocutionary forces are concerned there are five and only five fundamental types and thus five and only five illocutionary ways of using language. One can say how things are (assertives), one can try to get other people to do things (directives), one can commit oneself to doing things (commissives), one can bring about changes in the world through one's utterances (declarations), and one can express one's feelings and attitudes (expressives). Often one can do more than one of these things in the same utterance. Each of these five categories of illocutionary forces has one type of illocutionary point, and, as we said earlier, the idea of illocutionary point is the idea of the point or purpose of a type of illocution in virtue of its being an illocution of that type.

But why should there be these and only these illocutionary points? The illocutionary point of an illocutionary force always relates the propositional content of that illocutionary force to the world of the utterance, and there are a limited number of ways that propositional contents can be related to a world of utterance. The way in which a propositional content is related to a world of utterance we call its direction of fit. Intuitively the idea of direction of fit is the idea of responsibility for fitting. For example, in the case of a description, the propositional content of the speaker's utterance is supposed to match some independently existing state of affairs and to the extent that it does so we say that the description is true or false, accurate or inaccurate. But in the case of an order the propositional content is not supposed to match an independently existing reality but rather the hearer is supposed to change his behavior to match the propositional content of the order. To the extent that he does that we do not say that the order was true or accurate but rather that it was obeyed or disobeyed.

There are four and only four directions of fit[1] in language:

---

[1] The expression 'direction of fit' is due to J. L. Austin, *Philosophical Papers* (Oxford: Clarendon Press, 1962); but the idea is closer to G. E. M. Anscombe, *Intention* (Oxford: Blackwell, 1957).

The five illocutionary points

1. *The word-to-world direction of fit.*
   In achieving success of fit the propositional content of the illocution fits an independently[2] existing state of affairs in the world.

2. *The world-to-word direction of fit.*
   In achieving success of fit the world is altered to fit the propositional content of the illocution.

3. *The double direction of fit.*
   In achieving success of fit the world is altered to fit the propositional content by representing the world as being so altered.

4. *The null or empty direction of fit.*
   There is no question of achieving success of fit between the propositional content and the world, because in general success of fit is presupposed by the utterance.

The five different illocutionary points exhaust the different possible directions of fit between the propositional content and the world.

Utterances with the assertive point have the word-to-world direction of fit. In an assertive illocution the propositional content is expressed as representing an independently existing state of affairs in the world. Both the commissive and the directive illocutionary points have the world-to-word direction of fit. Part of the point of a commissive or directive illocution is to get the world to match the propositional content, and in a speech situation responsibility for bringing about success of fit can be placed on either the speaker or the hearer. In the case of a commissive illocution, responsibility for achieving success of fit rests with the speaker; in the case of a directive illocution it rests with the hearer. Speaker and hearer play such crucial roles in discourse that we distinguish between a speaker based world-to-word direction of fit (commissives) and a hearer based world-to-word direction of fit (directives). The double direction of fit is found in the declarative illocutionary point. In a declarative illocution the speaker makes the world match the propositional content simply by saying

---

2 'Independently', with the exception of self-referential speech acts where the state of affairs represented is not independent of its representation, e.g. 'This speech act is performed in English.'

that the propositional content matches the world. Finally, utterances with the expressive illocutionary point have the null direction of fit. The point of an expressive illocution is not to say that the propositional content matches the world, nor to get the world to match the propositional content, but it is simply to express the speaker's attitude about the state of affairs represented by the propositional content. (More about direction of fit later.)

We will now specify several laws governing the successful performance of illocutions with each of the five illocutionary points. These laws will state which general propositional content, preparatory, and sincerity conditions are determined by each illocutionary point, and will give some characteristic properties of these points.

1) *Assertive illocutionary forces.*

Assertive forces have the assertive point. They may differ from one another in respects such as their mode of achievement (the difference, for example, between arguing and testifying that P), their degree of strength of illocutionary point or of sincerity conditions (the difference, for example, between insisting that P and conjecturing that P), their propositional content conditions (the difference, for example, between a prediction and a report), their preparatory conditions (the difference, for example, between reminding and informing that P), or their sincerity conditions (the difference, for example, between asserting and complaining). There is no general propositional content condition common to all assertive illocutionary forces since any proposition P can be the content of an assertion. $\text{Prop}_{\|\text{assert}\|}(i) = \text{Prop}$. All assertive illocutionary forces have the preparatory condition that the speaker has reasons (or grounds or evidence) that count in favor of or support the truth of the propositional content. Thus, if $\Pi_F = \Pi_1$, $\rho a_i t_i P \in \Sigma_F(i, P)$. The stringency of this requirement may vary with variations in the degree of strength of the assertive. For example, one is required to have stronger grounds for what one swears to than for what one merely advances as a hypothesis. The psychological state expressed in all assertive illocutions is belief, again in varying degrees. A speaker who succeeds in performing an assertive illocutionary act of the form $F(P)$ is sincere only if he believes the propositions he expresses. Thus if $\Pi_F = \Pi_1$, then Bel $(P) \in \Psi_F(i, P)$.

2) *Commissive illocutionary forces.*

Commissive forces have the commissive point. Like assertive illocutionary forces, they may differ with respect to the mode of achievement of their illocutionary point, their degree of strength of illocutionary point or of sincerity conditions (the difference, for example, between vowing and consenting), their propositional content conditions, their preparatory conditions (the difference, for example, between a promise and a threat), and their sincerity conditions. Since commissive illocutions are by definition about the future actions of the speaker, they have precise constraints on the propositional content: the proposition must represent some future course of action by the speaker. The set $\text{Prop}_2(i)$ of all propositions that represent a future course of action of the speaker a_i of a context of utterance i satisfies the following clause: If for some proposition Q and for some moment of time $t > t_i$, $P = \delta a_i t Q$, then $P \in \text{Prop}_2(i)$. Moreover, Q_1 and $Q_2 \in \text{Prop}_2(i)$ iff $\sim Q_1$, and $(Q_1 \to Q_2) \in \text{Prop}_2(i)$. Thus, if $\Pi_F = \Pi_2$, $\text{Prop}_F(i) \subseteq \text{Prop}_2(i)$. All commissive illocutionary forces have the common preparatory condition that the speaker is capable of doing what he commits himself to doing. Consequently, if $\Pi_F = \Pi_2$ then $\Diamond P \in \Sigma_F(i, P)$. The psychological state expressed in all commissive illocutions is intention. All commissive forces have the general sincerity condition that the speaker intends to do what he commits himself to doing. Thus, if $\Pi_F = \Pi_2$, $\text{Int}(P) \in \Psi_F(i, P)$. Because all commissive illocutions are in one way or another undertakings, they create practical reasons for the speaker to do the action to which he commits himself. Thus when $i\Pi_2 P$, the proposition $\rho a_i t_i P$ is true in w_i.

3) *Directive illocutionary forces.*

Directive forces have the directive point. Like assertive and commissive illocutionary forces, they can differ in the mode of achievement of their illocutionary point (the difference, for example, between ordering and begging), their degree of strength of illocutionary point or of sincerity conditions (the difference, for example, between demanding and requesting or between beseeching and requesting), their propositional content conditions (the difference, for example, between asking a question and urging), their preparatory conditions (the difference, for example, between advising and recommending), or their sincerity conditions. Since all directive illocutions concern the future behavior of the hearer, directive illocutionary forces, like commissives, have quite precise constraints on their propositional content. They have the general propositional content condition that their propositional content represents a future course of action of the hearer. The set $\mathrm{Prop}_3(i)$ of all propositions that represent a future course of action of the hearer in a context i satisfies the following clause: If for some $Q \in \mathrm{Prop}$ and for some moment of time $t > t_i$, $P = \delta b_i t Q$, then $P \in \mathrm{Prop}_3(i)$. Moreover, Q_1 and $Q_2 \in \mathrm{Prop}_3(i)$ iff $\sim Q_1$ and $(Q_1 \rightarrow Q_2) \in \mathrm{Prop}_3(i)$. Thus, if $\Pi_F = \Pi_3$, $\mathrm{Prop}_F(i) \subseteq \mathrm{Prop}_3(i)$.

The directive illocutionary forces have the common preparatory condition that the hearer is capable of doing what he is directed to do. Consequently, if $\Pi_F = \Pi_3$ then $\diamondsuit P \in \Sigma_F(i, P)$. The psychological state expressed in all directive illocutions is want or desire, and it will be expressed in different degrees depending on the illocutionary force. All directive illocutionary forces have the general sincerity condition that the speaker wants or desires the hearer to do what he attempts to get him to do. Thus if $\Pi_F = \Pi_3$, then $\mathrm{Des}(P) \in \Psi_F(i, P)$. Finally, directive illocutions create reasons for the hearer to do the action that he is directed to do. Thus when $i\Pi_3 P$ the proposition $\rho b_i t_i P$ is true in w_i.

4) *Declarative illocutionary forces.*

Declarative forces have the declarative point. The illocutionary point of a declaration is to bring about changes in the world, so that the world matches the propositional content solely in virtue of the successful performance of the speech act. Normally, this is achieved by invoking some extralinguistic institution in such a way that within the institution the performance of the utterance act counts as bringing about the change in the world. Thus, when one adjourns a meeting, pronounces a couple man and wife, gives or bequeaths one's watch, or appoints a chairman, an extra-.

linguistic institution empowers an appropriately situated speaker to bring about a word–world match solely in virtue of his speech act. Exceptions to the general requirement of an extralinguistic institution for the successful performance of declarations are supernatural declarations and purely linguistic declarations. When God says "Let there be light!" He is making a declaration; and when a speaker says he abbreviates a certain long expression, as such and such, he is making a declaration. Neither sort of declaration requires an extralinguistic institution, in the one case because of supernatural powers, in the other because the declaration involves only language itself and not the world independent of language.

By definition, a declarative illocution is successful only if the speaker brings about the state of affairs represented by its propositional content in the world of the utterance. Thus, when $i\Pi_4 P$ the proposition $\delta a_i t_i P$ is true in w_i. Since $\delta a_i t_i P$ strictly implies P, this in turn implies that when the declarative point is achieved on a proposition, that proposition is true in the world of utterance. All successful declarations have a true propositional content and in this respect declarations are peculiar among speech acts in that they are the only speech acts whose successful performance is by itself sufficient to bring about a word–world fit. In such cases, "saying makes it so". There are no variations in degree of strength with which the declarative illocutionary point can be achieved: one either does it or one does not. Thus all declarative illocutionary forces F have the null degree of strength. If $\Pi_F = \Pi_4$, degree $(F) = \eta(F) = 0$. There are no general propositional content conditions on declaratives, though the range of subject matter over which declaratives can operate is obviously very restricted. All declarative illocutionary forces have the mode of achievement that the speaker invokes his power or authority to perform the declaration and the general preparatory condition that the speaker has that power or authority to change the world by the performance of the appropriate utterance act. Thus, if $\tau(i, P)$ is the proposition that is true in a world w iff $i\ [w/w_i]\Pi_4 P$ and $\Pi_F = \Pi_4$, then $\tau(i, P) \in \Sigma_F(i, P)$. The psychological states expressed in all declarations are belief and desire. A speaker who declares that P expresses simultaneously his desire to bring about the state of affairs represented by P and his belief that his utterance is bringing it about. Thus, the general sincerity conditions of all declarative illocutionary forces are: If $\Pi_F = \Pi_4$, then Bel $(\delta a_i t_i P)$ and Des $(\delta a_i t_i P) \in \Psi_F(i, P)$. A speaker cannot say successfully both "I declare that P" and "I do not believe that this utterance brings it about that P" or "I do not want to bring it about that P." Unlike assertives and commissives there is seldom any motivation for making an insincere declaration. Desire to succeed and belief in success normally go along with the intention of the speaker to achieve the declarative illocutionary point. As a consequence of this, successful declarations are in general (though not always) sincere.[3]

5) *Expressive illocutionary forces.*

The illocutionary point of an expressive illocution of form $F(P)$ is to express the speaker's attitude about the state of affairs that P. Though the point is the same, different attitudes are determined by different forces with content P. Thus, if I congratulate you on winning the race or apologize for stepping on your toe, the points of my utterances are respectively to express pleasure (about the state of affairs specified by the propositional content – that you won the race) and regret or remorse (about the state of affairs specified by the propositional content – that I stepped on your toe). As we noted before, the verb "express" is ambiguous between the sense of "express" in which humans express propositions and illocutionary forces and the sense of "express" in which they express their feelings and emotions. It is this latter sense in which people may be said to "express", "manifest", or "give vent to" feelings – whether or not they actually have the feeling that they express – which forms the basic notion of expressives. Since all psychological states can be expressed with varying degrees of strength, expressive illocutionary forces may differ with respect to degree of strength. Thus, for example, there

---

3 Here is an example of an insincere, though successful, declaration. Suppose I believe I am not empowered to perform marriage ceremonies but you and your partner believe I am. Suppose I want you both to believe that I am marrying you, so I go through the marriage ceremony. When I perform the declaration 'I now pronounce you man and wife', I neither believe that I am making you man and wife nor do I want to. But suppose that unknown to me I am empowered to marry you and as a result of my insincere speech act you are married.

is usually a difference of degree of strength between the expressive illocutionary forces of the two utterances "If only it would rain!" and "I wish to God it would rain!" As regards expressive illocutionary forces, the degree of strength of the illocutionary point, degree (F), and the degree of strength of the sincerity conditions, $\eta(F)$, are by definition identical, since the illocutionary point is achieved by expressing the sincerity conditions. Furthermore, the conditions of commitment to the expressive illocutionary point are identical with the conditions of commitment to certain psychological states. Thus, a speaker a_i is committed to the expressive illocutionary point Π_5 on a proposition P iff he commits himself to having some psychological states or attitudes about the state of affairs that P represents.

Particular expressive illocutionary forces have quite precise propositional content constraints, but there appears to be no general propositional content condition on the entire class of expressives. For most cases the propositional content must have something to do with the speaker or hearer. Most expressive illocutionary forces, in particular all expressive illocutionary forces with a psychological state that has a null direction of fit, have the preparatory condition that the propositional content is true in the world of the utterance. The speaker expresses a psychological state about a state of affairs that he presupposes to obtain in the world of the utterance. Thus for most, but not all, expressive illocutionary forces F, $P \in \Sigma_F(i, P)$.

So far we have defined five illocutionary points and the propositional content, sincerity, and preparatory conditions that they determine. These definitions together with the hypothesis of constructibility entail that there are in the set of illocutionary forces five primitive forces with the following logical form:

1. *The primitive assertive illocutionary force.*
By definition, the primitive assertive illocutionary force has the assertive illocutionary point; it has no special mode of achievement of illocutionary point, and no propositional content conditions; its preparatory conditions are simply that the speaker has reasons for accepting or evidence supporting the truth of the propositional content and its only psychological state is belief; it has medium degrees of strength of illocutionary point and of sincerity condi-

tions. The illocutionary force of assertion $\vdash$ is this primitive illocutionary force. It is defined as follows:

$$\Pi_\vdash = \Pi_1; \text{mode}(\vdash) = \Pi_1; \text{degree}(\vdash) = \eta(\vdash) = \mathrm{o}; \text{Prop}_\vdash(i)$$
$$= \text{Prop}, \Sigma_\vdash(i, P) = [\{\rho a_i t_i P\}] \text{ and } \Psi_\vdash(i, P) = [\{\text{Bel}(P)\}].$$

In English the primitive assertive illocutionary force is most nearly named by such performative verbs as "assert" and "state" and is expressed by the indicative mood.

2. *The primitive commissive illocutionary force.*

The primitive commissive illocutionary force has the commissive illocutionary point, no special mode of achievement of illocutionary point, and null degrees of strength. Its only propositional content condition is that the propositional content represents a future course of action of the speaker. Its sole preparatory condition is that the speaker is able (in the sense of $\diamondsuit$) to perform the act represented in the propositional content and its sole psychological state is intention. The illocutionary force $\perp$ of commitment to a future action is the primitive commissive illocutionary force. It is defined as follows:

$$\Pi_\perp = \Pi_2; \text{mode}(\perp) = \Pi_2; \text{degree}(\perp) = \eta(\perp) = \mathrm{o}; \text{Prop}_\perp(i) =$$
$$\text{Prop}_2(i); \Sigma_\perp(i, P) = [\{\diamondsuit P\}] \text{ and } \Psi_\perp(i, P) = [\{\text{Int}(P)\}].$$

There is no illocutionary force indicating device for the primitive commissive force in English. It is indirectly expressed by the modal auxiliary "will", as in such utterances as "I will fight it out on this line even if it takes all summer". The closest performative verb in English to name the primitive commissive is "commit" as in "I hereby commit myself to fighting it out on this line even if it takes all summer", but this is a somewhat unnatural locution. The more natural and frequently used commissive verbs such as "promise" and "vow" have additional special conditions attaching to them and so do not name the primitive commissive illocutionary force.

3. *The primitive directive illocutionary force.*

The primitive directive illocutionary force has the directive illocutionary point, no special mode of achievement of that illocutionary point, and null degrees of strength. Its only propositional content condition is that the propositional content represents a future course of action of the hearer. Its sole preparatory condition is that the hearer be able to carry out the course of action represented in the propositional content and its sole psychological state is desire. The illocutionary force of directives ! is the primitive directive illocutionary force. It is defined as follows:

$$\Pi_! = \Pi_3; \text{ mode } (!) = \Pi_3; \text{ degree } (!) = \eta(!) = o; \text{ Prop}_!(i) = \text{Prop}_3(i); \Sigma_!(i, P) = [\{ \Diamond P\}] \text{ and } \Psi_!(i, P) = [\{\text{Des }(P)\}].$$

In English the primitive directive illocutionary force is probably most nearly named by the performative "direct", as in e.g. "You are hereby directed to turn in your paper on Wednesday." The more natural directive verbs such as "order" and "request" have additional special conditions attaching to them and so do not name the primitive directive illocutionary force. The most natural way in English to express the primitive directive illocutionary force is with the imperative mood.

4. *The primitive declarative illocutionary force.*

The primitive declarative illocutionary force has the declarative illocutionary point, the mode of achievement that the speaker invokes his power to perform the declaration, and no propositional content conditions. Its sole preparatory condition is that the speaker be capable of bringing about the state of affairs represented in the propositional content solely in virtue of the performance of the speech act, and its sole psychological states are belief and desire. Its degree of strength of illocutionary point and its degree of strength of sincerity conditions are null. The illocutionary force of declaration T is the primitive declarative illocutionary force. It is defined as follows:

$$\Pi_T = \Pi_4; \text{ mode } (T) = \Pi_4; \text{ degree } (T) = o; \text{ Prop}_T(i) = \text{Prop};$$
$$\Sigma_T(i, P) = [\{ \Diamond \tau(i, P)\}]; \Psi_T(i, P) = [\{\text{Bel }(\delta a_i t_i P), \text{ Des }(\delta a_i t_i P)\}]$$
$$\text{and } \eta(T) = o.$$

In English this illocutionary force is named by the performative verb "declare" in one of its senses, and in French it is named by the verb "déclarer". The most natural way to express the illocutionary force of declaration is with a performative sentence.

5. *The primitive expressive illocutionary force.*

The primitive expressive illocutionary force has the expressive point, no special mode of achievement, and no propositional content, preparatory, and sincerity conditions. It is defined as follows:

$$\Pi_{\dashv} = \Pi_5; \text{mode}\,(\dashv) = \Pi_5; \text{degree}\,(\dashv) = \eta(\dashv) = \mathrm{o}; \text{Prop}_{\dashv}(i)$$
$$= \text{Prop}, \Sigma_{\dashv}(i, P) = \varnothing \text{ and } \Psi_{\dashv}(i, P) = \varnothing.$$

In English there is no special syntactical device for expressing that primitive illocutionary force as distinct from expressing particular expressive illocutionary forces with special sincerity conditions.

Given our analysis of the primitive forces, the conditions of success of illocutionary acts with a primitive force can now be stated precisely as follows:

An illocutionary act of the form $F(P)$ with a primitive illocutionary force F *is performed in a context of utterance i* iff the speaker in that context achieves the illocutionary point Π_F on P with the null degree of strength, if he expresses P and P satisfies the propositional content conditions of F with respect to i, if he presupposes that the preparatory conditions $\Sigma_F(i, P)$ and the propositional presuppositions $\sigma(P)$ obtain and finally if he expresses the psychological states $\Psi_F(i, P)$ with the null degree of strength. Because all propositional content, preparatory and sincerity conditions of a primitive force are determined by its point and because it is not possible to achieve an illocutionary point on a proposition without expressing that proposition and presupposing the propositional presuppositions, the conditions of success of illocutionary acts with a primitive force reduce to the achievement of the illocutionary point on the propositional content with the zero degree of strength. Thus, when F is primitive, an illocutionary act of the form $F(P)$ is performed in a context i iff $i\Pi_F^0 P$.

III. PRINCIPAL OPERATIONS ON
ILLOCUTIONARY FORCES.

The purpose of the last section was to define the primitive illocutionary forces. The purpose of this section is to define the operations by the application of which all illocutionary forces can be obtained from the primitive ones. These operations consist in adding propositional content, preparatory or sincerity conditions; in increasing or decreasing the degrees of strength of the illocutionary point and of the sincerity conditions and in restricting the mode of achievement. Each operation on illocutionary forces determines new conditions of success for the elementary illocutionary acts with the forces that can be obtained by applying that operation.

1) *The addition of propositional content conditions* (Operation θ).

As we said earlier, some illocutionary forces have more propositional content conditions than others with the same illocutionary point. Thus, for example, the illocutionary force of reports has one more propositional content condition than the illocutionary force of assertions, namely that its propositional content is a proposition about the past or the present. The illocutionary force of retrodiction has one more propositional content condition than the illocutionary force of reports, namely that its propositional content is a proposition about the past. Thus, $\mathrm{Prop}_{\|\mathrm{retrodict}\|}(i) \subseteq \mathrm{Prop}_{\|\mathrm{report}\|}(i) \subseteq \mathrm{Prop}_{\vdash}(i)$.

Propositional content conditions in illocutionary logic are determined by functions from contexts of utterance into sets of propositions. To each propositional content condition corresponds a function θ from I into $\mathscr{P}(\mathrm{Prop})$ that gives as value for each context i, a set of propositions $\theta(i)$ having a certain feature. For example, since a yes–no question is a directive by the speaker to the hearer to provide an answer, the propositional content conditions of the illocutionary force of asking a yes–no question are determined by that function θ_2 from I into $\mathscr{P}(\mathrm{Prop})$ that gives as value, for each context of utterance i, the set of all propositions whose truth conditions are that the hearer b_i performs after the time of utterance t_i a specific speech act, where the form of the yes–no question determines the propositional content of a possible appropriate answer.

Under certain conditions the operation of adding new propositional content conditions θ to an illocutionary force F generates a new illocutionary force $[\theta]F$ that differs from F only by the fact that an illocutionary act of the form $[\theta]F(P)$ has the additional condition of success that P satisfies the propositional content conditions determined by θ. Thus, an act of the form $[\theta]F(P)$ is performed in a context of utterance i iff $F(P)$ is performed in that context and $P \in \theta(i)$. Illocutionary force $[\theta]$ F differs from F by the fact that it has the stronger propositional content conditions $\text{Prop}_{[\theta]F}(i) = \text{Prop}_F(i) \cap \theta(i)$ with respect to each context of utterance i. The propositional content conditions of $[\theta]F$ are the intersection of the propositional content conditions of F and of the new propositional content conditions θ. Thus for example the illocutionary force of a yes–no question is $[\theta_?]\underset{\cdot}{!}$, i.e. is obtained from the illocutionary force of request[4] by adding propositional content conditions $\theta_?$. On this account a yes–no question is simply a request that the hearer perform a certain sort of speech act to the original speaker. Similarly, if $\theta_{\text{pres or past}}$ is a function from I into $\mathscr{P}(\text{Prop})$ such that $P \in \theta_{\text{pres or past}}(i)$ iff P is a proposition that is present or past with respect to the moment of time t_i, $\|\text{report}\| = [\theta_{\text{pres or past}}] \vdash$. On this account a report is simply an assertion about the past or the present. The operation of adding propositional content conditions to an illocutionary force F_1 restricts the set of propositions that satisfy the propositional content conditions of F_1: For each illocutionary force $F_2 = [\theta]F_1$, $\text{Prop}_{F_2}(i) \subseteq \text{Prop}_{F_1}(i)$.

Not just any addition of propositional content conditions to an illocutionary force F_1 will generate a new illocutionary force F_2. In order to generate a new force a proposed propositional content condition must meet certain requirements. A new propositional content condition θ must be relatively consistent with the propositional content conditions of F_1, i.e. for some contexts $i \in I$, $\theta(i) \cap \text{Prop}_{F_1}(i) \neq \varnothing$. Otherwise $[\theta]F_1$ would be an impossible illocutionary force; and all illocutionary acts of force F would be

---

4 For convenience, we will often use the symbols '$\underset{\cdot}{!}$', and '$\uparrow$', and 'Pr' for naming the paradigmatic illocutionary forces of request, order, and promise, respectively.

self-defeating. All illocutionary forces must serve some purpose and consequently they must be possible illocutionary forces.

Moreover, a new propositional content condition θ must be linguistically significant, that is, it must be based on such linguistically relevant categories as the time of utterance, the speaker, the hearer, or what is good or bad. Thus, for example, the obsolete English performative verb "macarize" (to call someone happy) does not name a different illocutionary force from assertion because the propositional content condition (that the propositional content is that the hearer is happy) has no special linguistic significance. It is not relevant to illocutionary force. In principle one can imagine all sorts of possible combinations of the features of the seven elements that go to make up illocutionary force. One could imagine a class of speech acts with the preparatory conditions that the speaker was standing on his head when the act was performed or that the propositional content was about a certain person. On the conception of illocutionary force that we are presenting here, such cases do not constitute new illocutionary forces because the features in these examples are of no linguistic significance. But what is meant by linguistic significance? Simply that in human linguistic practices there are certain categories that are pervasive and important for the structure of our discourse: time and place, the position of the speaker and the hearer, their relative abilities and statuses, what is or is not in their interest. And so on. However, there is nothing transcendentally necessary about such categories. One can imagine a class of beings different from human beings who perform illocutionary acts but for whom different categories altogether are linguistically significant. And in that sense the concept of linguistic significance is relative to human culture and to linguistic practices. One could adopt the approach of defining illocutionary forces in such a way that any new propositional content (or preparatory or sincerity) condition created a new illocutionary force. This would be formally elegant but the philosophical price of the elegance would be intolerably high. For example, it would have the consequence that no two different utterances ever had the same illocutionary force, because any two utterance tokens will always differ in some feature which could be treated as a condition on force.

2) *The addition of preparatory conditions*
(Operation Σ).

Some illocutionary forces also have more preparatory conditions than other forces with the same point. Thus, for example, the illocutionary force of accepting (a proposal, an invitation, etc.) has one more preparatory condition than the illocutionary force of commitment to a future action, namely that the speaker has been given a directive that allows for the possibility of refusal. Furthermore the illocutionary force of an act of consenting to do something has one more preparatory condition than the illocutionary force of acceptance, namely that the speaker has at least prima facie reasons for not doing what he consents to do. Preparatory conditions are determined in illocutionary logic by functions from possible contexts of utterance and propositions into sets of propositions. Thus, for example, the preparatory conditions of the illocutionary force of a promise are determined by that function that gives as value, for each context of utterance i and proposition P, the set that contains the two propositions $\diamondsuit P$ and that the state of affairs represented by P is good for the hearer b_i. Under certain conditions, the operation of adding new preparatory conditions Σ^* to an illocutionary force F generates a new illocutionary force $[\Sigma^*]F$ that differs from F only by the fact that an illocutionary act of the form $[\Sigma^*]F(P)$ has the additional condition of success that the speaker presupposes the preparatory conditions determined by Σ^*. Thus an act of the form $[\Sigma^*]F(P)$ is performed in a context of utterance i iff the speaker performs $F(P)$ in that context and presupposes the truth of all propositions belonging to $\Sigma^*(i, P)$. Thus, for example, if Σ_1 is that function from $I \times \text{Prop}$ into $\mathscr{P}(\text{Prop})$ such that $\Sigma_1(i, P) = \{$the proposition that the state of affairs represented by P is good for $b_i\}$, then the illocutionary force of advice $\|\text{advise}\| = [\Sigma_1]\|\text{suggest}\|$; for in one sense of the word "advise" to advise someone to do something is just to suggest to him to do it with the additional presupposition (and hence implication) that it is good for him. If Σ_2 is the preparatory condition such that $\Sigma_2(i, P) = \{$that the state of affairs that P is good$\}$ then the illocutionary force of recommendation $\|\text{recommend}\| = [\Sigma_2]\|\text{suggest}\|$ for to recommend to someone to do something is just to suggest to him to do it with the additional presupposition that it is a good thing to do. A new illocutionary force $[\Sigma^*]F$ differs from F by the fact that it has preparatory conditions $\Sigma_{[\Sigma*]F}(i, P) = [\Sigma_F(i, P) \cup \Sigma^*(i, P)]$ instead of $\Sigma_F(i, P)$ only. These preparatory conditions are the closure of the union of the preparatory conditions of F and of the new preparatory conditions Σ^*. The operation of addition preparatory conditions generates illocutionary forces with more and more special preparatory conditions: If $F_2 = [\Sigma]\ F_1$ then $\Sigma_{F_1}(i, P) \subseteq \Sigma_{F_2}(i, P)$.

Most special preparatory conditions of illocutionary forces concern linguistically significant features of the context of utterance such as (i) the respective status or position of the speaker and the hearer, (ii) their psychological states, (iii) their responsibilities and abilities, (iv) the surrounding discourse, (v) the way the propositional content relates to the interests of the hearer or speaker, or (vi) what is good or bad in general. Here are a few examples of illocutionary forces which have special preparatory conditions:

(i) $\Sigma_{\|testify\|}(i, P)/w/$ only if a_i is at a time $t \leqslant t_i$ a witness of P in w. In this case, the special preparatory condition is a particular status of the speaker.

(ii) $\Sigma_{\|inform\|}(i, P)/w/$ only if b_i does not know that P at time t_i in w. In this case a certain state of knowledge of the hearer is presupposed.

(iii) $\Sigma_{\|criticize\|}(i, P)/w/$ only if b_i is responsible for P in w. To criticize someone for something commits the speaker to the presupposition that the hearer is responsible for that thing.

(iv) $\Sigma_{\|accept\|}(i, P)/w/$ only if for some $j = \langle a, a_i, t_j, l, w \rangle$ such that $t_j \langle t_i, \downarrow(P)$ is performed in j. An acceptance by a speaker of a directive has the preparatory condition that the speaker has been given a directive that allows for the possibility of refusal. In this case a presupposition is made about the preceding discourse.

(v) $\Sigma_{\|threaten\|}(i, P)/w/$ only if P is bad for b_i at time t_i in w. To threaten someone to do something commits the speaker to the presupposition that the act is bad for the hearer.

3) *The addition of sincerity conditions* (Operation Ψ).

Some illocutionary forces have more sincerity conditions than others. Thus, for example, to lament that P is to assert P while expressing dissatisfaction and sadness that P. To boast that P is to assert P while expressing pride that P. Sincerity conditions of illocutionary forces in illocutionary logic are determined by functions from contexts of utterance and propositions into sets of psychological states. For example, the function Ψ_{dis} that associates with each pair (i, P) the singleton containing the psychological state of dissatisfaction with the existence of the state of affairs represented by P, determines a sincerity condition of the illocutionary forces of a complaint and of a lamentation. Under certain conditions, the operation of adding a new sincerity condition Ψ^* to an illocutionary force F generates a new illocutionary force $[\Psi^*]F$ that differs from F only by the fact that an illocutionary act of form $[\Psi^*]F(P)$ has the additional condition of success that the speaker expresses the sincerity conditions determined by Ψ^*. Thus, an illocutionary act $[\Psi^*]F(P)$ is performed in a context of utterance i iff $F(P)$ is performed in that context and the speaker expresses in i all psychological states $\Psi^*(i, P)$. For example, the illocutionary force of a complaint $\parallel$ complain $\parallel = [\Psi_{dis}] \vdash$ for to complain that P is just to assert P while expressing dissatisfaction for the state of affairs represented by P. The sincerity conditions of a new illocutionary force $[\Psi^*]F$ are the closure of the union of the sincerity conditions of F and of the new sincerity conditions Ψ^*. Thus, $\Psi_{[\Psi^*]F}(i, P) = [\Psi_F(i, P) \cup \Psi^*(i, P)]$. If it is not possible to express sincerity conditions Ψ^* without presupposing additional preparatory conditions Σ or expressing a propositional content satisfying certain conditions θ, then the addition of sincerity conditions Ψ^* to an illocutionary force F also constitutes an addition of these preparatory and propositional content conditions. Thus the preparatory conditions of a new illocutionary force $[\Psi^*]F$ are the closure of the union of the preparatory conditions of F and of all new preparatory conditions determined by Ψ^*, and its propositional content conditions are the intersection of the propositional content conditions of F and of all propositional content conditions determined by Ψ^*. For example, since a speaker cannot meaningfully express dissatisfaction with a state of affairs unless he presupposes that this state of affairs is in some sense bad, the illocutionary force of a complaint also has the preparatory condition that the state of affairs represented by the propositional content is bad. Similarly since a speaker can express pride only in the existence of a state of affairs which he believes has something to do with him, the illocutionary force of boasting which is obtained from assertion by adding the sincerity condition $\Psi(i, P) = \{\text{pride } (P)\}$ also has the propositional content condition that the state of affairs represented by the propositional content has something to do with the speaker.

4) *The restriction of the mode of achievement of the illocutionary point* (Operation μ).

The mode of achievement of illocutionary point restricts the set of conditions under which the illocutionary point can be achieved. Sometimes differences in modes of achievement express increased restrictions on these conditions. Thus for example the mode of achievement of commands is more restricted than the mode of achievement of orders; in an order the speaker achieves the directive illocutionary point by invoking a position of power or of authority over the hearer, in a command he must achieve the directive illocutionary point by invoking a position of authority. On this account, an order made from a position of power without authority is not a command, but every command is an order. The mode of achievement of an illocutionary point Π is determined in illocutionary logic by a function μ from $I \times \text{Prop}$ into truth values that gives the truth as value, for a pair (i, P) iff the speaker a_i in the context i achieves or is committed to the illocutionary point Π on proposition P in a certain mode. For example, the function μ_{beg} that gives the truth value 1 for a pair (i, P) iff the speaker a_i in the context i attempts or is committed to attempting in a very polite or humble way to get the hearer b_i to do P, determines a special mode of achievement of the directive illocutionary point. Later we will define the mode of achievement of an act of begging with the help of this function. In case each time the illocutionary point of an act $F(P)$ is achieved in a mode μ_1 it is also achieved in a mode μ_2 (i.e. when $\mu_1(i, P) = 1$ entails $\mu_2(i, P) = 1$), we will say that the mode of achievement μ_1 is a *restriction* of the mode of achievement

μ_2. Under certain conditions, the operation of restricting the mode of achievement of illocutionary point of an illocutionary force F by imposing an additional mode of achievement μ generates a new illocutionary force $[\mu]F$ that differs from F only by the fact that an illocutionary act of form $[\mu]F(P)$ has the additional condition of success that the illocutionary point Π_F is also achieved on P in the mode μ. An illocutionary act $[\mu]F(P)$ is performed in a context i iff illocutionary act $F(P)$ is performed in that context and $\mu(i, P) = 1$. Thus, for example, the illocutionary force $\|\text{beg}\| = [\mu_{\text{beg}}]\downarrow$ is obtained from the illocutionary force of request by adding mode of achievement μ_{beg}, for to beg is to request very politely or humbly. The mode of achievement of a new illocutionary force $[\mu]F$ is the conjunction of the mode of achievement of F and of the new mode of achievement μ. Thus mode $([\mu]F)(i, P) = 1$ iff mode $(F)(i, P) = \mu(i, P) = 1$. Its preparatory conditions are the closure of the union of the preparatory conditions of F and of all preparatory conditions Σ that are determined by μ.

When it is not possible to achieve an illocutionary point in a certain mode without presupposing certain preparatory conditions, the operation of restricting the mode of achievement by imposing that mode will also constitute an addition of these preparatory conditions. Thus, for example, since it is not possible to direct the hearer with the mode of achievement of a command without presupposing that one has a position of authority, the illocutionary force of commands also has the preparatory condition that the speaker is in a position of authority. Finally, the degree of strength, degree $([\mu]F)$, is equal to degree (F) except when $|\mu| >$ degree (F). In that case, degree $([\mu]F) = |\mu|$. The operation of restricting the mode of achievement of an illocutionary force will increase the degree of strength of illocutionary point of that force when the additional mode of achievement requires a greater degree of strength. Because it is not possible for a speaker to achieve an illocutionary point with a zero degree of strength without also expressing the sincerity conditions with the same degree, the operation of restricting the mode of achievement of an illocutionary force F will also increase the degree of strength of the sincerity conditions when $|\mu| \geqslant 0 > \eta(F)$. In that case indeed $\eta([\mu]F) \geqslant 0$.

5) *The operations of increasing or decreasing the degrees of strength of the illocutionary point and of the sincerity conditions* (Operations (+) and (−)).

Some illocutionary forces differ from others in the degree of strength with which their illocutionary point is achieved and in the degree of strength with which their psychological state is expressed. Thus, for example, the difference between suggesting to someone that he do something and directing him to do it is a difference in the degree of strength of the illocutionary point and of the sincerity conditions. The operation of increasing by one the degrees of strength of an illocutionary force F (where such an increase is possible given the other components) generates a new illocutionary force $[+1]F$ that differs from F only by the facts that degree $([+1]F) = $ degree$(F) + 1$, and $\eta([+1]F) = \eta(F) + 1$ when degree$(F) = \eta(F)$. When degree $(F) > \eta(F)$, on the other hand, the new illocutionary force $[+1]F$ differs from F only by the fact that $\eta([+1]F) = \eta(F) + 1$.[5] The operation of decreasing by one the degrees of strength of an illocutionary force F (where such a decrease is possible) generates on the other hand an illocutionary force $[-1]F$ that is such that $[+1][-1]F = F$. Thus, for example, $\|$ suggest $\| = [-1]!$. To suggest to someone that he do something is to make a weak attempt to get him to do it. $\|$pledge$\| = [+1]\perp$. To pledge to do something is to commit oneself strongly to a certain future course of action. An illocutionary act of the form $[+1]F(P)$ has simply one condition of success more than an illocutionary act of the form $F(P)$, namely that the speaker achieves illocutionary point Π_F on P and/or expresses the sincerity conditions with a greater degree of strength. One can increase the degrees of strength of the illocutionary force named by a performative by adding certain modifiers to that performative, e.g. "my humblest apologies", "heartfelt congratulations!", or "deepest thanks" (notice incidentally that nobody ever says "my most arrogant apologies", "unfelt congratulations", or "superficial thanks"). All of these expressive cases derive greater strength from the greater intensity of the psychological state expressed (for expressives: degree $(F) = \eta(F)$). An illocu-

---

5 This restriction is justified by the fact that we want degree (F) to be the maximum of $\eta(F)$ and $|\text{mode }(F)|$

tionary act of form $[-1]F(P)$ has weaker conditions of success than illocutionary act $F(P)$, since the speaker need achieve illocutionary point Π_F or express the sincerity conditions Ψ_F with only the smaller degrees of strength degree $(F) - 1$ and $\eta(F) - 1$.

The operations on illocutionary forces are simple operations that usually affect only one component of illocutionary force and do not change the illocutionary point. All illocutionary forces that are obtained by the application of one operation to an illocutionary force keep the same illocutionary point as that force. As we pointed out earlier, not just any application of one operation on an illocutionary force generates a new illocutionary force. In order that a new force be obtained, certain general conditions must obtain. First, the additional mode of achievement, propositional content, preparatory, and sincerity conditions must be linguistically significant in the sense previously mentioned. Secondly, the nature of the different components of an illocutionary force limits the set of possible applications of these operations that generate a new force. Since the result of an application of an operation to force F_1 is force F_2 only if F_2 is possible, i.e. only if at least one illocutionary act of force F_2 is performable, the special mode of achievement, propositional content, preparatory, or sincerity conditions added to F_1 in an application of an operation must be consistent with the features already present in F_1. If, for example, mode of achievement μ is relatively inconsistent with the mode of achievement of F_1, i.e. if $\mu(i, P) \neq$ mode $(F_1)(i, P)$ then the operation of restricting the mode of achievement of F_1 by requiring the additional mode μ does not generate a new illocutionary force. Similarly if sincerity conditions Ψ are relatively inconsistent with the sincerity conditions of F_1, i.e. if it is not possible for a speaker to have simultaneously all the psychological states $\Psi(i, P) \cup \Psi_{F_1}(i, P)$, then the operation of adding sincerity conditions Ψ to F_1 does not generate a new illocutionary force; for illocutionary acts with relatively inconsistent sincerity conditions are self-defeating. Thirdly, since there are various logical relations that hold between the components of illocutionary forces (for example, certain sincerity conditions determine certain preparatory conditions), the application of one operation to force F_1 may change several components of F_1. Finally, all operations on illocutionary forces are recursive, i.e. their application can be reiterated indefinitely. Certain illocutionary forces F_2 are obtained from an illocutionary force F_1 by applying successively several operations: The illocutionary force of advice ‖ advise ‖ for example is obtained from the primitive directive ! by two successive applications of operation ($-$ 1) and operation (Σ). ‖ advise ‖ differs from ! only by the fact that, first, degree (‖ advise ‖) $= \eta$(‖ advise ‖) $=$ degree (!) $-$ 1; and, secondly, $\Sigma_{\parallel\text{advise}\parallel}(i, P) = [\Sigma_!(i, P) \cup \{$the state of affairs that P is good for $b_i\}]$. Thus if $\Sigma_*(i, P) = \{$the state of affairs that P is good for $b_i\}$, ‖ advise ‖ $= [\Sigma_*][-1]$!.

Notice that the illocutionary force $[-1]$! is named in English by the performative "suggest". But not all illocutionary forces have a corresponding illocutionary verb or illocutionary force indicating device in English. For example there is no English illocutionary verb or performative for the directive illocutionary force $[+1][\Sigma_*]$! of strong advice. "Urge" is the closest English verb, but, unlike "advise", "urge" does not necessarily imply that the action urged is presupposed to be in the hearer's interest.

Chapter 4

CONDITIONS OF SUCCESS OF ILLOCUTIONARY ACTS AND ILLOCUTIONARY COMMITMENTS

In this chapter we will give an inductive definition of the necessary and sufficient conditions for the successful performance of illocutionary acts and for illocutionary commitments. We will also state the axioms that determine the relation of illocutionary commitment between illocutionary acts.

I. DEFINITIONS OF THE SET OF ALL ILLOCUTIONARY ACTS AND OF THEIR CONDITIONS OF SUCCESS.

The set of illocutionary acts that we discuss in this book is the smallest set Act which (1) contains all elementary illocutionary acts of form $F(P)$ where $F \in \Phi$ and $P \in \text{Prop}$ and (2) contains all complex acts of form $(\mathscr{A}_1 \,\&\, \mathscr{A}_2)$, $\neg \mathscr{A}$ and $(P \Rightarrow \mathscr{A})$, when $\mathscr{A}$ $\mathscr{A}_1, \mathscr{A}_2$ belong to Act and $P \in \text{Prop}$. $(\mathscr{A}_1 \,\&\, \mathscr{A}_2)$ is the conjunctive illocutionary act which consists in performing both $\mathscr{A}_1$ and $\mathscr{A}_2$; $\neg \mathscr{A}$ is the illocutionary denegation of $\mathscr{A}$, and $(P \Rightarrow \mathscr{A})$ is the conditional illocutionary act which consists in performing $\mathscr{A}$ on the condition that P. If all operations on illocutionary acts can be reduced to conjunction, illocutionary negation, and the illocutionary conditional, then there are no other kinds of complex illocutionary acts than those listed above. The degree of complexity of an illocutionary act can be measured by the length of its formulation in canonical notation, i.e. by the number of occurrences of $\neg$, $\&$ and $\Rightarrow$ within its canonical representation. On this criterion, elementary illocutionary acts are the simplest as their length is zero.

Since illocutionary acts are expressed by speakers in the utterance of sentences there is a function φ^* from I into $\mathscr{P}(\text{Act})$ that gives as value, for each context of utterance i, the set $\varphi^*(i)$ of all illocutionary acts that the speaker a_i expresses in that context with the intention of performing them. A speaker expresses an illocutionary act with the intention of performing it in a context of utterance iff he utters in that context a sentence that expresses, whether literally or not, that act – or a stronger one – with respect to that context. Thus, for example, a speaker who utters seriously and literally the sentence: "Paris is the capital of France" or the corresponding performative sentence "I assert that Paris is the capital of France" expresses and *eo ipso* attempts to perform the act of asserting that Paris is the capital of France. The speaker may express a non-literal illocutionary act as when he says, for example, "You'd better do it" and means it as an order. In such indirect speech acts, the speaker relies on features of the conversational background that are part of the common knowledge of the speaker and hearer and on the principles of conversation to communicate to the hearer his intention to perform a non-literal act.

The expression of an illocutionary act is a necessary but not a sufficient condition for its successful performance. It is necessary because in order for a speaker to perform an illocutionary act he must utter a sentence (or produce some other symbolic device), whether he is speaking literally or nonliterally, which expresses that act – or a stronger one – relative to that context. But it is not sufficient, because a speaker might express an act and thus try to perform it, but fail, if for example he is not in a position to perform it.

The conditions of success of illocutionary acts are defined by induction in illocutionary logic, i.e. we first define the conditions of success of elementary acts and then the conditions of success of complex acts in terms of the conditions of success of their constituent parts. The definition of the conditions of success of an illocution $\mathscr{A}$ is thus an induction on the length of $\mathscr{A}$.

1) *Definition of the conditions of success of an illocutionary act.*

A speaker a_i *succeeds in performing an illocutionary act* $\mathscr{A}$ in a context of utterance i (for short: $\mathscr{A}(i) = 1$) iff his utterance satisfies the following conditions:

Basis: $\mathscr{A}$ is an elementary illocutionary act of the form $F(P)$.
An elementary illocutionary act of the form $F(P)$ is performed in a context of utterance i iff the speaker a_i in that context (1) succeeds

in achieving the illocutionary point of F on P with the characteristic mode of achievement and degree of strength of F, (2) performs the propositional act which consists in expressing P and P satisfies the propositional content conditions of F with respect to i, (3) presupposes that the preparatory conditions of $F(P)$ and the propositional presuppositions obtain, and, finally, (4) expresses the psychological states specified by the sincerity conditions of $F(P)$ with the characteristic degree of strength of sincerity conditions of F. Thus an elementary illocutionary act $F(P)$ is performed in i iff $i\Pi_F^{\text{degree}\,(F)}P$ and mode $(F)(i, P) = 1$; a_i expresses P in i and $P \in \text{Prop}_F(i)$; a_i presupposes in i all propositions $Q \in \Sigma_F(i, P) \cup \sigma(P)$; and a_i expresses in i with degree of strength $\eta(F)$ all psychological states $\Psi_F(i, P)$.

Induction step: $\mathscr{A}$ is a complex illocutionary act.

Case 1. $\mathscr{A}$ is a conjunction of the form $(\mathscr{A}_1 \,\&\, \mathscr{A}_2)$.
A conjunction of two illocutionary acts is performed in a context of utterance iff both conjuncts are performed in that context. Thus, $(\mathscr{A}_1 \,\&\, \mathscr{A}_2)$ is performed in context i iff $\mathscr{A}_1$ and $\mathscr{A}_2$ are performed in i. For example, a speaker performs the complex act expressed by the sentence "I apologize for what I have done and I promise not to do it again" in a context of utterance iff in that context he makes both the apology and the promise.

Case 2. $\mathscr{A}$ is an act of illocutionary denegation of the form $\neg\mathscr{A}'$.
An act of illocutionary denegation of the form $\neg\mathscr{A}'$ is performed in a context of utterance i iff the speaker in that context performs an act whose aim is to make explicit his non-performance of $\mathscr{A}'$. Using the relation of compatibility we can say he performs such an act iff he expresses in that context the denegation of act $\mathscr{A}'$ and as a result of his utterance all possible contexts that are compatible with the context of utterance are contexts where $\mathscr{A}'$ is not performed. Thus, $\neg\mathscr{A}'$ is performed at i iff $\neg\mathscr{A}' \in \varphi^*(i)$ and, for no $j \in I$ such that $i > j$, $\mathscr{A}'$ is performed at j. Indeed, if $\mathscr{A}'$ is performable and is not performed in any possible context that is compatible with the context of the utterance, then the speaker must have succeeded in performing in that context the denegation of $\mathscr{A}'$ if he has expressed that denegation. If $\mathscr{A}'$ is self-defeating, then it is both necessary and sufficient that a_i has expressed in i the

denegation of $\mathscr{A}'$ in order to have performed $\neg\mathscr{A}'$, since by definition no matter what happens in i, $\mathscr{A}'$ is not performed in any possible context of utterance $j \in I$.

Notice that this definition implies the following two laws which explain certain features of illocutionary denegation. First, the law of non-contradiction holds for illocutionary negation, that is to say any illocutionary act is relatively incompatible with its denegation since the relation of compatibility $>$ is reflexive.

Second, as we noted earlier, illocutionary negation is not success-functional, i.e. it is not the case that $\neg\mathscr{A}$ is performed at i iff $\mathscr{A}$ is not performed at i. From the fact that, for example, one does not promise that P it does not follow that one has explicitly refused to promise that P. A speaker might not have performed an illocutionary act in a context of utterance simply because he does not say anything in that context or because the act is self-defeating. But in order to make it explicit that he does not perform an illocution, he needs to do something, namely to express and perform a speech act that restricts the set of all possible contexts that are compatible with the context of his utterance. For example he might say "I do not promise."

Case 3: $\mathscr{A}$ is a conditional illocutionary act of the form $(P \Rightarrow \mathscr{A}')$.
A conditional illocutionary act of the form $(P \Rightarrow \mathscr{A}')$ is performed in a context of utterance iff the speaker in that context performs an act whose purpose is to perform act $\mathscr{A}'$ on the condition that P is true. Using the relation of compatibility we can say that a speaker performs such an act in a context of utterance i iff he expresses in that context that act with the intention of performing it, and as a result of his utterance all contexts of utterance that are compatible with i are contexts where $\mathscr{A}'$ is performed when P is true. Thus, $(P \Rightarrow \mathscr{A}')$ is performed at i iff $(P \Rightarrow \mathscr{A}') \in \varphi^*(i)$; and, for all $j \in I$, if P is true in w_j and $i > j$ then $\mathscr{A}'$ is performed at j.

Several general laws that explain features of conditional illocutionary acts follow from this definition. First, the conditional occurring in conditional acts is neither truth- nor success-functional. It is not the case that $(P \Rightarrow \mathscr{A}')$ is performed at i iff P is false in w_i or $\mathscr{A}'$ is performed at i. Thus if a speaker has performed a conditional speech act of the form $(P \Rightarrow \mathscr{A}')$, then he must actually have expressed a speech act of that form. It is not enough that the antecedent of the conditional P be false or that it be true that he has performed the speech act $\mathscr{A}'$ named in the consequent. Otherwise, every speaker would automatically have performed every speech act with an impossible antecedent; and every performance of a speech act would automatically be the performance of an infinite number of conditional speech acts. Secondly, conditional illocutionary acts obey the law of *modus ponens*. If a speaker performs a conditional illocutionary act of the form $(P \Rightarrow \mathscr{A}')$ and the antecedent P is true in the world of utterance, then he is committed to $\mathscr{A}'$. Thus, for example, a speaker who offers to do something for a hearer is committed to doing it if the hearer accepts the offer just as though he had promised it outright, since an offer is a promise that is conditional on acceptance by the hearer.

2) *Definition of a non-defective performance of an illocution.*

A non-defective performance is a successful performance in which all the propositional presuppositions and the preparatory and sincerity conditions are satisfied. Thus, an elementary illocution of the form $F(P)$ is *non-defectively performed* in a context of utterance i when $F(P)$ is performed in i, $\sigma(P) \cup \Sigma_F(i, P)/w_i/$ and for all $m(P) \in \Psi_F(i, P)$, ma_it_iP is true in w_i.

3) *Definitions of the relations of strong commitment and of strict equivalence.*

An illocutionary act $\mathscr{A}_1$ *strongly commits the speaker to* an illocutionary act $\mathscr{A}_2$ (for short $\mathscr{A}_1 \rhd \mathscr{A}_2$) iff it is not possible to perform the first without thereby performing the second. Thus, $\mathscr{A}_1 \rhd \mathscr{A}_2$ when, for all contexts $i \in I$, if $\mathscr{A}_1$ is performed at i, $\mathscr{A}_2$ is also performed at i. Two illocutionary acts $\mathscr{A}_1$, $\mathscr{A}_2$ are *strictly equivalent* (for short $\mathscr{A}_1 \equiv \mathscr{A}_2$) when they have both the same conditions of success, i.e. when $\mathscr{A}_1 \rhd \mathscr{A}_2$ and $\mathscr{A}_2 \rhd \mathscr{A}_1$. Thus for example a yes–no question of the form "Is Julius here?" is strictly equivalent to the request "Please tell me whether Julius is here!" because the question is just a request that the hearer perform such an assertion.

4) *Definitions of simultaneous performability and related notions.*

A set $\Gamma \subseteq$ Act of illocutionary acts is *simultaneously performed* in a context of utterance i iff for all $\mathscr{A} \in \Gamma$, $\mathscr{A}$ is performed at i. Γ is *simultaneously performable* when there is at least one possible context of utterance $i \in I$ where it is simultaneously performed. Two acts $\mathscr{A}_1$ and $\mathscr{A}_2$ are *relatively incompatible* (for short: $\mathscr{A}_1 > < \mathscr{A}_2$) when the set $\{\mathscr{A}_1, \mathscr{A}_2\}$ is not simultaneously performable. A *self-defeating* illocution is one that is relatively incompatible with itself.

5) *Definition of a failure to perform an illocutionary act.*

For the purposes of illocutionary logic we define *failure* not as non-performance but in terms of the distinction between utterance acts and illocutionary acts. When a speaker utters a sentence that expresses a certain act with the intention of performing it, he may fail because the other conditions necessary for successful performance are not met. Such cases of failure are of interest to illocutionary logic. In real life people also try and fail to perform speech acts for all sorts of other reasons which are irrelevant to illocutionary logic – e.g. laryngitis, deafness in the hearer, etc. In illocutionary logic we will say that a speaker fails to perform an illocutionary act when he utters a sentence which expresses that act with the intention of performing it, but the other conditions of success do not obtain. Thus, the law of excluded middle does not apply to success and failure as it applies to truth and falsity. Failure to perform an illocutionary act can be defined formally in terms of φ^* and its conditions of success as follows:

A speaker a_i *fails to perform the illocutionary act $\mathscr{A}$ in a context of utterance i* when $\mathscr{A} \in \varphi^*(i)$ but $\mathscr{A}$ is not performed in i.

Since, for each illocutionary act $\mathscr{A}$ and possible context of utterance i, three disjoint possibilities hold – (1) the speaker performs $\mathscr{A}$ in i or (2) he fails or (3) he neither succeeds nor fails, because he does not try – each illocutionary act $\mathscr{A}$ induces a function $|\mathscr{A}|$ from possible contexts of utterance into a set of three values $\{1, 2, 3\}$ representing respectively success, failure, and neither success nor failure. By definition, $|\mathscr{A}|_i = 1$ if $\mathscr{A}$ is performed at i, $|\mathscr{A}|_i = 2$ if the speaker fails to perform at i, and $|\mathscr{A}|_i = 3$ otherwise.

6) *Definition of the conditions of commitment to illocutionary acts.*

The conditions of commitment to illocutionary acts are also defined by induction in illocutionary logic. A speaker a_i *is committed to an illocutionary act* in a context of utterance i (for short: $\rhd \mathscr{A}$) under the following conditions:

Case 1. $\mathscr{A}$ is an elementary act of the form $F(P)$.

A speaker is committed to an elementary illocutionary act $F(P)$ in a context of utterance i iff in that context (1) he is committed to the illocutionary point Π_F on P with the mode of achievement and degree of strength of illocutionary point of F; (2) he is committed to presupposing the preparatory conditions $\Sigma_F(i, P)$ and the propositional presuppositions $\sigma(P)$; (3) he is committed to having the psychological states $\Psi_F(i, P)$ with the degree of strength of sincerity conditions of F; and, finally, (4) if P satisfies the propositional content conditions of F with respect to the context of utterance.

Case 2. $\mathscr{A}$ is a complex illocutionary act of the form $(\mathscr{A}_1 \,\&\, \mathscr{A}_2)$.
A speaker is committed to a conjunction of two illocutionary acts iff he is committed to both conjuncts. Thus $\rhd (\mathscr{A}_1 \,\&\, \mathscr{A}_2)$ iff both $\rhd \mathscr{A}_1$ and $\rhd \mathscr{A}_2$.

Case 3. $\mathscr{A}$ is an act of denegation of the form $\neg \mathscr{A}'$.
A speaker is committed to an act of illocutionary denegation of the form $\neg \mathscr{A}'$ iff he performs an illocutionary act that is relatively incompatible with $\mathscr{A}'$. Thus, $\rhd \neg \mathscr{A}'$ iff, for some $\mathscr{A}''$, $\mathscr{A}''$ is performed at i and the set $\{\mathscr{A}', \mathscr{A}''\}$ is not simultaneously performable. For example, a speaker who performs a denial that P is committed to the denegation of an assertion that P because a denial and an assertion of the same proposition cannot be successfully performed simultaneously.

Case 4. $\mathscr{A}$ is a conditional illocutionary act of the form $(P \Rightarrow \mathscr{A}')$.
A speaker is committed to a conditional illocutionary act of the form $(P \Rightarrow \mathscr{A}')$ iff he performs an illocutionary act that commits him to $\mathscr{A}'$ in case P is true. He performs such an act when and only

when he performs an illocution $\mathcal{A}''$ that it is not possible to perform in a context where P is true without being committed to $\mathcal{A}'$. Thus $\triangleright (P \Rightarrow \mathcal{A}')$ iff, for some $\mathcal{A}''$, $\mathcal{A}''$ is performed at i and, for all $j \in I$, if $\mathcal{A}''$ is performed at j and P is true in w_j, then $\triangleright \mathcal{A}'$.

7) *Definition of a non-empty context.*

We shall hereafter call a context of utterance i in which the speaker a_i has at least one illocutionary commitment to an illocutionary act a *non-empty* context of utterance. In symbols: $\triangle$.

8) *Definition of illocutionary consistency.*

A set of illocutionary acts $\Gamma \subseteq \mathrm{Act}$ is said to be *consistent* iff there is at least one possible context of utterance $i \in I$ where the speaker is committed to all acts $\mathcal{A} \in \Gamma$. Otherwise it is *inconsistent*. An illocutionary act $\mathcal{A}$ is *consistent* iff the set $\{\mathcal{A}\}$ is consistent; otherwise it is *inconsistent*.

9) *Definition of the relation of illocutionary commitment between illocutionary acts.*

An illocutionary act $\mathcal{A}_1$ commits the speaker to an illocution $\mathcal{A}_2$ (for short: $\mathcal{A}_1 \triangleright \mathcal{A}_2$) iff it is not possible for a speaker to perform $\mathcal{A}_1$ without being committed to $\mathcal{A}_2$. Thus, $\mathcal{A}_1 \triangleright \mathcal{A}_2$ iff for all $i \in I$, if $\mathcal{A}_1$ is performed at i then the speaker is committed to $\mathcal{A}_2$ in i.

A conjunction of two illocutionary acts, for example, commits the speaker to both conjuncts. Similarly, any illocutionary act $\mathcal{A}$ commits the speaker to the denegation of its denegation $\neg \neg \mathcal{A}$ – e.g. "I promise" – commits the speaker to "I'm not saying that I do not promise."

10) *Definition of illocutionary congruence.*

The introduction of the notion of illocutionary commitment enables us to define the notion of illocutionary congruence. Intuitively the idea of illocutionary congruence is that two illocutionary acts are *congruent* iff each commits the speaker to the other. Illocutionarily congruent acts have in this sense the same illocutionary value. Thus two illocutionary acts $\mathscr{A}_1$ and $\mathscr{A}_2$ are congruent (for short: $\mathscr{A}_1 \simeq \mathscr{A}_2$) iff both $\mathscr{A}_1 \rhd \mathscr{A}_2$ and $\mathscr{A}_2 \rhd \mathscr{A}_1$. Illocutionary congruence is an equivalence relation ($\simeq$ is at the same time reflexive, symmetric, and transitive). Two examples of congruent illocutionary acts are: First, an assertion of a conjunction of two propositions is congruent with a conjunction of two assertions of the conjuncts, i.e. $\vdash (P \,\&\, Q) \simeq (\vdash (P) \,\&\, \vdash (Q))$; and, secondly an illocutionary act that is conditional on the truth of a disjunction $((P_1 \lor P_2) \Rightarrow \mathscr{A})$ is congruent with a conjunction of two illocutionary acts conditional on the truth of each disjunct $(P_1 \Rightarrow \mathscr{A}) \,\&\, (P_2 \Rightarrow \mathscr{A})$.

II. SOME AXIOMS GOVERNING ILLOCUTIONARY COMMITMENT AND STRICT EQUIVALENCE.

A primary task of illocutionary logic is to characterize the formal properties of the relations of strong and weak illocutionary commitment between illocutions. Here are the axioms that characterize these relations.

1. *The law of transitivity of illocutionary commitment.*

If $\mathscr{A}_1 \rhd \mathscr{A}_2$ and $\mathscr{A}_2 \rhd \mathscr{A}_3$ then $\mathscr{A}_1 \rhd \mathscr{A}_3$.

The set of all successful illocutionary commitments of a speaker is transitive, i.e. a speaker is committed to all illocutions to which the illocutionary acts to which he is committed commit him.

By the transitivity of $\rhd$, any two illocutionarily congruent illocutionary acts commit the speaker to the same acts. This explains why their performances have the same illocutionary value.

2. *The law of identity for illocutionary forces.*

For any two illocutionary forces F_1, F_2, $F_1 = F_2$ iff, for all propositions P, $F_1(P) \equiv F_2(P)$.

If two illocutionary forces F_1, F_2 are such that all acts of form $F_1(P)$, $F_2(P)$ have the same conditions of success, those two illocutionary forces are identical and consequently have the same components.

There is a correlation between the components of illocutionary force, the conditions of success of illocutionary acts, and the linguistic purposes served by types of illocutionary acts. Different components would determine different conditions of successful performance and would serve different linguistic purposes. Strict equivalence therefore provides a criterion of identity for illocutionary forces. This law is similar to an axiom of extensionality for illocutionary forces.

3. *The law of propositional identity.*

For all propositions P_1, $P_2 \in \text{Prop}$, $P_1 = P_2$ iff for all F, $F(P_1) \equiv F(P_2)$.

If two propositions P, Q are such that it is not possible for a speaker, for any illocutionary force F, to perform an illocution of the form $F(P)$ without also performing an illocution of the form $F(Q)$ and conversely, then $P = Q$. Illocutionary interchangeability is thus a necessary and sufficient condition of identity for propositions. It entails necessary equivalence. This conception of propositional identity relates the two notions of force and of propositional content. A difference at the level of content between two propositions must be reflected in a difference of use at the illocutionary level.

4. *The law of identity for elementary illocutionary acts.*

If $F_1(P_1) \equiv F_2(P_2)$ then $F_1(P_1) = F_2(P_2)$ when $F_1(P_1)$ is performable.

Performable elementary illocutionary acts with the same conditions of success are identical. Strict equivalence also provides us with a criterion of identity for illocutionary acts that are performable. Different performable illocutionary acts must be performed under different conditions. This law of identity is not valid for illocutionary acts in general in our logic because not all self-defeating elementary illocutionary acts are identical. Consider, for example, the two self-defeating speech acts "I declare that henceforth squares be circles" and "I assert that I never make assertions." They are not identical although the sets of context of utterance where they are performed are both identical with the empty set.

For performable elementary illocutionary acts, on the other hand, strict equivalence amounts to identity because if there is any difference in logical form between two performable illocutionary acts this difference must be reflected in their conditions of success.

5. *Laws of identity for complex illocutionary acts.*

$\neg \mathscr{A}_1 = \neg \mathscr{A}_2$ iff $\mathscr{A}_1 = \mathscr{A}_2$, $(P_1 \Rightarrow \mathscr{A}_1) = (P_2 \Rightarrow \mathscr{A}_2)$ iff $P_1 = P_2$ and $\mathscr{A}_1 = \mathscr{A}_2$ and $(\mathscr{A}_1 \& \mathscr{A}_2) = (\mathscr{A}_3 \& \mathscr{A}_4)$ when $\{\mathscr{A}_1, \mathscr{A}_2\} = \{\mathscr{A}_3, \mathscr{A}_4\}$.

Complex illocutionary acts are identical iff they have the same components. Thus, two acts of illocutionary denegation are identical iff they are denegations of the same act. Two conditional illocutionary acts are identical if they consist in performing the same act under the same conditions. Finally, two conjunctions of illocutionary acts are identical iff the sets of their conjuncts are identical.

Definition of a strong speech act.

Certain illocutionary acts performed in a context of utterance are such that they commit the speaker to all the illocutionary acts to which he is committed in that context. We shall hereafter call such illocutionary acts the *strong illocutions* performed in that context. In any real-life context these would normally be conjunctions of speech acts since an elementary speech act would not normally be sufficient to commit the speaker to all the illocutions he is committed to in that context. Thus an illocutionary act $\mathscr{A}$ is a strong illocutionary act performed in i [for short: $\mathscr{A} \triangleright$] iff $\mathscr{A}$ is performed at i and for all $\mathscr{A}'$ such that $\triangleright \mathscr{A}'$, $\mathscr{A} \triangleright \mathscr{A}'$. On this definition, a strong illocutionary act in a context i is an act which is successfully performed in i and can be taken as the starting point of all chains of illocutionary commitments of the speaker a_i in i. By a *chain of illocutionary commitments* of a speaker a_i in a context i we mean a set Γ of illocutionary acts to which a_i is committed in i that is totally ordered by the relation $\triangleright$ of illocutionary commitment. Thus, for any pair of illocutionary acts $\mathscr{A}_1$, $\mathscr{A}_2 \in \Gamma$, both $\triangleright \mathscr{A}_1$ and $\triangleright \mathscr{A}_2$ and either $\mathscr{A}_1 \triangleright \mathscr{A}_2$ or $\mathscr{A}_2 \triangleright \mathscr{A}_1$.

6. *The law of foundation.*

If the context of utterance i is non-empty then for some $\mathscr{A}^*$, $\mathscr{A}^* \rhd$ and for all $\mathscr{A}$, if $\mathscr{A} \rhd$ then $\mathscr{A}^* \simeq \mathscr{A}$.

There is at least one strong illocutionary act that is performed in each context of utterance where a speaker has a successful illocutionary commitment, and this strong illocutionary act is unique modulo illocutionary congruence (i.e. it is unique if we treat all illocutionarily congruent acts performed in that context as identical). Axiom 6 is a law of foundation for $\rhd$ because it states that all chains of successful illocutionary commitments of a speaker a_i in a context of utterance i have a starting point. That is to say: there is no infinitely descending chain of successful illocutionary commitments to non-congruent illocutionary acts of form $\mathscr{A}_1$, $\mathscr{A}_2, \mathscr{A}_3, \ldots, \mathscr{A}_k, \ldots$ which is such that for each k, $\mathscr{A}_{k+1} \rhd \mathscr{A}_k$. Moreover, all chains of illocutionary commitments of a speaker in a context of utterance have a *common* starting point which is *unique* modulo illocutionary congruence. Intuitively, the idea of a strong illocutionary act is reasonably clear. The strong illocutionary act in a context of utterance, when the utterance is successful and literal, is the speech act expressed by the sentence used by the speaker in that context. In case the speaker utters a series of sentences, we will construe the series as a conjunction.

7. *The operations on illocutionary forces preserve strict equivalence.*

If $F_1(P) \equiv F_1(Q)$ and F_2 is obtained from F_1 by applying one operation on illocutionary forces, then $F_2(P) \equiv F_2(Q)$. Thus, if $F(P) \equiv F(Q)$ then $[-1]F(P) \equiv [-1]F(Q)$, $[+1]F(P) \equiv [+1]F(Q)$, $[\theta]F(P) \equiv [\theta]F(Q)$, $[\mu]F(P) \equiv [\mu]F(Q)$, $[\Sigma]F(P) \equiv [\Sigma]F(Q)$, and $[\Psi]F(P) \equiv [\Psi]F(Q)$.

Strict equivalence is thus a weak relation of identity between illocutionary acts.

The law of propositional identity together with axiom 6 entail that two propositions P and Q are identical iff, for the primitive forces F, the elementary acts $F(P)$ and $F(Q)$ are equivalent. Illocutionary interchangeability within illocutionary acts with a primitive force is thus a necessary and sufficient condition for propositional identity in illocutionary logic.

The seven preceding axioms are the only proper axioms of illocutionary logic. We prefer to use the term "postulate" for the various clauses that state laws for the components of illocutionary force such as the transitivity of degree of strength. Axiom 1 states an essential property of illocutionary commitment, namely transitivity. Axioms 2–5 state laws of identity for the basic entities of the theory, namely illocutionary forces, propositional contents and illocutionary acts. The axiom of foundation states that all chains of illocutionary commitments of a speaker have a common unique starting point. Finally, axiom 7 imposes restrictions on the nature of components of illocutionary force. In a forthcoming book on the semantics of speech acts, D. Vanderveken develops a model–theoretical semantics for languages with illocutionary force indicating devices and illocutionary connectives where all these axioms are valid.

Chapter 5

ON THE LOGICAL FORM OF THE VARIOUS COMPONENTS OF ILLOCUTIONARY FORCE

The first aim of this chapter is to explain further four features of illocutionary forces: illocutionary point, direction of fit, degree of strength, and sincerity conditions. The second aim is to state various postulates governing these notions that will explain many of the logical relations between speech acts.

I. ILLOCUTIONARY POINT.

The most important component of illocutionary force and indeed the one which forms the basis of our analysis is *illocutionary point*. As we said earlier, illocutionary point is the internal point or purpose of a type of illocution. Illocutionary point always determines direction of fit; that is the illocutionary point determines how the propositional content is presented as relating to the world of utterance. For example, the fact that the propositional content of an assertion is supposed to match the world of the utterance is a consequence of the fact that the illocutionary point of an assertion is to say how things are. Assertions therefore have the word-to-world direction of fit. In the case of a pledge, on the other hand, the speaker's subsequent behavior is supposed to match the propositional content of his pledge. And this is a consequence of the fact that the illocutionary point of a pledge is to commit the speaker to a future course of action. Pledges therefore have the world-to-word direction of fit.

For logical purposes, it is important to note that different types of illocutions are often logically related by their illocutionary point. Consider, for example, the relation between a promise by a speaker to do act A and an assertion by that speaker that he will not do A. These two illocutions are incompatible – that is, they cannot both be successfully performed at the same time because there is an assertive commitment in the achievement of the commissive illocutionary point. Similarly, a declaration commits the speaker to an assertion with the same propositional content because there is an assertive commitment in the achievement of the declarative point. Many cases of illocutionary commitment or of relative incompatibility between illocutions are due to properties of their illocutionary point. The following postulates concerning illocutionary points explain some general features of illocutionary commitment and relative incompatibility between speech acts.

1. *The law of restricted compatibility of strict implication with respect to illocutionary point.*

In certain (but not all) cases where a propositional content P strictly implies a proposition Q, a speaker who achieves an illocutionary point Π on proposition P is thereby committed to the same point on Q. For example, a speaker who makes an attempt to get the hearer to carry out the future course of action represented by a conjunction $P \& Q$ is committed to attempting to get him to carry out the courses of action represented by both conjuncts P and Q. This compatibility of strict implication with respect to illocutionary point is restricted. For example, although any proposition P strictly implies the disjunction $P \lor Q$, it is not the case that any attempt by a speaker to get the hearer to carry out the future course of action represented by a proposition P will commit him to attempting to get the hearer to carry out the disjunctive course of action represented by $(P \lor Q)$ for any proposition Q.

This law can be stated as follows:

If a speaker achieves in a context of utterance i with a degree of strength k an illocutionary point Π on a proposition P and that proposition strictly implies another proposition Q then he is committed with the same degree of strength k to Π on Q in those cases and only those cases where the satisfaction of the propositional content and sincerity conditions determined by Π is preserved. Thus if P strictly implies Q then $\{i/i\Pi^k P\} \subseteq \{i/i\Pi^k Q\}$ iff 1) for all propositional content conditions θ determined by Π, $P \in \theta(i)$ only if $Q \in \theta(i)$, and 2) for all sincerity conditions Ψ determined by Π, $\Psi(i, P) \rhd \Psi(i, Q)$.

Thus, for example, in making an attempt to get a hearer to carry out the future course of action represented by a conjunction a speaker necessarily also attempts to get him to carry out the future courses of action represented by both conjuncts – because if a conjunction represents a future course of action of a hearer in a context of utterance so do the conjuncts and also because if a speaker desires that $(P \& Q)$ he is committed to desiring both P and Q. This is a strong illocutionary commitment (i.e. $i\Pi_3^k (P \& Q)$ entails $i\Pi_3^k P$) because of the strong propositional attitude commitment (a desire that $P \& Q$ contains a desire that P).

A speaker who achieves the illocutionary point Π on the proposition P is thereby only weakly committed to that point on Q if the following conditions hold: $P \dashv Q$ is true, Q satisfies the propositional content conditions determined by Π when P does, and the psychological states $\Psi(i, P)$ expressed in the achievement of Π on P weakly commit the speaker to the psychological states $\Psi(i, Q)$ expressed in the achievement of Π on Q but their possession does not involve the possession of psychological states $\Psi(i, Q)$. Thus for example a speaker who makes an attempt to get a hearer to carry out the future course of action represented by $P \& (P \to Q)$ is weakly committed to attempting to get him to carry out the future action represented by Q, because if a speaker desires that $P \& (P \to Q)$ he is committed to desiring Q, but he need not actually possess that desire.

The law of restricted compatibility of strict implication explains why the law of compatibility of strict implication with respect to illocutionary commitment fails. If $P \dashv Q$ is true, it is not necessarily the case that $F(P) \rhd F(Q)$ because in some cases $\Psi_F(i, P) \not\rhd \Psi_F(i, Q)$ and $P \in \mathrm{Prop}_F(i)$ does not entail $Q \in \mathrm{Prop}_F(i)$. It thus connects the laws of distribution of illocutionary points with the laws of distribution of their propositional content and sincerity conditions. For example, a speaker who makes an attempt to get the hearer to carry out a future course of action will not be committed to attempting to get him to carry out the disjunctive course of action represented by a proposition of form $P \vee Q$, although P strictly implies $P \vee Q$. This is because, first, if Q does not represent a future course of action of the hearer, $P \vee Q$ does not satisfy the propositional content conditions of a directive; and second because it is sometimes possible for a speaker to express a desire for P without being committed to having a desire for $(P \vee Q)$ when, for example, he does not want it to be the case that Q.

According to the law of restricted compatibility of strict implication with respect to illocutionary point, there is a strong parallelism between illocutionary commitment and propositional attitude commitment. We will now generalize that law in order to define under which conditions a speaker is committed to an illocutionary point.

A speaker is committed with the degree of strength k to an illocutionary point Π on a proposition Q in a context i (for short: $i\widehat{\Pi}^k Q$) iff in that context he achieves that illocutionary point or a stronger one Π' with that degree on a proposition P that strictly implies Q, and Q satisfies the propositional content conditions determined by Π if P satisfies those determined by Π' and the psychological states expressed in the achievement of Π' on P commit the speaker to those determined by Π about Q. Thus $i\widehat{\Pi}^k Q$ iff for some Π', $i\Pi'^k P$, $P \dashv Q$ is true, and the intersections θ, θ' of all propositional content conditions determined respectively by Π', Π, and the unions Ψ', Ψ of all sincerity conditions determined respectively by Π', Π, are such that if $P \in \theta'(j)$ then $Q \in \theta(j)$ and $\Psi'(i, P) \rhd \Psi(i, Q)$.

Thus, for example, a speaker who commits himself to doing something is committed to the assertion that it is possible for him to do it, because if a speaker expresses an intention to do something, he is committed to believing that it is possible for him to do it, and because the assertive point does not determine any propositional content conditions.

Later in this chapter we will formulate some hypotheses concerning psychological states that imply laws of introduction and elimination of logical constants in illocutionary points.

2. *The non-deniability of preparatory conditions.*

A speaker cannot simultaneously presuppose and deny that a proposition P is true in the world of its utterance.

Thus, if P is presupposed by a speaker in a context of utterance i then it is not the case that he achieves the assertive illocutionary point Π_1 on $\sim P$ in that context. To represent a state of affairs as nonexistent is to make an overt commitment to the negation of the proposition that represents that state of affairs. Presuppositions are also commitments, although unlike assertions they are not overt commitments. This is the reason why it is not possible for a speaker to presuppose that a proposition P is true in the world of the utterance and to succeed at the same time in representing as not actual the state of affairs that P represents. In consequence an illocutionary act $F(P)$ and an assertive illocution whose propositional content is that some preparatory conditions of $F(P)$ do not hold are relatively incompatible. This explains why utterances of sentences of the form "I command you to do this and I have no authority to give you such a command" or "I promise to do this but I am absolutely unable to do it" are self-defeating.

3. *The non-deniability of the sincerity conditions.*

A speaker cannot simultaneously express a psychological state and deny that he has that state. Thus, if he expresses a psychological state $m(P)$ in a context i then it is not the case that he achieves the assertive point on proposition $\sim ma_i t_i P$ in that context. To express a psychological state is to commit oneself to having that state and this commitment implies a commitment to the truth of the proposition that one has that psychological state. This postulate explains Moore's paradox. An illocutionary act $F(P)$ and an assertive illocution whose propositional content is that a sincerity condition of $F(P)$ does not hold are relatively incompatible. Thus for example one cannot say: "I promise to do A and I do not intend to do it."

4. *The existence of an assertive commitment in the achievement of the commissive and of the declarative illocutionary points.*

A speaker who commits himself to performing a future course of action A is committed to the assertive that he will perform A, and a speaker who makes a declaration that P is committed to the assertive that P.

Why? In the case of commissives, the commitment to the performance necessarily involves a commitment to the truth of the proposition that he will so perform. There is no way, for example, that a speaker can consistently make a promise and deny that he will carry it out because his commitment to carry out a future action commits him to having the belief that he will carry it out. A speaker who commits himself to doing something cannot be sincere without believing that he will keep his commitment. Furthermore the making of the promise necessarily creates a reason for the speaker to perform the action and thus creates a *prima facie* reason for his believing that he will do it. In the case of the declaration that P, the speaker brings about the state of affairs that P by representing it as being brought about and thus he represents that state of affairs as actual in the world of the utterance. It is not possible, for example, that a speaker can consistently declare the meeting adjourned and deny that the meeting is adjourned. Furthermore, since his action makes it the case that P, he has a good reason for believing that P. A speaker who sincerely declares that P must believe that P, because the belief that he brings about the state of affairs represented by the propositional content contains the belief that this state of affairs obtains.

5. *The impossibility of achieving the directive point on a contradiction P & $\sim P$.*

A rational speaker might desire with respect to one set of reasons that his hearer perform a certain action, and with respect to another set of reasons that he does not perform it. But even though such conflicting desires are possible, a speaker cannot succeed in issuing a directive to a hearer both to perform and not to perform the same action. The reason for this is that a directive by definition is an attempt to get a hearer to do something and a speaker cannot coherently attempt to get a hearer to do something that he knows to be impossible.

II. DIRECTION OF FIT.

In Chapter 3, we briefly introduced the notion of direction of fit, and in this section we will attempt to explain it more fully. Some illocutions, as part of their illocutionary point, have the aim of getting their propositional content to match the world of the utterance, others to get the world of the utterance to match their propositional content. For example, if I make the prediction that you will leave the room, then it is a consequence of the illocutionary point of my prediction that the propositional content is supposed to match an independently existing reality. If you leave the room my prediction is said to be true, if you fail to leave the room it is said to be false. If on the other hand I order you to leave the room, then it is part of the illocutionary point of my order to get you to act in such a way as to match your behavior to the propositional content of the order. If you do leave the room by way of carrying out the order, the order is not said to be true, but rather to have been obeyed, and if you fail to leave the room the order is not said to be false, but rather to have been disobeyed.

When the illocutionary point of the utterance is to get the propositional content to match the world of the utterance, as with the assertive illocutions, we say that the utterance has the *word-to-world direction of fit*. The words "true" and "false" are the most common terms in English for assessing success in achieving the word-to-world direction of fit. When the illocutionary point of the utterance is to get the world of the utterance to match the propositional content, as with directives and commissives, we will say that the utterance has the *world-to-word direction of fit*. Some words in English used to assess success in achieving the world-to-word direction of fit are: "obeyed", "disobeyed", "complied with", "kept", "fulfilled", and "broken" (as in "broken promise"). For both directions of fit the criterion of success of direction of fit between the propositional content P of an illocution and the world of utterance w is that P is true in w. The relation of fit is, of course, symmetrical: If the proposition fits the world then the world fits the proposition; but it is still essential in illocutionary logic to distinguish the two directions of fit, because an essential part of the illocutionary point in each of the cases is to achieve the fit from different directions. If the illocution has the word-to-world direction of fit, the success of fit is due to the fact that the world of the utterance is as the speaker says it is. He has correctly represented an independently existing state of affairs. In the world-to-word direction of fit, the success is due to the fact that one of the protagonists of the utterance, the speaker or the hearer, has changed the world by acting in such a way as to bring about a fit between his action and the propositional content of the illocution. Intuitively the idea of the direction of fit of an utterance can be clarified by pointing out that if the propositional content fails to match reality, one side or the other is at fault. If my statement fails to match reality, it is my statement and not reality that is at fault.

Statements can be said to be true or false, and statements and other members of the assertive class are said to have the word-to-world direction of fit. But if my order is disobeyed or my promise is not carried out, it is not my order or promise which is at fault but rather reality in the person of the hearer who disobeyed the order or myself who failed to carry out the promise. Such utterances are said to have the world-to-word direction of fit. Exactly analogous distinctions can be made for psychological states such as beliefs, intentions, and desires. Beliefs have the mind-to-world direction of fit, desires and intentions have the world-to-mind direction of fit. In general, the direction of fit of an illocution is the same as that of its expressed psychological state – though some expressives are exceptions to this principle. Expressive illocutionary acts have no direction of fit but some are expressions of beliefs and desires both of which have a direction of fit. This point will be explained in more detail later.

We can summarize the relations between illocutionary forces and directions of fit as follows:

(i) Assertive illocutionary forces have the word-to-world direction of fit↓. The point of an assertive illocution is to represent how the world is.

(ii) Commissive and directive illocutionary forces have the world-to-word direction of fit↑. It is a consequence of the illocutionary point of the commissive/directive illocutions that they create reasons for the speaker/hearer to change the world by acting in such a way as to bring about success in achieving direction of fit.

(iii) Expressive illocutionary forces have the null or empty direction of fit. Nearly all of the words in English which name expressive illocutionary acts (e.g. apologize, congratulate, thank) name illocutions which are expressions of psychological states which have no direction of fit. In each case the psychological state contains a belief, and a desire; the belief has the mind-to-world direction of fit and the desire has the world-to-mind direction of fit, but the point of the speech act is not to express that belief and desire but rather to express the state of sorrow, pleasure, gratitude, etc., which presupposes the truth of that belief and involves an expression of that desire. In such cases the truth of the proposition is presupposed and there is no direction of fit of the complex psychological state in addition to the direction of fit of the belief and desire. The exceptions to the principle that the directions of fit of the illocutionary point and of the sincerity condition are identical are cases where the illocutionary point of the expressive is to express a psychological state which has a direction of fit, even though the expressive speech act itself has no direction of fit. For example some speech acts are simply expressions of desire or belief. Consider the English sentence "If only John would come!" or a sentence in the old optative mood "Would that John came." Utterances of such sentences function as expressions of desires, and they are therefore expressives, but they are exceptions to the general rule that the directions of fit of the illocutionary point and of the sincerity conditions are identical, since each of these expresses a psychological state with a world-to-mind direction of fit even though the point of the utterance is not to bring about success of fit. Similarly, when a church congregation recites the Apostles' Creed ("I believe in God the Father Almighty . . ."), the illocutionary point of this utterance is to express their common faith, even though in this case, unlike the case of desire, there is no special syntactical device for this purpose, and the expression is done as an indirect speech act performed by way of making an assertion to the effect that they do so believe.

(iv) Declarations have both directions of fit simultaneously, because the point of a declaration is to bring about a change in the world by representing the world as so changed. These are not two independent directions of fit, but one illocutionary point that achieves both. The double direction of fit peculiar to declarations$\updownarrow$ is not to be confused with both directions of fit independently construed ($\updownarrow \neq \downarrow \& \uparrow$).

As we noticed in Chapter 3, the fact that there are four and only four directions of fit, with two possible agents for achieving the world-to-word direction of fit, either speaker or hearer, provides us with a rationale for the view that there are five and only five illocutionary points.

In light of these facts we can define the success and failure of fit of an illocution as follows:

We shall say that an illocution $F(P)$ with a non-empty direction of fit performed in a context of utterance *has success (or failure) of fit* iff the propositional content P is true (or false) in the world of the utterance. The notions of success and of failure of fit are thus derived notions of illocutionary logic. They are connected with a family of derived *properties* of illocutions such as the properties of being a true or false assertive illocution, the properties of being a kept or broken promise, and the properties of being an obeyed or disobeyed order.

When the propositional presuppositions are false we will say there is a failure of fit. This enables us to continue to use the principle of bivalence for success and failure of fit and is in accord with our treatment of propositional presupposition failure in Chapter 2. This is strictly for logical convenience. An alternative method would have been to treat presupposition failure (à la Frege–Strawson) in such a way that propositions suffering from such failures are neither true nor false and illocutionary acts containing such propositions have neither success nor failure of fit.

(i) *True or false assertive illocutions.*

In both ordinary speech and philosophical contexts there are at least two uses of the notions of truth and of falsity. We speak of true and false propositions, independently of whether or not the proposition has been asserted, and also of true or false assertive illocutions – statements, conjectures, etc. These two uses are necessarily connected. Propositions by definition are true in certain worlds and false in others; true or false illocutions are simply assertives with true or false propositional contents. Though etymologically the use of "true" with assertives would appear to be primary, logically speaking its use with propositions is primary, for a true assertive illocutionary act is an illocutionary act whose propositional content is true in the world of the utterance. There is no way to explain what a statement is without explaining what a proposition is, and there is no way to explain what a proposition is without explaining what a true proposition is. Thus there is no way to explain what a statement is without explaining what a true statement is, and there are analogous internal relations between the notion of an order and the notion of obedience to an order, the notion of a promise and the notion of keeping a promise, etc.

(ii) *Kept or broken commissive illocutions.*

A commissive illocutionary act is kept iff the speaker makes its propositional content true by carrying out the future course of action that it represents; otherwise it is broken.

(iii) *Fulfilled or unfulfilled directive illocutions.*

A directive illocutionary act is fulfilled iff the hearer makes its propositional content true by carrying out the future course of action that it represents.

Usually one says of a fulfilled (or unfulfilled) directive illocution with a mode of achievement that leaves an option of refusal to the hearer that it is *granted* (or refused), and of a fulfilled (or unfulfilled) directive illocution with a mode of achievement that does not leave any option of refusal to the hearer that it is *obeyed* (or disobeyed).

The notions of obeying an order or keeping a promise, however, have one further important formal difference from the notion of the truth of a statement. A statement is true if the propositional content is successful in word-to-world direction of fit no matter how that success of fit came about, but in the full sense an order is obeyed or a promise kept only if the agent brings about the successful world-to-word direction of fit *by way of* obeying the order or keeping the promise. In the full sense the agent obeys the order or keeps the promise only if he acts *because of* the order or promise, and in this sense the conditions of success of fit of orders and promises are self-referential, since they require that the success of the direction of fit be achieved *in order to* satisfy the order or the promise. To put the point precisely: the propositional content conditions of an order are that the hearer perform a future course of action *by way of* obeying the order and the propositional content conditions of a promise are that the speaker perform a future course of action *by way of* keeping the promise.

As an argument for these points, notice that if I am given the order to leave the room I might respond by saying that I was going to leave the room anyhow but was not doing so in obedience to the order. In such a case I perform the future course of action, but do not strictly speaking obey the order. After a sequence of such cases I could not, for example, be described as an obedient person.

Similarly if I promise to come and see you on Wednesday and then forget all about the promise, but on Wednesday I show up on your doorstep to borrow some money, I have not strictly speaking kept my promise, though I have carried out the future course of action promised.

(iv) *Successful or unsuccessful declarations.*

Since the *successful* performance of a declaration brings about the truth of its propositional content, a successful declaration always has success of fit. For commissives, directives, and declarations, unlike assertives, the achievement of success of fit always involves the speech act itself in the achievement of success of fit. However, to incorporate this point into illocutionary logic complicates the formalism enormously. Therefore for the sake of simplicity we will continue to treat orders as obeyed iff the hearer performs the act he is ordered to perform, promises as kept iff the speaker performs the act he promised to perform, etc.

Using this simplifying assumption we can then define the conditions of success and failure of fit of an illocution of the form $F(P)$ as follows:

(1) Illocutionary act $F(P)$ has *success of fit* in context i iff $F(P)$ is performed at i and P is true in w_i.

(2) Illocutionary act $F(P)$ has *failure of fit* in context i iff $F(P)$ is performed at i and P is false in w_i.

Thus, when $\Pi_F = \Pi_1$, $F(P)$ is performed at i and P is true in w_i, a *true* assertive illocution $F(P)$ is performed at i. When $\Pi_F = \Pi_2$, $F(P)$ is performed at i and P is true in w_i, a *kept* commissive illocution $F(P)$ has been made in context i. When $\Pi_F = \Pi_3$, $F(P)$ is performed at i and P is true in w_i, the directive illocution $F(P)$ performed at i has been *fulfilled*.

III. DEGREE OF STRENGTH.

Most illocutionary points can be achieved with different degrees of strength in the world of utterance. As a consequence of this, degree of strength is another component of illocutionary force. Since there are various sources of difference in the degree of strength of the illocutionary point, it is difficult to get a realistic ordering of degrees of strength of illocutionary point of the forces expressed by actual English illocutionary verbs. However there is a clear intuitive difference within, for example, the directive illocutionary forces between the strength of illocutionary point expressed by such strong verbs as "order", "command", and "insist", and the strength of illocutionary point of the forces named by such weak verbs as "suggest", "advise" and "recommend", and somewhere between these two classes lie forces expressed by such intermediate verbs as "ask" and "request". With some idealization therefore we will group the illocutionary forces named by most assertive, commissive, and directive verbs, into three classes: strong, weak, and intermediate; and we will take as our medium, or zero intermediate point for measuring degrees of strength, the characteristic degrees of strength of the corresponding primitive illocutionary forces. All other forces F named by performative verbs with those illocutionary points have a degree of strength 0, 1, -1 when the degree of strength with which their illocutionary point is achieved, is respectively equal to, greater than, or smaller than the degree of strength of the corresponding primitives. The degree of strength of illocutionary point can be further increased by adding modifiers to the performative expressions, e.g. "I sincerely promise", "I do solemnly swear."

The approximate scale of degrees of strength established by this procedure on the following sets of English assertives, commissives, and directives is:

1) *Assertives.*

Degree $(\|\text{swear}\|) = $ degree $(\|\text{testify}\|) = $ degree $(\|\text{insist}\|) = $ degree $(\|\text{assure}_1\|) = +1$;

degree $(\|\text{assert}\|) = $ degree $(\|\text{claim}\|) = $ degree $(\|\text{state}\|) = $ degree $(\|\text{affirm}\|) = $ degree $(\|\text{accuse}\|) = $ degree $(\|\text{report}\|) = $ degree $(\|\text{notify}\|) = $ degree $(\|\text{inform}\|) = $ degree $(\|\text{criticize}\|) = $ degree $(\|\text{predict}\|) = $ degree $(\|\text{boast}\|) = $ degree $(\|\text{retrodict}\|) = $ degree $(\|\text{confess}\|) = $ degree $(\|\text{admit}\|) = $ degree $(\|\text{remind}\|) = 0$; and

degree $(\|\text{suggest}\|) = $ degree $(\|\text{hypothesize}\|) = $ degree $(\|\text{conjecture}\|) = $ degree $(\|\text{opine}\|) = -1$.

2) *Commissives.*

Degree ($\|$swear (to)$\|$) = degree ($\|$vow$\|$) = degree ($\|$pledge$\|$)
= degree ($\|$assure$_2$$\|$) = degree ($\|$promise$\|$) = + 1; and
degree ($\|$commit$\|$) = degree ($\|$threaten$\|$) = degree ($\|$accept$\|$)
= degree ($\|$consent$\|$) = 0.

It is not surprising that there is a shortage of weak commissive verbs in English: the whole point of a commissive is to commit the speaker to a future course of action. But there is not much point in having a special name for ways of doing that unless the commissive act in question is fairly serious, such as a promise, vow, or threat. Notice further that one says "I solemnly promise" but never "I frivolously promise" or "I half-heartedly promise." In real life when we want to make an explicitly weak commitment we often do it indirectly, sometimes even with an illocutionary denegation of the strong commissive. Thus, for example, one says "I intend to do it, but I can't promise to." For most illocutionary forces expressed by actual English assertive and commissive verbs, the degrees of strength of the illocutionary point and of the sincerity conditions are the same. Most strong assertives express a strong belief of the speaker. Most strong commissives express a strong intention of the speaker, and weak assertives express a weak belief.

3) *Directives.*

For directives, as we said earlier, there are at least two independent sources of degree of strength – the intensity of the speaker's desire that the hearer should do the directed act, and the extent of the speaker's authority or power over the hearer. Thus, for example, the degree of strength of begging or beseeching the hearer to do something exceeds that of merely asking or requesting him to do it by way of the intensity of the expressed desire. One would invoke such an intensity of desire in cases where the speaker thought it was a matter of great seriousness that the hearer do the directed act, or the hearer had reasons for not doing the act which the speaker is trying to overcome by the strength of his directive. Similarly, the degree of strength of ordering and commanding that someone do something exceeds that of merely asking or requesting him to do it; but here the increased degree of strength comes from the fact that the speaker invokes some position of power or authority over the hearer.

Thus the following illustrates degrees of desire.

Degree ($\|$implore$\|$) = degree ($\|$entreat$\|$) = degree ($\|$plead$\|$) = degree ($\|$beseech$\|$) = degree ($\|$beg$\|$) = degree ($\|$pray$\|$) = $+1$ because $\eta(\|$implore$\|$) = $\eta(\|$pray$\|$) = $+1$.

On the other hand, strength derived from the position of the speaker is illustrated by:

Degree ($\|$order$\|$) = degree ($\|$command$\|$) = degree ($\|$require$\|$) = $+1$ because $|$mode ($\|$order$\|$)$|$ = $|$mode ($\|$command$\|$)$|$ = degree ($\|$demand$\|$) = $|$mode ($\|$require$\|$)$|$ = $|$mode ($\|$demand$\|$)$|$ = $+1$.

Degree ($\|$ask$\|$) = degree ($\|$tell to$\|$) = degree ($\|$request$\|$) = 0; degree ($\|$suggest$\|$) = degree ($\|$advise$\|$) = degree ($\|$recommend$\|$) = -1.

Though the degree of strength of the illocutionary point and the mode of achievement are independent parameters, they do not always function independently. For example, a person in authority does not have to entreat or implore as long as his authority is recognized. In such a case, as in many others, degree of strength is determined by the mode of achievement of the illocution. In fact, there are some quite elegant interrelationships among the three factors of preparatory conditions, mode of achievement, and degree of strength as our much-used example of a command will illustrate. A preparatory condition on giving a command is that the speaker must be in a position of authority over the hearer but the position of authority enters into the achievement of the illocutionary point: the mode of achievement of the directive illocutionary point in this case is precisely that the speaker achieves it in the authority mode, which determines its degree of strength. A command is stronger than a mere request, and not necessarily because of any greater intensity of the desire expressed. Similarly, an order is stronger than a request, *qua* mode of achievement, regardless of how intense a desire is expressed.

IV. SINCERITY CONDITIONS.

Since sincerity conditions are an intrinsic part of illocutionary acts, illocutionary logic requires at least some principles of a logic of psychological states. A full characterization of a logic of psychological states expressible in the performance of illocutionary acts would be the task of a separate logic of propositional attitudes. In many respects such a logic would parallel illocutionary logic. Some of the questions it would deal with are: What is the logical form of the various psychological states? What are the necessary and sufficient conditions for having each type of psychological state? What are the logical relations between the various types? In particular when does the possession of one psychological state necessarily involve the possession of another? Similarly, when does the expression of one psychological state commit the speaker to the possession of another? Which ones are relatively incompatible and why? Are there basic types of psychological states, and if so how and to what extent are the others composed of the basic ones?

These questions are relevant for illocutionary logic both because of the fact that in the performance of an illocutionary act the speaker necessarily expresses a certain psychological state and because an illocutionary act commits the speaker to another only if in the performance of the first he commits himself to having the psychological states specified by the sincerity conditions of the second. Furthermore, a logic of propositional attitudes has a special relevance to the class of expressive forces, since to each operation on types of psychological states there corresponds an operation on the expressive illocutionary force generating more and more complex expressive illocutionary forces.

Though we do not here try to develop such a logic we will state a few hypotheses concerning beliefs, desires, and intentions. These together with the law of restricted compatibility of strict implication with respect to illocutionary points entail laws of introduction and elimination of the logical constants within illocutionary points.

Parallel to our distinction between strong and weak illocutionary commitments there is a distinction between strong and weak psychological commitments. In a strong illocutionary commitment a speech act strongly commits the speaker to another iff in the performance of the first he necessarily performs the second. Thus for example $\vdash (P \,\&\, Q)$ strongly commits the speaker to $\vdash (Q)$. Analogously in a strong psychological commitment a psychological state commits the speaker to another iff in the possession of the first he necessarily possesses the second. Thus for example Bel $(P \,\&\, Q)$ strongly commits the speaker to Bel (Q). In weak illocutionary commitments a speech act commits the speaker to another, even though the second has not been explicitly performed. Thus for example $\vdash (P \rightarrow Q)$ and $\vdash (P)$ weakly commit the speaker to $\vdash (Q)$. Analogously in a weak psychological commitment the possession of one state or set of states commits the speaker to another state, even though the possession of the first does not entail the possession of the second. Thus for example Bel $(P \rightarrow Q)$ together with Bel (P) weakly commit the speaker to Bel (Q).

Notice further that we need to distinguish both of these forms of commitment from logical relations between speech acts and psychological states on the one hand and facts in the world on the other. Thus for example if a man performs $\vdash (P)$ and it is independently the case that $(P \rightarrow Q)$ he is not so far committed to Q, even though, given the facts as they are, his assertion cannot be true unless Q is true. Analogously if a man has Bel (P) and it is independently the case that $(P \rightarrow Q)$ he is not so far committed to Q, even though, given the facts as they are, his belief cannot be true unless Q is true.

With these distinctions in mind let us now turn to the laws of introduction and elimination.

1. *Introduction of & in beliefs, desires, and intentions.*
   If $m = $ Bel, Int, or Des, $\{m(P), m(Q)\} \rhd m(P \,\&\, Q)$.
A speaker believes in the truth of a conjunction $(P \,\&\, Q)$ if he believes in the truth of each conjunct P and Q. A speaker who both desires that P and desires that Q desires that $(P \,\&\, Q)$. A speaker who both intends that P and intends that Q intends that $(P \,\&\, Q)$.

2. *Elimination of & in beliefs, desires, and intentions.*
   $m(P \,\&\, Q) \rhd m(P)$ and $m(P \,\&\, Q) \rhd m(Q)$.
If a speaker believes in the truth of a conjunction $(P \,\&\, Q)$, he believes in the truth of each conjunct P and Q. If a speaker desires

that $(P \& Q)$ he both desires that P and desires that Q. Similarly for intention.

Apparent counter-examples to this principle are, we believe, cases where there are implied hypotheticals in the statement of the conjunction. Thus, for example, if it is true that "Bill wants to die and go to heaven" or "Sally wants to get married and have children" do not imply *simpliciter* "Bill wants to die" or "Sally wants to have children", that is because there may be an implied hypothetical of the form, "Bill wants to die *only if* he goes to heaven", or "Sally wants to have children *only if* she gets married." Similar considerations apply to intentions.

3. *Elimination of* $\vee$.
   If $m = $ Bel, Des, or Int, and both $m(P_1) \rhd m(Q)$ and $m(P_2) \rhd m(Q)$, then $m(P_1 \vee P_2) \rhd m(Q)$ and similarly for weak commitment $\rhd$.
   If it is not possible for u to believe P_1 or to believe P_2 without believing Q then the belief that $(P_1 \vee P_2)$ contains the belief that Q. The same holds for intention and desire.

4. *Elimination of* $\sim$.
   If $m = $ Bel or Int, it is not the case that $mut(P \& \sim P)$ is true in a world w.
   No speaker can believe in the truth of a conjunction of a proposition P and its truth-functional negation $\sim P$. No speaker can intend both to carry out and not to carry out the same course of action under the same description.
   Nothing could be more obvious than that people unknowingly hold inconsistent beliefs, beliefs which cannot all be true. They hold beliefs of the form $(P \& Q)$ where unknown to them Q is inconsistent with P. However a criterion of rationality is that one does not knowingly hold two mutually self-contradictory beliefs of the form $(P \& \sim P)$ and this is true even in cases where one might have independent evidence supporting the truth of each. The situation with desire is different. Because of the different direction of fit of desire, i.e. because of the fact that the content of a desire does not purport to represent how things are but how one would like them to be, one can consistently hold desires that one knows to be inconsistent. Thus relative to one set of reasons one

might desire to be in Berkeley all day Wednesday and relative to another set of reasons one might desire not to be in Berkeley all day Wednesday.

The fact that one can have two inconsistent desires, together with the fact that desire is closed under conjunction, entails (what is independently known to be true anyway) that one can desire what one knows to be impossible. But this is not true for intentions. If I intend to do something I must believe it is possible for me to do it, and therefore even in cases where I might knowingly desire to carry out two mutually inconsistent courses of action I could not knowingly intend to carry them out. Thus for m = Bel or Int, one cannot rationally have a propositional content of the form $(P \& \sim P)$ but one can have such a form where m = Des.

5. *Elimination of → in beliefs, desires, and intentions.*
    If m = Bel, Des, or int, $\{m(P), m(P \rightarrow Q)\} \triangleright m(Q)$.
A person who has the belief (intention, desire) that P and the belief (intention, desire) that $(P \rightarrow Q)$ is committed to the belief (intention, desire) that Q. Notice that unlike the first three cases, this is a case of weak commitment. The person is committed to the belief that Q but his beliefs in the premises of a *modus ponens* argument do not contain the belief in the conclusion in the way that his belief in a conjunction contains a belief in both conjuncts.

Chapter 6

AXIOMATIC PROPOSITIONAL
ILLOCUTIONARY LOGIC

The main aim of this chapter is to present an axiomatization of the theory of illocutionary acts. We will formulate all definitions, independent axioms and postulates governing the central notions of illocutionary logic. Such an axiomatization has the advantage of making our commitments fully explicit. All of the laws that have been stated so far, as well as all others that will be stated in the following chapters, can be derived from these definitions and axioms. The axiomatization, however, is not intended to be complete because there are laws for illocutionary forces that do not follow from these axioms. A more complete axiomatization would require a more powerful formal apparatus as well as further formal developments of the logic of propositional attitudes and of the modal theory of types of intensional logic.[1]

I. BASIC SET-THEORETICAL ENTITIES OF
ILLOCUTIONARY LOGIC.

I) *The set of all possible contexts of utterance.*

Five basic sets of illocutionary logic are: the set I_1 of all possible speakers, the set I_2 of all possible hearers, the set I_3 of all moments of time, the set I_4 of all possible places of utterance, and the set W of all possible worlds in which utterance acts take place. These sets have the following structure. There is a linear ordering $\leqslant$ on I_3 and a reflexive relation of accessibility R on W. There is also a function U with domain $W \times I_3$ that gives as value, for each pair $w \in W$, $t \in I_3$, the set $U_t(w)$ of all individual objects that exist at time t in w. $U(w) \underset{\text{def}}{=} \bigcup_{t \in I_3} U_t(w)$ and $\hat{U} \underset{\text{def}}{=} \bigcup_{w \in W} U(w)$. The set

---

1 The formalization will be pursued in a later book on the model-theoretical semantics of illocutionary acts by Daniel Vanderveken.

$\hat{U}$ is the *universe of discourse* of illocutionary logic. The set I of all possible contexts of utterance is a proper subset of the Cartesian product $I_1 \times I_2 \times I_3 \times I_4 \times W$; if $a \in I_1$, $b \in I_2$, $t \in I_3$, $l \in I_4$ and $w \in W$, $\langle a,b,t,l,w \rangle \in I$ only if $\{a,b\} \subseteq U_t(w)$. There is a binary reflexive and symmetric relation of compatibility $\geqslant$ on the set I. By definition, $i \geqslant j$ iff all illocutionary acts performed in i and in j are simultaneously performable in a possible context of utterance. If $i \in I$, a_i, b_i, t_i, l_i, and w_i are hereafter respectively the first, second, third, fourth, and fifth component of i.

2) *The sets of all propositions and propositional attitudes.*

The set Prop of all propositions is a sixth basic set of illocutionary logic. By definition, each proposition $P \in \text{Prop}$ has a truth value $P(w)$ in each possible world $w \in W$. We will use the set $2 = \{1,0\}$ to represent alternatively truth values and success values: 1 is truth and 0 is falsehood when propositions are evaluated and 1 is success and 0 is failure or lack of success when illocutionary acts are evaluated. There is a function σ from Prop into $\mathscr{P}(\text{Prop})$ that gives as value, for each proposition P, the set $\sigma(P)$ of all propositional presuppositions of P: $P(w) = 1$ only if for all $Q \in \sigma(P)$, $Q(w) = 1$.

To each possible world w corresponds a unique maximal set $\hat{w}$ of elementary propositions that are true in w. The set Prop of all propositions contains all elementary propositions $P \in \bigcup_{w \in W} \hat{w}$ and is closed under the following operations: If P and $Q \in \text{Prop}$, $t \in I_3$ and $u \in \hat{U}$ then $\sim P$, $\square P$, $(P \to Q)$, $\diamondsuit P$, δutP and ρutP are new propositions belonging to Prop. The truth conditions of these propositions are defined as follows: If P is an elementary proposition, $P(w) = 1$ iff $P \in \hat{w}$; $\sim P(w) = 1$ iff $P(w) = 0$; $\square P(w) = 1$ iff, for all $w' \in W$, $P(w') = 1$; $(P \to Q)(w) = 1$ iff $P(w) = 0$ or $Q(w) = 1$; $\diamondsuit P(w) = 1$ iff, for some $w' \in W$, wRw' and $P(w') = 1$. $\delta utP(w) = 1$ iff u at time t in w acts so as to bring about the state of affairs represented by P and $\rho utP(w) = 1$ iff u at time t in w has reasons for bringing about the state of affairs that P or for supposing it is the case that P.

Propositional attitudes also figure in illocutionary logic. There is a seventh basic set M that contains all of the types of psychological states that have propositions as contents. To each type of psychological state $m \in M$ there corresponds an operation on propositions that determines the following truth conditions: If $m \in M$, $mutP$ is a new proposition such that $mutP(w) = 1$ iff individual u at time t in w has the psychological state of type m with the propositional content that P. The set M contains three designated types Bel, Des, and Int for respectively belief, desire, and intention.

Abbreviations: &, $\vee$, $\leftrightarrow$, and $\dashv$ are defined in the usual way. If $\Gamma \subseteq \text{Prop}$, $\Gamma/w/ \underset{\text{def}}{=}$ for all $P \in \Gamma$, $P(w) = 1$.

3) *Relations and functions on the sets I, Prop, and M.*

Since in the performance of speech acts the speaker presupposes or is committed to presupposing certain propositions in certain contexts, there are two primitive relations on $I \times \text{Prop}$: *the relation of presupposing a proposition P in a context i* and *the relation of being committed to presupposing a proposition P in a context i*. By definition, the speaker is committed to presupposing all propositions that he presupposes.

Since the speaker expresses certain psychological states in certain contexts there is also in illocutionary logic one primitive relation on $I \times (M \times \text{Prop})$, namely *the relation of expressing a psychological state m(P) in a context of utterance i*. This relation is indexed by the set Z of all integers and satisfies the following postulates:

(i) *The postulate of possible sincerity.*
If a speaker expresses psychological states $\Gamma \subseteq M \times \text{Prop}$ in a context of utterance i, then for at least one $w \in W$, for all $m(P) \in \Gamma$, $ma_i t_i P(w) = 1$. It is possible for the speaker to be sincere in expressing a psychological state.

(ii) *The postulate of transitivity of degree of strength of sincerity conditions.*
If a speaker a_i expresses with degree of strength $k + 1$ a psycho-

logical state $m(P)$ in a context of utterance i, then he also expresses $m(P)$ with degree k in that context.

Weak and strong propositional attitude commitment can now be defined as follows:

> The *psychological states* $\Gamma \subseteq M \times Prop$ *commit the speaker to the psychological states* Δ (for short: $\Gamma \rhd \Delta$) iff it is not possible for a speaker to express psychological states Γ with a degree k in a possible context of utterance without being committed to having the psychological states Δ with the same degree in that context. The psychological states Γ *strongly commit the speaker to* the psychological states Δ (for short $\Gamma \rhd \Delta$) iff it is not possible for a speaker to have psychological states Γ without also having the psychological states Δ. Thus $\Gamma \rhd \Delta$ iff for all possible worlds w, if for all $m_1(P_1) \in \Gamma$, $m_1 ut P_1(w) = 1$ then for all $m_2(P_2) \in \Delta$, $m_2 ut P_2(w) = 1$. A speaker *is committed to having a psychological state* $m(P)$ with the degree of strength k in a context of utterance i iff in that context he expresses with that degree of strength some psychological states Γ that commit him to $m(P)$.

For the purpose of this study we accept the laws of elimination and of introduction of the logical constants in beliefs, intentions, and desires that were stated as hypotheses at the end of Chapter 5 and the following postulate for strong propositional attitude commitment:

(iii) *The law of inclusion of sincerity conditions.*

If a speaker expresses psychological states Γ with degree of strength k in a context i and $\Gamma \rhd \Delta$, then he also expresses the psychological states Δ with that degree in that context.

Abbreviations: If $\Gamma \subseteq Prop$, $[\Gamma] \underset{\text{def}}{=} \{P / \text{in all contexts } i \text{ where the speaker presupposes } \Gamma \text{ he also presupposes } P\}$. If $\Gamma \subseteq M \times Prop$, $[\Gamma] \underset{\text{def}}{=} \{m(P) / \Gamma \rhd - m(P)\}$.

II. DEFINITIONS OF THE SET OF ALL ILLOCUTIONARY FORCES AND OF THE CONDITIONS OF SUCCESS OF ILLOCUTIONARY ACTS.

The main proper task of illocutionary logic is to specify materially and formally adequate definitions of the set of all illocutionary forces and of the conditions of success of illocutionary acts. These definitions make use of the following primitive notions of speech act theory:

1) *Illocutionary points.*

There are five primitive relations Π_1, Π_2, Π_3, Π_4, and Π_5 on $I \times$ Prop that determine respectively the conditions of achievement of the assertive, the commissive, the directive, the declarative, and the expressive illocutionary points. These relations determining the conditions of achievement of the five illocutionary points are indexed by the set Z of all integers. By definition if $k \in Z$, $i\Pi^k P$ iff a_i achieves in i illocutionary point Π on P with degree of strength k.

The illocutionary points obey the following postulates:

(i) *Each illocutionary point is achieved with a maximal degree of strength.*
If $i\Pi P$ then there is a greatest $k \in Z$ such that $i\Pi^k P$. In particular, the declarative illocutionary point is always achieved with the null degree of strength. $\Pi_4^k \neq \varnothing$ iff $k = 0$.

(ii) *There is a transitivity of degree of strength of illocutionary point.*
If $\Pi \neq \Pi_4$, $\{i/i\Pi^{k+1}P\} \subset \{i/i\Pi^k P\}$.

(iii) *A speaker who achieves an illocutionary point on a proposition presupposes the propositional presuppositions.*
If $i\Pi P$ then a_i presupposes $\sigma(P)$ in i.

(iv) *The preparatory conditions cannot be denied.*
If a_i presupposes P in i, then it is not the case that $i\Pi_1 \sim P$.

(v) *The sincerity conditions cannot be denied.*
If a_i expresses $m(P)$ in i, then it is not the case that $i\Pi_1 \sim ma_it_iP$.

(vi) *A speaker achieves the expressive point on a proposition iff he expresses a psychological state about the state of affairs that it represents.*
$i\Pi_5^k P$ iff, for some $m \in M$, a_i expresses with degree of strength k $m(P)$ in i.

(vii) *The achievement of the declarative point on a proposition P brings about the state of affairs that P represents.*
If $i\Pi_4 P$ then $\delta a_i t_i P(w_i) = 1$.

(viii) *A speaker cannot achieve the directive point on a contradiction of the form* $(P \, \& \sim P)$.
$\{i / i\Pi_3 P \, \& \sim P\} = \emptyset$.

2) *Propositional content, preparatory and sincerity conditions.*

Three sets of functions $\Xi \subseteq (\mathscr{P}(\text{Prop}))^I$, $\Lambda \subseteq (\mathscr{P}(\text{Prop}))^{I \times \text{Prop}}$ and $\chi \subseteq (\mathscr{P}(M \times \text{Prop}))^{I \times \text{Prop}}$ determine respectively in illocutionary logic all (linguistically significant) propositional content, preparatory and sincerity conditions. They contain respectively the empty propositional content condition θ such that $\theta(i) = \text{Prop}$ and the empty preparatory and sincerity conditions Σ and Ψ such that $\Sigma(i, P) = \Psi(i, P) = \emptyset$. These sets are closed under the operations of union, intersection, and complementarity. Thus, for example, if θ_1 and θ_2 are two propositional content conditions belonging to Ξ then the intersection $\theta_1 \cap \theta_2$, the union $\theta_1 \cup \theta_2$, and the complement $\bar{\theta}_1$ are new propositional content conditions of Ξ such that $\theta_1 \cap \theta_2(i) = \theta_1(i) \cap \theta_2(i), \theta_1 \cup \theta_2(i) = \theta_1(i) \cup \theta_2(i)$, and $\bar{\theta}_1(i) = \text{Prop} - \theta_1(i)$. Among the members of Ξ there are two functions Prop_2 and Prop_3 that give, respectively, as values, for each $i \in I$, the sets of all propositions representing courses of actions of the speaker a_i and of the hearer b_i that are future with respect to the moment of time t_i. If Σ is a preparatory condition, there exists another preparatory condition $[\Sigma]$ called *the closure of* Σ such that $[\Sigma](i, P) = [\Sigma(i, P)]$. Similarly if Ψ is a sincerity condition, there exists another sincerity condition $[\Psi]$ such that $[\Psi](i, P) = [\Psi(i, P)]$.

3) *Modes of achievement.*

To each illocutionary point Π corresponds a set of functions Mode $(\Pi) \subseteq 2^{I \times \text{Prop}}$ determining (linguistically significant) modes of achievement of that point. By definition, if $\mu \in \text{Mode}(\Pi)$ and it is not the case that for all i and P, $\mu(i, P) = 0$, there exists a greatest degree of strength of illocutionary point determined by μ. This degree $|\mu|$ is the greatest k such that if $i\Pi P$ and $\mu(i, P) = 1$ then $i\Pi^k P$. For each $n \in Z$, the empty mode of achievement μ such that $\mu(i, P) = 1$ iff $i\hat{\Pi}^n P$ belongs to Mode (Π).

All other modes of achievement are special. If μ, μ_1 and $\mu_2 \in$ Mode (Π), then the complement of mode μ and the conjunction of modes μ_1 and μ_2 are new modes of achievement $\bar{\mu}$ and μ_1 & $\mu_2 \in$ Mode (Π) such that for all i and P, $\bar{\mu}(i, P) \neq \mu(i, P)$ and μ_1 & $\mu_2(i, P) = 1$ iff $\mu_1(i, P) = \mu_2(i, P) = 1$.

As we noted earlier, some components of illocutionary force determine other components. A propositional content condition θ, a preparatory condition Σ, and a sincerity condition Ψ are *determined by an illocutionary point* Π when for all i and P, if $i\Pi^0 P$ then $P \in \theta(i)$ and the speaker in i presupposes propositions $\Sigma(i, P)$ and expresses psychological states $\Psi(i, P)$. Similarly, a propositional content condition θ, a preparatory condition Σ, and a sincerity condition Ψ are determined by a mode of achievement μ of a point Π and a sincerity condition Ψ^* when for all i and P, if the speaker achieves Π on P with the mode $\bar{\mu}$ or expresses psychological states $\Psi^*(i, P)$ in i then $P \in \theta(i)$ and a_i also presupposes propositions $\Sigma(i, P)$ and expresses psychological states $\Psi(i, P)$ in i.

Symbolism.

We will often write θ_Π, θ_μ, and θ_Ψ to indicate that propositional content conditions θ are determined respectively by illocutionary point Π, by mode of achievement μ, and by sincerity conditions Ψ. We will write Σ_Π and Ψ_Π to indicate that preparatory conditions Σ and sincerity conditions Ψ are determined by point Π, and we will write Σ_μ and Ψ_μ when they are determined by mode μ, and similarly for the other cases.

The following five postulates specify which components are determined by each of the five illocutionary points:

(ix) *The assertive point determines the empty propositional content condition, the preparatory condition that the speaker has reasons in support of the truth of the propositional content and the sincerity condition that he believes the propositional content.*

$\bigcap \theta_{\Pi_1}(i) = \text{Prop}$, $\bigcup \Sigma_{\Pi_1}(i, P) = [\{a_i t_i P\}]$, and $\bigcup \Psi_{\Pi_1}(i, P) = [\{\text{Bel}(P)\}]$.

(x) *The commissive point determines the condition that the propositional content represents a future course of action of the speaker, the preparatory condition that the speaker is capable of carrying out that* course of action, and the sincerity condition that he intends to carry it out.

$$\bigcap \theta_{\Pi_2}(i) = \mathrm{Prop}_2(i),\ \bigcup \Sigma_{\Pi_2}(i, P) = [\{\Diamond P\}]\text{ and } \bigcup \Psi_{\Pi_2}(i, P) = [\{\mathrm{Int}(P)\}].$$

(xi) *The directive point determines the condition that the propositional content represents a future course of action of the hearer, the preparatory condition that the hearer is capable of carrying out that course of action, and the sincerity condition that the speaker wants or desires him to carry out that action.*

$$\bigcap \theta_{\Pi_3}(i) = \mathrm{Prop}_3(i),\ \bigcup \Sigma_{\Pi_3}(i, P) = [\{\Diamond P\}],\text{ and } \bigcup \Psi_{\Pi_3}(i, P) = [\{\mathrm{Dev}\,(P)\}].$$

(xii) *The declarative point determines the empty propositional content condition, the preparatory condition that the speaker has the power or authority to bring about the state of affairs represented by the propositional content in his utterance and the sincerity condition that he believes that he brings it about and that he desires to do so.*

$$\bigcap \theta_{\Pi_4}(i) = \mathrm{Prop},\ \bigcup \Sigma_{\Pi_4}(i, P) = [\{\text{the proposition }\Diamond Q \text{ such that } Q(w) = 1 \text{ iff } i[w/w_i]\Pi_4 P\}],\text{ and } \bigcup \Psi_{\Pi_4}(i,\ P) = \{\mathrm{Bel}(\delta a_i t_i P), \mathrm{Des}(\delta a_i t_i p)\}].$$

(xiii) *The expressive point determines empty propositional content, preparatory and sincerity conditions.*

$$\bigcap \theta_{\Pi_5}(i) = \mathrm{Prop},\ \bigcup \Sigma_{\Pi_5}(i, P) = \bigcup \Psi_{\Pi_5}(i, P) = \varnothing.$$

All illocutionary points obey the following laws with regard to the relation of determination:

(xiv) *If a speaker achieves an illocutionary point with the zero degree of strength then he also necessarily expresses the sincerity conditions determined by that point with the same degree.*

O is the greatest integer k such that if $i\Pi^0 P$ then the speaker a_i expresses psychological states $\Psi_\Pi(i, P)$ with degree k in i.

(xv) *There is a restricted compatibility of strict implication with respect to illocutionary point.*

If $P \quad Q(w) = 1$ then $\{i/i\Pi^k P\} \subseteq \{i/i\Pi'^k Q\}$ iff, for all $i \in I$ first, if $P \in \bigcap \theta_\Pi(i)$ then $Q \in \bigcap \theta_{\Pi'}(i)$, and, secondly, $\bigcup \Psi_\Pi(i, P) \rhd \bigcup \Psi_{\Pi'}(i, Q)$.

In achieving an illocutionary point Π on a proposition P with degree k in a context i a speaker also necessarily achieves an illocutionary point Π' on a proposition Q with that degree when P strictly implies Q; Q satisfies the propositional content conditions determined by Π' when P satisfies those determined by Π; and the psychological states that are expressed in the achievement of Π on P strongly commit the speaker to those of Π' on Q.

A speaker *is committed to an illocutionary point* Π' on a proposition Q with a degree of strength k (for short: $i\widehat{\Pi}'^k Q$) iff for some point Π, $i\Pi^k P$, $P \dashv Q(w) = 1$, and, first, if $P \in \bigcap \theta_\Pi(i)$ then $Q \in \bigcap \theta_{\Pi'}(i)$ and, secondly, $\bigcup \Psi_\Pi(i, P) \rhd \bigcup \Psi_{\Pi'}(i, Q)$.

4) *Definition of the set of all illocutionary forces.*

The set Φ of all illocutionary forces is defined recursively as follows: First, Φ contains the five primitive illocutionary forces $\vdash, \perp, !, T,$ and $\dashv$ that determine the following conditions of success:

An illocutionary act of the form $\vdash (P)$ is performed in a context of utterance i iff $i\Pi_1^0 P$.

An illocutionary act of the form $\perp (P)$ is performed in a context of utterance i iff $i\Pi_2^0 P$.

An illocutionary act of the form $!(P)$ is performed in a context of utterance i iff $i\Pi_3^0 P$.

An illocutionary act of the form $T(P)$ is performed in a context of utterance i iff $i\Pi_4^0 P$.

An illocutionary act of the form $\dashv (P)$ is performed in a context of utterance i iff $i\Pi_5^0 P$.

All other illocutionary forces belonging to Φ are obtained from these primitive illocutionary forces by a finite number of applications of the following operations:

(i) *Adding propositional content conditions.*
If $F \in \Phi$ and θ is a function from I into $\mathscr{P}(\text{Prop})$ determining certain (linguistically significant) propositional content conditions, the result of adding propositional content conditions θ to F is an illocutionary force $[\theta]F$ such that an illocutionary act of the form

$[\theta]F(P)$ is performed in a context of utterance i iff $F(P)$ is performed in that context and $P \in \theta(i)$, when $[\theta]F$ has the same illocutionary point as F.

The *illocutionary point* Π_F of a force F is the intersection of all illocutionary points Π such that if an illocutionary act of the form $F(P)$ is performed in a context of utterance i, then $i\Pi P$.

(ii) *Adding preparatory conditions.*

If $F \in \Phi$ and Σ is a function from $I \times$ Prop into $\mathscr{P}(\text{Prop})$ determining (linguistically significant) preparatory conditions, the result of adding preparatory conditions Σ to F is an illocutionary force $[\Sigma]F$ such that an illocutionary act of the form $[\Sigma]F(P)$ is performed in a context of utterance i iff $F(P)$ is performed in that context and the speaker a_i presupposes propositions $\Sigma(i, P)$ in i, when $[\Sigma]F$ has the same illocutionary point as F.

(iii) *Adding sincerity conditions.*

If $F \in \Phi$, and Ψ is a function from $I \times$ Prop into $\mathscr{P}(M \times \text{Prop})$ determining (linguistically significant) sincerity conditions, the result of adding sincerity conditions Ψ to F is an illocutionary force $[\Psi]F$ such that an illocutionary act of the form $[\Psi]F(P)$ is performed in a context of utterance i iff $F(P)$ is performed in that context and the speaker a_i expresses psychological states $\Psi(i, P)$ with degree $\eta(F)$ in i, when $[\Psi]F$ has the same illocutionary point as F.

The degree of strength of the sincerity conditions $\eta(F)$ of force F is defined as follows from the conditions of success of the acts with that force:

> The *sincerity conditions* Ψ_F of a force F are the union of all sincerity conditions Ψ such that if an illocutionary act of the form $F(P)$ is performed in a context i then the speaker a_i expresses psychological states $\Psi(i, P)$ in i; and the *degree of strength of the sincerity conditions of* F, $\eta(F)$, is the greatest integer k such that if an illocutionary act of the form $F(P)$ is performed in a context i, the speaker a_i expresses psychological states $\Psi_F(i, P)$ with degree k.

(iv) *Restricting the mode of achievement.*

If $F \in \Phi$ and μ is a function from $I \times$ Prop into 2 determining a (linguistically significant) mode of achievement of the illocutionary point of F, the result of restricting the mode of achievement of F by imposing additional mode μ is a new illocutionary force $[\mu]F$ such that an illocutionary act of the form $[\mu]F(P)$ is performed in a context of utterance i iff $F(P)$ is performed in i and $\mu(i, P) = 1$, when $[\mu]F$ has the same illocutionary point as F.

(v) *Increasing the degrees of strength.*

If $F \in \Phi$, the result of increasing by one the degrees of strength of illocutionary point and of sincerity conditions of F is a new illocutionary force $[+1]F$ such that an illocutionary act of the form $[+1]F(P)$ is performed in a context of utterance i iff $F(P)$ is performed in that context and the speaker a_i expresses in i psychological states $\Psi_F(i, P)$ with degree of strength $\eta(F) + 1$, when $[+1]F$ has the same illocutionary point as F.

(vi) *Decreasing the degrees of strength.*

If $F \in \Phi$, the result of decreasing by one the degrees of strength of illocutionary point and of sincerity conditions of F is a new illocutionary force $[-1]F$ such that $[+1][-1]F = F$ when $[-1]F$ has the same illocutionary point as F. (This operation is the only operation on illocutionary forces which decreases the degrees of strength.)

We will often write hereafter $[+n]F$ and $[-n]F$ as the abbreviations for $\underbrace{[+1] \ldots [+1]}_{n \text{ times}}F$ and $\underbrace{[-1] \ldots [-1]}_{n \text{ times}}F$.

The other components of an illocutionary force are defined as follows from the conditions of success that it determines:

The *propositional content conditions* Prop_F of a force F are the intersection of all propositional content conditions θ such that if an illocutionary act of the form $F(P)$ is performed in a context of utterance i then $P \in \theta(i)$.

The *preparatory conditions* Σ_F of a force F are the union of all preparatory conditions Σ such that if an illocutionary act of the form $F(P)$ is performed in a context i then the speaker a_i presupposes in i propositions $\Sigma(i, P)$.

The *mode of achievement* mode (F) of a force F is the conjunction of all modes of achievement μ of the illocutionary point of F such that if an illocutionary act of the form $F(P)$ is performed in a context i then $\mu(i, P) = 1$.

The *degree of strength of the illocutionary point,* degree (F), of a force F is the greatest degree k such that if an illocutionary act of the form $F(P)$ is performed in a context of utterance i, then $i\Pi_F^k P$.

Each illocutionary force $F \in \Phi$ is identified in illocutionary logic with the septuple $\langle \Pi_F, \text{mode}(F), \text{degree}(F), \text{Prop}_F, \Sigma_F, \Psi_F, \eta(F) \rangle$ consisting of its seven components.

It is a postulate of illocutionary logic that the degree of strength of the illocutionary point of an illocutionary force is the maximum of the degree of strength of its sincerity conditions and of the degree of strength of illocutionary point determined by its mode of achievement. The degree (F) is the maximum of $\eta(F)$ and $|\text{mode}(F)|$.

5) *Definitions of the set of all illocutionary acts and of their conditions of success.*

The set of all illocutionary acts that we discuss in this book is the smallest set Act that contains all elementary illocutionary acts of the form $F(P)$ where $F \in \Phi$ and $P \in \text{Prop}$, and contains also the complex illocutionary acts $\neg\mathcal{A}$, $\mathcal{A}_1 \,\&\, \mathcal{A}_2$ and $(P \Rightarrow \mathcal{A})$ when $\mathcal{A}$, $\mathcal{A}_1$, and $\mathcal{A}_2$ belong to it and $P \in \text{Prop}$. There is a function ϕ^* from I into $\mathscr{P}(\text{Act})$ that gives as value, for each context of utterance i, the set $\phi^*(i)$ of all illocutionary acts that the speaker expresses with the intention of performing them in that context. By definition if $i\Pi P$, then for some F such that $\Pi_F = \Pi$, $F(P) \in \phi^*(i)$. A speaker who achieves an illocutionary point intends to perform an act with a force with that point. Moreover, if $\mathcal{A}_1 \,\&\, \mathcal{A}_2 \in \phi^*(i)$ then both $\mathcal{A}_1$ and $\mathcal{A}_2 \in \phi^*(i)$. A speaker who intends to perform a conjunction of two illocutionary acts intends to perform both conjuncts.

The conditions of *successful performance* of all illocutionary acts are defined by induction on their length.

An illocutionary act $\mathcal{A}$ *is performed* in a context i (for short $\mathcal{A}(i) = 1$) under the following conditions:

Case 1. $\mathcal{A}$ is an elementary illocutionary act of the form $F(P)$.
The conditions of success of elementary illocutionary acts of form $F(P)$ are determined in the definition of their force. Thus, if F is

primitive, $F(P)(i) = 1$ iff $i\Pi_F^0 P$. $[\theta]F(P)(i) = 1$ iff $F(P)(i) = 1$ and $P\in\theta(i)$ and so on as in the preceding section.

Case 2. $\mathscr{A}$ is a conjunction of the form $\mathscr{A}_1$ & $\mathscr{A}_2$
  $\mathscr{A}_1$ & $\mathscr{A}_2(i) = 1$ iff $\mathscr{A}_1(i) = \mathscr{A}_2(i) = 1$.

A speaker performs a conjunction of two illocutionary acts in a context of utterance iff he performs in that context both conjuncts.

Case 3. $\mathscr{A}$ is an act of illocutionary denegation of the form $\neg\mathscr{A}'$
  $\neg\mathscr{A}'(i) = 1$ iff $\neg\mathscr{A}'\in\phi^*(i)$ and for no $j\in I$, both $i > j$ and $\mathscr{A}'(j) = 1$.

An act of illocutionary denegation of form $\neg\mathscr{A}'$ is performed in a context of utterance i iff the speaker in that context expresses act $\mathscr{A}'$ with the intention of performing its denegation and all possible contexts of utterance that are compatible with i are contexts where $\mathscr{A}'$ is not performed.

Case 4. $\mathscr{A}$ is a conditional illocutionary act of the form $(P\Rightarrow\mathscr{A}')$.
  $(P\Rightarrow\mathscr{A}') = 1$ iff $(P\Rightarrow\mathscr{A}')\in\phi^*(i)$ and for all $j\in I$, such that $i > j$, if $P(w_j) = 1$ then $\mathscr{A}'(j) = 1$.

A conditional illocutionary act of form $(P\Rightarrow\mathscr{A}')$ is performed in a context of utterance i iff the speaker in that context expresses act $\mathscr{A}'$ with the intention of performing it on the condition P and all possible contexts of utterance that are compatible with i are contexts where $\mathscr{A}'$ is performed when P is true.

A speaker *fails to perform* an illocutionary act $\mathscr{A}$ in a context i iff $\mathscr{A}\in\phi^*(i)$ but $\mathscr{A}(i) \neq 1$, i.e. when he expresses that act with the intention of performing it but the conditions of success do not obtain. An illocutionary act of form $F(P)$ is *non-defectively performed* in a context of utterance i iff $F(P)(i) = 1$, $\sigma(P)\cup\Sigma_F(i, P)/w_i/$, and for all $m(P)\in\Psi_F(i, P)$, $ma_i t_i P(w_i) = 1$.

A set of illocutionary acts $\Gamma \subset \text{Act}$ is said to be *simultaneously performed* in a context of utterance i iff for all $\mathscr{A}\in\Gamma$, $\mathscr{A}(i) = 1$. Γ is *simultaneously performable* if it is simultaneously performed in at least one possible context of utterance $i\in I$. An illocutionary act $\mathscr{A}_1$ *strongly commits the speaker* to an illocutionary act $\mathscr{A}_2$ (for short, $\mathscr{A}_1 \triangleright \mathscr{A}_2$) when $\{i/\mathscr{A}_1(i) = 1\} \subseteq \{i/\mathscr{A}_2(i) = 1\}$. Two illocutionary acts $\mathscr{A}_1$, $\mathscr{A}_2$ are *strictly equivalent* (for short $\mathscr{A}_1 \equiv \mathscr{A}_2$) when each of them strongly commits the speaker to the other. A force F_1 *illocutionarily entails* a force F_2 (for short $F_1 \triangleright F_2$) iff, for all propositions P, $F_1(P) \rhd F_2(P)$. Two illocutionary acts are *relatively incompatible* (for short, $\mathscr{A}_1 > < \mathscr{A}_2$) when the set $\{\mathscr{A}_1, \mathscr{A}_2\}$ is not simultaneously performable. A *self-defeating* illocutionary act is an act that is relatively incompatible with itself (in symbols: $> \mathscr{A} <$).

6) *Definition of the conditions of commitment to illocutionary acts.*

The conditions of commitment to illocutionary acts are also defined by induction on their length. A speaker *is committed to* an illocutionary act $\mathscr{A}$ in a context i (for short $\rhd \mathscr{A}$) under the following conditions:

Case 1. $\mathscr{A}$ is an elementary illocutionary act of the form $F(P)$.
    If F is primitive, $\rhd F(P)$ iff $i\Pi_F^0 P$.
A speaker is committed to an elementary illocutionary act with a primitive force iff he is committed to the illocutionary point on the propositional content with the degree of strength o.

$\rhd [\Sigma]F(P)$ iff $\rhd F(P)$ and the speaker a_i is committed to presupposing propositions $\Sigma(i, P)$ in i.
$\rhd [\theta]F(P)$ iff $\rhd F(P)$ and $P \in \theta(i)$.
$\rhd [\Psi]F(P)$ iff $\rhd F(P)$ and the speaker a_i is committed to having with degree $\eta(F)$ psychological states $\Psi(i, P)$ in i.
$\rhd [\mu]F(P)$ iff $\rhd F(P)$ and $\mu(i, P) = 1$.
$\rhd [+1]F(P)$ iff $\rhd F(P)$ and the speaker a_i is committed to having psychological states $\Psi_F(i, P)$ with degree $\eta(F) + 1$ in i.

Case 2. $\mathscr{A}$ is a conjunctive illocutionary act of the form $\mathscr{A}_1$ & $\mathscr{A}_2$.
    $\rhd \mathscr{A}_1$ & $\mathscr{A}_2$ iff $\rhd \mathscr{A}_1$ and $\rhd \mathscr{A}_2$.
A speaker is committed to a conjunction of two illocutionary acts iff he is committed to both conjuncts.

Case 3. $\mathscr{A}$ is an act of illocutionary denegation of the form $\neg \mathscr{A}'$.
    $\rhd \neg \mathscr{A}'$ iff, for some $\mathscr{A}''$, $\mathscr{A}''(i) = 1$ and the set $\{\mathscr{A}', \mathscr{A}''\}$ is not simultaneously performable.
A speaker is committed to an act of illocutionary denegation of the form $\neg \mathscr{A}'$ iff he performs an illocutionary act that is relatively incompatible with $\mathscr{A}'$.

Case 4. $\mathscr{A}$ is a conditional illocutionary act of the form $(P \Rightarrow \mathscr{A}')$.

$\triangleright (P \Rightarrow \mathscr{A}')$ iff, for some $\mathscr{A}'', \mathscr{A}''(i) = 1$ and, for all $j \in I$, if $\mathscr{A}''(j) = 1$ and $P(w_j) = 1$ then $\triangleright \mathscr{A}'$.

A speaker is committed to a conditional illocutionary act of the form $(P \Rightarrow \mathscr{A}')$ iff he performs an act that it is not possible to perform in a context where P is true without being committed to $\mathscr{A}'$.

An illocutionary act $\mathscr{A}_1$ *commits the speaker* to an illocutionary act $\mathscr{A}_2$ (for short $\mathscr{A}_1 \triangleright \mathscr{A}_2$) iff for all $i \in I$, if $\mathscr{A}_1(i) = 1$ then $\triangleright \mathscr{A}_2$. Two illocutionary acts $\mathscr{A}_1$ and $\mathscr{A}_2$ are *congruent* (for short $\mathscr{A}_1 \simeq \mathscr{A}_2$) when each of them commits the speaker to the other.

A set of illocutionary acts $\Gamma \subseteq \text{Act}$ is *illocutionarily consistent* when there is at least one possible context of utterance $i \in I$ such that for all $\mathscr{A} \in \Gamma$, $\triangleright \mathscr{A}$. Otherwise Γ is *illocutionarily inconsistent*.[2] A set of illocutionary acts Γ commits the speaker to an illocutionary act $\mathscr{A}$ (for short $\Gamma \triangleright \mathscr{A}$) iff for some $\mathscr{A}_1, \ldots, \mathscr{A}_n \in \Gamma$, $\mathscr{A}_1 \& \ldots \& \mathscr{A}_n \triangleright \mathscr{A}$. A context of utterance is *non-empty* or *actualized* (for short $\triangle$) iff for some illocution $\mathscr{A}$, $\triangleright \mathscr{A}$. An illocutionary act $\mathscr{A}$ is *strong* in a context of utterance $i(\mathscr{A} \triangleright)$ iff $\mathscr{A}(i) = 1$ and for all $\mathscr{A}'$, if $\triangleright \mathscr{A}'$ then $\mathscr{A} \triangleright \mathscr{A}'$.

7) *Definition of the conditions of satisfaction of elementary illocutionary acts.*

An illocutionary act of the form $F(P)$ is *satisfied* in a context of utterance i iff $P(w_i) = 1$ and is *not satisfied* otherwise in i.

III. AXIOMS OF ILLOCUTIONARY LOGIC.

A few fundamental axioms govern the primitive notions of illocutionary logic. Each of them states a law concerning the conditions of success of or the conditions of commitment to illocutionary acts. These axioms are:

Axiom I. *The law of transitivity of $\triangleright$.*

If $\mathscr{A}_1 \triangleright \mathscr{A}_2$ and $\mathscr{A}_2 \triangleright \mathscr{A}_3$ then $\mathscr{A}_1 \triangleright \mathscr{A}_3$.

2 Henceforth when we say 'consistent' and 'inconsistent' we mean illocutionarily consistent and illocutionarily inconsistent.

The set of all successful commitments of a speaker is transitive.

Axiom II. *The law of identity for illocutionary forces.*

For all F, $F' \in \Phi$, $F = F'$ iff for all propositions $P \in \text{Prop}$, $F(P) \equiv F'(P)$.

If any two illocutionary acts with forces F and F' and the same propositional content have the same conditions of success, the two forces are identical.

Axiom III. *The law of propositional identity.*

For all P, $P' \in \text{Prop}$, $P = P'$ iff, for all illocutionary forces $F \in \Phi$, $F(P) \equiv F(P')$.

If any two illocutionary acts with the same force that have propositional contents P and Q have identical conditions of success, the two propositions are identical.

Axiom IV. *A law of identity for elementary illocutionary acts.*

$F_1(P_1) = F_2(P_2)$ iff $F_1(P_1) \equiv F_2(P_2)$ when $F_1(P_1)$ is performable.

Two performable elementary illocutionary acts are identical iff they have the same conditions of success.

Axiom V. *Laws of identity for complex illocutionary acts.*

$\neg \mathscr{A}_1 = \neg \mathscr{A}_2$ iff $\mathscr{A}_1 = \mathscr{A}_2$, $(P_1 \Rightarrow \mathscr{A}_1) = (P_2 \Rightarrow \mathscr{A}_2)$ iff $P_1 = P_2$ and $\mathscr{A}_1 = \mathscr{A}_2$ and $(\mathscr{A}_1 \,\&\, \mathscr{A}_2) = (\mathscr{A}_3 \,\&\, \mathscr{A}_4)$ when $\{A_1, \mathscr{A}_2\} = \{A_3, \mathscr{A}_4\}$.

Two acts of illocutionary denegation are identical iff they are denegations of the same act. Two conditional illocutionary acts are identical iff they set the same condition on the performance of the same act. Finally, two conjunctions of illocutionary acts are identical iff the sets of their conjuncts are identical.[3]

3 A more advanced and simpler formalization of illocutionary logic is possible if we admit, as D. Vanderveken does in 'A model-theoretical semantics for illocutionary forces', an axiom of extensionality for all elementary illocutionary acts whether performable or not. Indeed if $F_1(P_1) = F_2(P_2)$ in case $F_1(P_1) \equiv F_2(P_2)$, each illocutionary act can be identified with the function from possible contexts of utterance into success values that gives the value success for a possible context i iff that act is successfully performed in that context. In such a logic, each illocutionary force F can then be identified with the function from Prop into $(2)^I$ that gives as value for each proposition P, the function from contexts into success values corresponding to elementary illocutionary act $F(P)$.

Axiom VI. *The law of foundation.*

If $\triangle$ then for some $\mathscr{A}$, $\mathscr{A} \triangleright$ and for all $\mathscr{A}'$ such that $\mathscr{A}' \triangleright$, $\mathscr{A} \simeq \mathscr{A}'$.

In each non-empty context of utterance, the speaker performs a strong speech act that commits him to all illocutions to which he is committed in that context. This strong speech act is unique modulo congruence.

Axiom VII. *The operations on illocutionary forces preserve strict equivalence.*

If F_2 is obtained from F_1 by applying one operation and $F_1(P) \equiv F_1(Q)$ then it is also the case that $F_2(P) \equiv F_2(Q)$.

Chapter 7

GENERAL LAWS OF ILLOCUTIONARY LOGIC

The laws of illocutionary logic state regularities concerning successful performances of and commitments to illocutionary acts. In this chapter we will enumerate some of these laws. We will emphasize those that are philosophically significant for the foundations of a formal theory of speech acts. These laws follow from the definitions, postulates, and axioms of propositional illocutionary logic stated in the last chapter.

One condition of adequacy on illocutionary logic is that its laws must be consistent with the facts of natural languages. Though the theory is formal, the empirical facts of natural language are relevant to it. The existence of regularities corresponding to the laws of the system is a form of empirical confirmation of the adequacy of the theory, and conversely the absence of such regularities is a form of disconfirmation of the theory. Furthermore the fact that the unified mathematical theory imposes a certain unified form of description to the facts of natural languages enables us to make predictions and offer explanations of regularities which would not be readily observable or apparent without the theory.

The laws of illocutionary logic can be classified according to their level of generality. First, the most general laws are those that hold for all illocutionary acts whether elementary or complex. An example is the law of the relative incompatibility of an illocution and its denegation. For all illocutionary acts $\mathscr{A}$, $\mathscr{A} > < \neg\mathscr{A}$.

Secondly, there are those laws of illocutionary logic that hold for all or most illocutionary forces. These state regularities concerning elementary illocutionary acts of the form $F(P)$. Thus, for example, for any non-expressive illocutionary force F there is the following law of elimination of truth-functional negation: $F(\sim P) \triangleright \neg F(P)$. A propositional negation commits the speaker to an illocutionary denegation.

Thirdly, there are the laws of illocutionary logic that hold only for primitive or for simple illocutionary forces such as, for example, the law of distribution of primitive illocutionary forces with respect to truth-functional conjunction: if F is primitive then $(F(P) \& F(Q)) \equiv F(P \& Q)$.

Fourthly, there are the laws of illocutionary logic that follow from the analysis of the five illocutionary points and hold only for all illocutionary forces with a given illocutionary point, e.g. for assertive forces or for commissive forces. An example of such a law is the law of the truth of the propositional content of a successful declaration. For all illocutionary forces F, if $\Pi_F = \Pi_4$ and $F(P)$ is performed in i then P is true in w_i.

Finally, the laws of least generality in illocutionary logic are those which govern specific illocutionary forces and follow from the definitions of the components of these forces. Thus, for example, if a speaker urges a hearer to do something he is committed to requesting him to do it because urging is obtained from requesting by adding the preparatory condition that the future course of action represented by the propositional content is important to the speaker or hearer.

In this chapter, we will discuss only the more general laws of illocutionary logic, i.e. the laws that hold for all illocutionary acts and for all illocutionary forces. In the next chapter, we will discuss the laws that hold for primitive and simple illocutionary forces and for each different type of illocutionary force. In Appendix 1, we will be concerned with the illocutionary entailments that follow from the semantical analysis of illocutionary verbs of English.

I. LAWS FOR THE COMPONENTS OF ILLOCUTIONARY FORCE.

It follows from the definitions of the set of all illocutionary forces and of the conditions of success of elementary illocutionary acts that the various components of an illocutionary force have certain general properties and stand in certain logical relations. For example, the degree of strength of illocutionary point of an illocutionary force of the form $[\mu]F$ is not smaller than the degree of strength of the illocutionary point of F and the degree of strength determined by the mode of achievement μ. The following are some general laws that state such properties of the components of illocutionary force that are in accordance with the hypothesis of constructibility.

1.1 *Each primitive illocutionary force has one illocutionary point, no special mode of achievement of that point, null degree of strength and only the propositional content, preparatory and sincerity conditions determined by that point.*

If F is primitive, mode $(F) = \Pi_F$, $|$mode $(F)| = 0$, $\text{Prop}_F = \bigcap \theta_{\Pi_F}$, $\Sigma_F = \bigcup \Sigma_{\Pi_F}$, $\Psi_F = \bigcup \Psi_{\Pi_F}$, and degree $(F) = \eta(F) = 0$

Proof:

Use the definition of the conditions of success of elementary illocutionary acts with a primitive force, the definitions of the components of an illocutionary force, the postulate of transitivity of degree of strength of the illocutionary point, and the fact that the degree of strength of the illocutionary point is the maximum of the degree of strength of the sincerity conditions and of the degree of strength determined by the mode of achievement.

1.2 *An illocutionary force of the form* $[\mu]F$ *has the following components:* $\Pi_{[\mu]F} = \Pi_F$, mode $([\mu]F) =$ mode (F) & μ, degree $([\mu]F) \geqslant$ the maximum of degree (F) and $|\mu|$, $\text{Prop}_{[\mu]F} = \text{Prop}_F \cap \bigcap \theta_\mu$, $\Sigma_{[\mu]F} = [\Sigma_F \cup \bigcup \Sigma_\mu]$, $\Psi_{[\mu]F} = [\Psi_F \cup \bigcup \Psi_\mu]$, and $\eta([\mu]F) \geqslant \eta(F)$.

An illocutionary force of the form $[\mu]F$ has the illocutionary point of F. Its mode of achievement is the conjunction of the mode of achievement of F and of the new mode μ. Its degree of strength of illocutionary point is not smaller than the degree of strength of illocutionary point of F and the degree of strength of illocutionary point determined by mode μ. Its propositional content conditions are the intersection of the propositional content conditions of F and of all propositional content conditions determined by μ. Its preparatory conditions are the closure of the union of the preparatory conditions of F and of all preparatory conditions determined by μ. Its sincerity conditions are of the closure of the union of the sincerity conditions of F and of all sincerity conditions determined by μ. Its degree of strength of sincerity conditions is not smaller than the degree of strength of sincerity conditions of F.

The operation of restricting the mode of achievement of an

illocutionary force F by imposing a new mode of achievement μ increases the degree of strength of the sincerity conditions when it is not possible to achieve the point with that mode without expressing the sincerity conditions of F with a greater degree of strength. Thus for example if we apply the operation of restricting the mode of achievement to the illocutionary force of a suggestion $[-1]$! by imposing the special mode of achievement of an order, we obtain an illocutionary force $[\text{mode}\,(\|\text{order}\|)]\,[-1]$! with the greater degree of strength of sincerity conditions o because the degree of strength of illocutionary point determined by that mode, $|\text{mode}\,(\|\text{order}\|)| = +1$; and it is not possible to achieve the directive point with the degree of strength $+1$ without expressing the sincerity conditions determined by that mode with at least the degree of strength o.

1.3 *An illocutionary force of the form* $[\Psi^*]F$ *has the following components:*

$\Pi_{[\Psi^*]F} = \Pi_F$, $\Psi_{[\Psi^*]F} = [\Psi_F \cup \Psi^*]$, $\Sigma_{[\Psi^*]F} = [\Sigma_F \cup \bigcup \Sigma_{\Psi^*}]$, mode $([\Psi^*]F) = \text{mode}\,(F)$ & $\wedge \mu_{\Psi^*}$, degree $[\Psi^*]F \geqslant$ the maximum of degree (F) and $|\wedge \mu_{\Psi^*}|$ and $\eta([\Psi^*]F) \geqslant (F)$, where $\wedge \mu_{\Psi^*}$ is the conjunction of all modes of achievement of Π_F determined by Ψ^*, and $\text{Prop}_{[\Psi^*]F} = \text{Prop}_F \cap \bigcap \theta_{\Psi^*}$.

An illocutionary force $[\Psi^*]F$ has the illocutionary point of F. Its sincerity conditions are the closure of the union of the sincerity conditions of F and of the new sincerity conditions Ψ^*. Its propositional content conditions are the intersection of the propositional content conditions of F and of all propositional content conditions determined by Ψ^*. Its preparatory conditions are the closure of the union of the preparatory conditions of F and of all preparatory conditions determined by Ψ^*. Its mode of achievement is the conjunction of the mode of achievement of F and of all modes of achievement of the illocutionary point of F determined by Ψ^*. Its degree of strength of illocutionary point is not smaller than the degree of strength of illocutionary point of F and the degree of strength of illocutionary point determined by the modes of achievement determined by Ψ^*, and its degree of strength of sincerity conditions is not smaller than $\eta(F)$.

1.4 *An illocutionary force of the form* $[\Sigma^*]F$ *has the following components:*

$\Pi_{[\Sigma^*]F} = \Pi_F$, $\Sigma_{[\Sigma^*]F} = [\Sigma_F \cup \Sigma^*]$, mode $([\Sigma^*]F) =$ mode (F)
& $\wedge \ \mu_{\Sigma^*}$, $\Psi_{[\Sigma^*]F} = [\Psi_F \cup \bigcup \Psi_{\Sigma^*}]$, $\mathrm{Prop}_{[\Sigma^*]F} = \mathrm{Prop}_F \cap \bigcap \theta_{\Sigma^*}$,
degree $([\Sigma^*]F) \geqslant$ the maximum of degree (F) and $| \wedge \ \mu_{\Sigma^*}|$ and
$\eta([\Sigma^*])F) \geqslant \eta(F)$.

An illocutionary force $[\Sigma^*]F$ has the illocutionary point of F. Its preparatory conditions are the closure of the union of the preparatory conditions of F and of the new preparatory conditions Σ^*. Its mode of achievement is the conjunction of the mode of achievement of F and of all modes of achievement determined by Σ^*. Its sincerity conditions are the closure of the union of the sincerity conditions of F and of all sincerity conditions determined by Σ^*. Its proportional content conditions are the intersection of the propositional content conditions of F and of all propositional content conditions determined by Σ^*. Its degree of strength of illocutionary point is not smaller than the degree of strength of illocutionary point of F and the degree of strength of illocutionary point determined by the modes of achievement that Σ^* determines and its degree of strength of the sincerity conditions is not smaller than $\eta(F)$.

1.5 *An illocutionary force of the form* $[\theta]F$ *has the following components:*

$\Pi_{[\theta]F} = \Pi_F$, $\mathrm{Prop}_{[\theta]F} = \mathrm{Prop}_F \cap \theta$, mode $([\theta]F) =$ mode (F) &
$\wedge \ \mu_\theta$, $\Sigma_{[\theta]F} = [\Sigma_F \cup \bigcup \Sigma_\theta]$, $\Psi_{[\theta]F} = [\Psi_F \cup \bigcup \Psi_\theta]$, degree$([\theta]F)$
$\geqslant$ the maximum of degree (F) and $| \wedge \ \mu_\theta|$ and $\eta([\theta]F) \geqslant \eta(F)$.

An illocutionary force $[\theta]F$ has the illocutionary point of F. Its propositional content conditions are the intersection of the propositional content conditions of F and of the new propositional content conditions θ. Its mode of achievement is the conjunction of the mode of achievement of F and of all modes of achievement determined by θ. Its preparatory conditions are the closure of the union of the preparatory conditions of F and of all preparatory conditions determined by θ. Its sincerity conditions are the closure of the union of the sincerity conditions of F and of all sincerity conditions determined by θ. Its degree of strength of illocutionary point is not smaller than the degree of strength of illocutionary point of F and the degree of strength of illocutionary point determined by the modes of achievement that θ determines, and its degree of strength of the sincerity conditions is not smaller than $\eta(F)$.

1.6 *An illocutionary force of the form* $[+_I]F$ *has the illocutionary point, mode of achievement, propositional content, preparatory and sincerity conditions of F. Its degree of strength of illocutionary point is the immediate successor of the degree of strength of illocutionary point of F when degree* $(F) = \eta(F)$, *and is identical with that of F otherwise. Its degree of strength of the sincerity conditions is the immediate successor of the degree of strength of the sincerity conditions of F.*

1.7 *An illocutionary force of the form* $[-_I]F$ *has the illocutionary point and some propositional content, preparatory and sincerity conditions of F. Its degree of strength of illocutionary point is the immediate predecessor of the degree of strength of illocutionary point of F when $|$mode $(F)| \neq$ degree (F) and is identical with degree (F) otherwise. Its degree of strength of the sincerity conditions is the immediate predecessor of the degree of strength of the sincerity conditions of F.*

1.8 *There is a normal form for each illocutionary force.*

Each illocutionary force F is of the form [mode (F)] $[\Psi_F]$ [Prop$_F$] $[\Sigma_F]$ $[\eta(F)]$ F^* is the primitive illocutionary force with illocutionary point Π_F.

Proof:

If F and F^* have the same illocutionary point then $F =$ [mode (F)] ... $[\eta(F)]F^*$ because both forces have the same components.

It can easily be proved that the order of the prefixes [mode (F)] $[\Psi_F]$ [Prop$_F$] $[\Sigma_F]$ $[\eta(F)]$ in a normal form has an importance. Thus for example F is not always identical with $[\eta(F)]$ [mode (F)] $[\Sigma_F]$ $[\Psi_F]$ [Prop$_F$]F^*.

The law that there is a normal form for each illocutionary force has the following obvious corollaries about the conditions of success of and the conditions of commitment to elementary illocutionary acts:

Corollary 1: An elementary illocutionary act has the following conditions of success:

$F(P)(i) = 1$ iff $i\Pi_F^{\text{degree}(F)}P$ and mode $(F)(i, P) = 1$, $P\in\text{Prop}_F(i)$, a_i presupposes in i propositions $\Sigma_F(i, P)\cup\sigma(P)$ and expresses in i with degree $\eta(F)$ psychological states $\Psi_F(i, P)$.

An illocutionary act $F(P)$ is performed in a context of utterance i iff the speaker in that context achieves the illocutionary point Π_F with the mode of achievement and degree of strength of illocutionary point of F on the propositional content P and P satisfies the propositional content conditions of F with respect to i, if he presupposes the preparatory conditions and the propositional presuppositions, and finally if he expresses with the required degree of strength the psychological states determined by the sincerity conditions of F.

Corollary 2: A speaker is committed to an elementary illocutionary act under the following conditions:

$\triangleright F(P)$ iff $i\Pi_F^{\text{degree }(F)}P$ and mode $(F)(i, P) = 1$; $P\in\text{Prop}_F(i)$; and a_i is committed in i to presupposing $\Sigma_F(i, P)$ and to having with degree of strength $\eta(F)$ the psychological states $\Psi_F(i, P)$.

A speaker is committed to an elementary illocutionary act $F(P)$ in a context of utterance i iff in that context (1) he is committed to the illocutionary point Π_F on P with the characteristic mode of achievement and degree of strength of F, (2) he is committed to presupposing the preparatory conditions, (3) he is committed to having the psychological states determined by the sincerity conditions with the required degree of strength of F, and finally (4) if P satisfies the propositional content conditions of F with respect to the context of utterance.

As the preceding theorems show, the recursive definition of the set of all illocutionary forces and the definitions of the conditions of success of and of the conditions of commitment to elementary illocutionary acts formulated in Chapter 6 are in accordance with the hypothesis of constructibility and with the earlier definitions of success and of commitment.

II. ILLOCUTIONARY ENTAILMENT.

Certain pairs of illocutionary force F_1, F_2 are such that it is not possible for a speaker to perform an illocutionary act of the form $F_1(P)$ without also performing an act of the form $F_2(P)$. In such a case, we say that F_1 *illocutionarily entails* F_2 and we write $F_1 \rhd F_2$. Thus, $F_1 \rhd F_2$ iff, for all propositions P, all conditions of success of $F_2(P)$ are conditions of success of $F_1(P)$, i.e. $\{i/F_1(P)$ is performed in $i\} \subseteq \{i/F_2(P)$ is performed in $i\}$.

The relation of illocutionary entailment is a relation of ordering on $\mathbf{\Phi}$, i.e. (1) it is reflexive: $F_1 \rhd F_1$; (2) it is anti-symmetric: if $F_1 \rhd F_2$ and $F_2 \rhd F_1$ then $F_1 = F_2$ (by the law of identity of illocutionary forces); (3) it is transitive: if $F_1 \rhd F_2$ and $F_2 \rhd F_3$ then $F_1 \rhd F_3$.

Of course, illocutionary entailment is a partial order on the set of all illocutionary forces, for there are illocutionary forces F_1, F_2 such that neither $F_1 \rhd F_2$ nor $F_2 \rhd F_1$. Indeed, it is not the case that for any pair of illocutionary forces F_1, F_2, $F_1(P) \rhd F_2(P)$ or $F_2(P) \rhd F_1(P)$. Consider, for example, the illocutionary forces $\|\text{inform}\|$ and $\|\text{call}\|$.

The set $\mathbf{\Phi}$ of all illocutionary forces has a strong logical structure with respect to illocutionary entailment, as the following theorems show:

2.1 *An illocutionary force that is the result of the application of one operation to an illocutionary force either illocutionarily entails or is illocutionarily entailed by that illocutionary force.*

$$[+1]F \rhd F, \; F \rhd [-1]F, \; [\mu]F \rhd F, \; [\theta]F \rhd F, \; [\Sigma]F \rhd F,$$
$$[\Psi]F \rhd F.$$

The following are instances of each of the possible cases of illocutionary entailment:

(*1*) *Illocutionary entailment by way of the degree of strength.*

$$[+1]F \rhd F, \; F \rhd [-1]F.$$

If two illocutionary forces F_1, F_2 differ only by the fact that the degrees of strength of illocutionary point or of sincerity conditions of F_1 are the successors of the degrees of strength of illocutionary point or of sincerity conditions of F_2, then all illocutionary acts of the form $F_1(P)$ strongly commit the speaker to an illocutionary act of the form $F_2(P)$.

Thus, for example, the illocutionary force of directives illocutionarily entails the directive illocutionary force of suggestion $\|\text{suggest}\|$ since $\|\text{suggest}\| = [-1]!$. Similarly the illocutionary force of a pledge entails the primitive commissive since $\|\text{pledge}\| = [+1]\perp$.

(2) Illocutionary entailment by way of the mode of achievement.

$$[\mu]\,F \rhd F.$$

If two illocutionary forces F_1 and F_2 differ only in that the mode of achievement of illocutionary point of F_1 is a restriction of the mode of achievement of F_2 so that the illocutionary point of F_2 cannot be achieved in the mode required by F_2 without also being achieved in the mode required by F_1, then all illocutionary acts of form $F_1(P)$ strongly commit the speaker to an illocutionary act of form $F_2(P)$. Thus, for example, a request commits the speaker to a directive because a request is just a directive illocutionary act that allows for the possibility of refusal. $\overset{.}{\downarrow}$ differs from ! only by the fact that mode $(\overset{.}{\downarrow})(i, P) = 1$ iff mode $(!)(i, P) = 1$ and a_i gives b_i in i option of refusing P. Consequently $\overset{.}{\downarrow} \rhd !$.

(3) Illocutionary entailment by way of propositional content conditions.

$$[\theta]\,F \rhd F.$$

If two illocutionary forces F_1 and F_2 differ only by the fact that F_1 has more propositional content conditions than F_2, then all illocutionary acts of the form $F_1(P)$ strongly commit the speaker to $F_2(P)$.

For example, a yes or no question ? (i.e. a question which one can answer by "yes" or "no") illocutionarily entails the illocutionary force or request: $? \geqslant \overset{.}{\downarrow}$, for a question is a request that the hearer perform a certain speech act. ? differs from $\overset{.}{\downarrow}$ only by the fact that it has the additional propositional content condition that the propositional content represents a future speech act of the hearer directed at the speaker.

(4) Illocutionary entailment by way of preparatory conditions.

$$[\Sigma^*]\,F \rhd F.$$

If two illocutionary forces F_1 and F_2 differ only in the fact that

F_1 has more preparatory conditions than F_2, then all illocutionary acts of form $F_1(P)$ strongly commit the speaker to an illocutionary act of the form $F_2(P)$.

For example, the commissive illocutionary force of acceptance illocutionarily entails the primitive commissive illocutionary force $\perp$, for to accept a directive to do something is simply to commit oneself to doing it while presupposing that one has been given a directive to do it that allows for the possibility of refusal.

(5) *Illocutionary entailment by way of sincerity conditions.*

$$[\Psi^*] F \rhd F.$$

If two illocutionary forces F_1, F_2 differ only by the fact that F_1 has more sincerity conditions than F_2, then all illocutionary acts of the form $F_1(P)$ strongly commit the speaker to an act of the form $F_2(P)$.

Thus, for example, the illocutionary force of a complaint illocutionarily entails that of an assertion because a complaint is an assertion with the additional sincerity condition that the speaker is dissatisfied with the state of affairs represented by the propositional content.

A consequence of all this by the transitivity of illocutionary entailment is the following:

2.2 *If an illocutionary force F_2 is obtained from another illocutionary force F_1 by applying the operations which consist in restricting the mode of achievement, increasing the degrees of strength, and adding new propositional content, preparatory or sincerity conditions, then F_2 illocutionarily entails F_1.*

For example, the illocutionary force of promise Pr illocutionarily entails the primitive commissive illocutionary force, for ∥promise∥ is obtained from the primitive commissive illocutionary force $\perp$ by applying successively operation (Σ) and operation (μ). A promise is a commissive with the special preparatory condition that what the speaker commits himself to doing is good for the hearer and the special mode of achievement of putting the speaker under an obligation to do what he commits himself to doing. This special mode of achievement increases the degree of strength of the illocutionary point. Thus, the illocutionary force

Pr differs from $\perp$ only by the fact that 1) mode $(\text{Pr})(i, P) = 1$ iff mode $(\perp)(i, P) = 1$ and a_i puts himself under an obligation to carry out the action represented by P; 2) degree $(\text{Pr}) = $ degree $(\perp) + 1$; and 3) $\Sigma_{\text{Pr}}(i, P) = \Sigma_{\perp}(i, P) \cup \{$the proposition that it is good for b_i that $P\}$. Consequently, $\text{Pr} \rhd \perp$.

Successive applications of operation (μ), operation $(+)$, operation (Σ), operation (θ), and operation (Ψ) to an illocutionary force F_1 generate illocutionary forces F_2 that illocutionarily entail F_1. Thus, when an illocutionary force F_3 is obtained by applying one of these operations to an illocutionary force F_2 that is itself also obtained by the same operations from another illocutionary force F_1, $F_3 \rhd F_2 \rhd F_1$. For example, if $F_3 = [\theta] F_2$ and $F_2 = [\mu] F_1$ then $F_3 \rhd F_2 \rhd F_1$. Thus, a question ? commits the speaker to a request which commits him to a directive: $? \rhd \downarrow \rhd !$.

The following are therefore cases of illocutionary entailment between two illocutionary forces with the same illocutionary point:

F_1 entails F_2 in case F_1 and F_2 differ at most by the fact that

(1) the mode of achievement of the illocutionary point of F_1 is a restriction of the mode of achievement of F_2:

$$\{(i, P)/\text{mode } (F_1)(i, P) = 1\} \subseteq \{(i, P)/\text{mode } (F_2)(i, P) = 1\}; \text{ or}$$

(2) the degrees of strength of the illocutionary point and of the sincerity conditions of F_1 are greater than the degree of strength of the illocutionary point of the sincerity conditions of F_2:

degree $(F_1) \geqslant$ degree (F_2) or $\eta(F_1) \geqslant \eta(F_2)$; or

(3) F_1 has more propositional content conditions than F_2:

For all i, $\text{Prop}_{F_1}(i) \subseteq \text{Prop}_{F_2}(i)$; or

(4) F_1 has more preparatory conditions than F_2:

For all i, $\Sigma_{F_2}(i, P) \subseteq \Sigma_{F_1}(i, P)$; or

(5) F_1 has more sincerity conditions than F_2:

For all i, $\Psi_{F_2}(i, P) \subseteq \Psi_{F_1}(i, P)$.

The converse of theorem 2.2 is also true in illocutionary logic when F_1 and F_2 have the same illocutionary point.

2.3 *A completeness theorem.*
An illocutionary force F_1 illocutionarily entails an illocutionary force F_2 with the same point iff it can be obtained from F_2 by applying the operations which consist in restricting the mode of achievement, increasing the degrees of strength, and adding new propositional content, preparatory or sincerity conditions.

The proof that for any two illocutionary forces F_1, F_2 such that $\Pi_{F_1} = \Pi_{F_2}$, $F_1 \rhd F_2$ only if F_1 can be obtained from F_2 by applying the operations mentioned above, is made by using the law that there is a normal form for each illocutionary force. According to that law $F_1 = [\text{mode } (F_1)][\Psi_{F_1}][\Sigma_{F_1}][\text{Prop}_{F_1}][\eta(F_1)]F^*$ and $F_2 = [\text{mode } (F_2)][\Psi_{F_2}][\Sigma_{F_2}][\text{Prop}_{F_2}][\eta(F_2)]F^*$ where F^* is the primitive force with illocutionary point Π_{F_1}. Now if $F_1 \rhd F_2$ by the definition of the components of an illocutionary force, there exists a mode of achievement μ^* such that mode $(F_1) = \text{mode } (F_2) \& \mu^*$, there exists a propositional content condition θ^* such that $\text{Prop}_{F_1} = \text{Prop}_{F_2} \cap \theta^*$, there exists a preparatory condition Σ^* such that $\Sigma_{F_1} = \Sigma_{F_2} \cup \Sigma^*$, there exists a sincerity condition Ψ^* such that $\Psi_{F_1} = \Psi_{F_2} \cup \Psi^*$, and there exists a positive or null integer k such that $\eta(F_1) = \eta(F_2) + k$. Consequently, $F_1 = [\text{mode } (F_2) \& \mu^*][\Psi_{F_2} \cup \Psi^*][\Sigma_{F_2} \cup \Sigma^*][\text{Prop}_{F_2} \cap \theta^*][\eta(F_2) + k]F^*$. But by definition $[\mu_1 \& \mu_2]F = [\mu_1][\mu_2]F, [\theta_1 \cap \theta_2]F = [\theta_1][\theta_2]F$, $[\Psi_1 \cup \Psi_2]F = [\Psi_1][\Psi_2]F$. Consequently, $F_1 = [\mu^*][\Psi^*][\Sigma^*][\theta^*][k][\text{mode } (F_2)][\Psi_{F_2}][\Sigma_{F_2}][\text{Prop}_{F_2}]\eta(F_2)F^* = [\mu^*][\Psi^*][\Sigma^*][\theta^*][k]F_2$. In other words, F_1 is obtained from F_2 by applying the operations which consist of imposing the mode of achievement μ^*, increasing by k the degrees of strength, and adding propositional content conditions θ^*, preparatory conditions Σ^*, and sincerity conditions Ψ^*.

The preceding theorem is important because it establishes the completeness of our set of operations on illocutionary forces in relation to illocutionary entailment. The reason it is restricted to cases of illocutionary entailment between forces with the same point is that the operations on illocutionary forces do not affect illocutionary point. Thus for example each non-expressive force illocutionarily entails an expressive force which consists of expressing its sincerity condition (e.g. $\vdash \rhd [\Psi] \dashv$ where $\Psi(i, P) = \{\text{Bel}(P)\}$) although it cannot be derived from it since its illocutionary point is not expressive and is not reducible to an expressive point.

The completeness theorem has many strong consequences, such as:

2.4 *Each finite set of illocutionary forces with the same point has a lower bound.*

If for all $F \in \Gamma$, $\Pi_F = \Pi$ and Γ is finite and non-empty then there exists an illocutionary force F_0, such that for all $F \in \Gamma$, $F \rhd F_0$.

For each finite non-empty set of illocutionary forces with the same illocutionary point there exists an illocutionary force that is illocutionarily entailed by all illocutionary forces of that set.

Proof:

Let F be the illocutionary force such that $F_0 = [\underset{F \in \Gamma}{V} \text{mode} (F)][\bigcup \text{Prop}_{F \in \Gamma}][\bigcap \Sigma_{F \in \Gamma}][\bigcap \Psi_{F \in \Gamma}][k]F^*$ where F^* is the primitive illocutionary force from which all F can be derived, k is the smallest degree of strength of sincerity conditions and V mode (F) is the disjunction of all modes of achievement of a force $F \in \Gamma$.

2.5 *Illocutionary entailment of simple illocutionary forces.*

If F_2 is a simple illocutionary force, then for all illocutionary forces F_1, such that $\Pi_{F_1} = \Pi_{F_2}$, degree $(F_1) \geqslant$ degree (F_2) and $\eta(F_1) \geqslant \eta(F_2)$, $F_1 \rhd F_2$.

A simple illocutionary force is illocutionarily entailed by all illocutionary forces F with the same illocutionary point that have greater or equal degrees of strength of illocutionary point and of sincerity conditions.

Thus, for example, all directive illocutionary forces F with degree (F) and $\eta(F) \geqslant -1$ entail the weak directive $\|\text{suggest}\|$. In particular, if F_2 is a primitive illocutionary force, then for all simple illocutionary forces F_1 such that $\Pi_{F_1} = \Pi_{F_2}$ and degree (F_1), $\eta(F_1) \geqslant 0$, $F_1 \rhd F_2$. Thus, for example, all simple commissive illocutionary forces F with degree (F), $\eta(F) \geqslant 0$ entail the primitive commissive force $\perp$.

Proof:
The proof of this theorem is based on the transitivity of degree of strength and on the fact that simple illocutionary forces have no special mode of achievement, and only preparatory, propositional content, and sincerity conditions determined by their illocutionary point.

Corollary 1. Each set (finite or infinite) of illocutionary forces with the same point which contains an illocutionary force with a smallest degree of strength has a lower bound.

If $\Gamma \subseteq \Phi$, for all $F \in \Gamma$, $\Pi_F = \Pi$, and for some $F' \in \Gamma$, for all $F \in \Gamma$ $\eta(F) \geqslant \eta(F')$ and degree $(F) \geqslant$ degree (F'), then there exists an illocutionary force $F_0 \in \Phi$ such that for all $F \in \Gamma$, $F \rhd F_0$

Proof:
Take F_0 to be the simple illocutionary force with illocutionary point Π and degree $(F_0) = \eta(F_0) = \eta(F')$.

2.6 *No set which contains all illocutionary forces with a given illocutionary point has an upper bound.*
It is not the case that a set containing all illocutionary forces with the same illocutionary point has an upper bound because it contains relatively incompatible forces. If, for example, F_1 and F_2 are two illocutionary forces with relatively inconsistent modes of achievement of illocutionary point, i.e. if mode $(F_1)(i, P) \neq$ mode $(F_2)(i, P)$, then an illocutionary force F_3 such that $F_3 \rhd F_1$ and $F_3 \rhd F_2$ would have an impossible mode of achievement: mode $(F_3)(i, P) = 0$ for all i and P. Consequently, F_3 would not be a possible illocutionary force.

2.7 *There exists a least element in certain sets of illocutionary forces.*

If $\Gamma = \{F/\Pi_F = \Pi \text{ and degree}(F) \text{ and } \eta(F) \geqslant k\} \neq \varnothing$ then there exists a unique illocutionary force $F_0 \in \Gamma$ such that for all $F \in \Gamma$, $F \rhd F_0$.

Each set that contains all illocutionary forces with a given illocutionary point whose degrees of strength are equal to or greater than a given integer contains an illocutionary force that is illocutionarily entailed by all others.

Proof:

Clearly, by corollary 1 of theorem 2.5, all illocutionary forces $F \in \Gamma$ entail the simple illocutionary force F_0 with degrees of strength degree $(F_0) = \eta(F_0) = k$, and by definition $F_0 \in \Gamma$. Now by the anti-symmetry of $\triangleright$, if there is an illocutionary force F_1 such that $F_0 \triangleright F_1$, $F_1 = F_0$. Consequently, F_0 is the unique least element of Γ.

Thus, for example, the set of all declarative illocutionary forces has a least element that is entailed by all declarative forces, namely the primitive illocutionary force of declaration T. The set of all commissive illocutionary forces with degrees of strength equal to or greater than $+1$ has a least element which is the illocutionary force $\|\text{pledge}\| = [+1]\perp$.

Illocutionary entailment is not a well ordering on sets of illocutionary forces with the same illocutionary point since there are such sets of illocutionary forces which do not contain a smallest element. This is the case, for example, for all sets of the form $\{F_1, F_2\}$ where $\Pi_{F_1} = \Pi_{F_2}$ and neither $F_1 \triangleright F_2$ nor $F_2 \triangleright F_1$.

2.8 *A Church–Rosser theorem for illocutionary entailment.*

If $\Pi_{F_1} = \Pi_{F_2}$ and both $F \triangleright F_1$ and $F \triangleright F_2$ then there exists some F_3 such that both $F_1 \triangleright F_3$ and $F_2 \triangleright F_3$.

If an illocutionary force F illocutionarily entails two illocutionary forces F_1, F_2 with the same illocutionary point, then there exists a third one F_3 which is illocutionarily entailed by those two illocutionary forces F_1 and F_2. Thus, if an illocutionary act $F(P)$ strongly commits the speaker to two illocutionary acts $F_1(P)$ and $F_2(P)$ then there exists a third illocutionary act $F_3(P)$ to which those two illocutionary acts $F_1(P)$ and $F_2(P)$ strongly commit him.

Proof:

Let F_3 be the expressive force $[\Psi_{F_1} \cap \Psi_{F_2}][k] \dashv$ where k is the minimum of the degrees of strength of sincerity conditions of F_1 and F_2.

III. LAWS OF IDENTITY FOR DERIVED ILLOCUTIONARY
FORCES.

3.1 $[+1]F_1 = [+1]F_2$ iff $F_1 = F_2$; $[-1]F_1 = [-1]F_2$ iff
$F_1 = F_2$.
Two illocutionary forces obtained by increasing (or decreasing)
the degrees of strength of two other illocutionary forces are
identical iff these two illocutionary forces are identical.

A propositional content condition θ, a preparatory condition Σ,
and a sincerity condition Ψ are said hereafter to be *new* with respect
to an illocutionary force F when they are not included in the
propositional content, preparatory and sincerity conditions of F,
i.e. when $\theta(i) \nsubseteq \mathrm{Prop}_F(i)$ $\Sigma(i, P) \nsubseteq \Sigma_F(i, P)$ and $\Psi(i, P) \nsubseteq \Psi_F(i, P)$
and do not determine any condition or mode that is part of a
component of F and when their addition does not increase the
degrees of strength of F.

3.2 When θ is new with respect to F_1 and F_2, $[\theta]F_1 = [\theta]F_2$
iff $F_1 = F_2$. When Σ is new with respect to F_1 and F_2, $[\Sigma]F_1 =$
$[\Sigma]F_2'$ iff $F_1 = F_2$.
Two illocutionary forces obtained by adding, respectively, to two
forces F_1, F_2 new propositional content conditions θ or new
preparatory conditions Σ are identical iff $F_1 = F_2$.

3.3 When Ψ is new with respect to F_1 or F_2, $[\Psi]F_1 = [\Psi]F_2$
iff $F_1 = F_2$.
Two illocutionary forces obtained by adding respectively new
sincerity conditions to two illocutionary forces F_1, F_2 are identical
iff $F_1 = F_2$.

The reason that $[\Psi]F_1 = [\Psi]F_2$ entails $F_1 = F_2$ only if Ψ is
new is that the addition of sincerity conditions Ψ to an illocutionary
force may also constitute the addition of preparatory conditions Σ
in case Ψ determines Σ. In such a case, there may be two illocutionary forces $F_1 \neq [\Sigma]F_1$ such that $[\Psi]F_1 = [\Psi][\Sigma]F_1$.

3.4 When μ is new with respect to F_1 and F_2, $[\mu]F_1 = [\mu]F_2$
iff $F_1 = F_2$.
Two illocutionary forces obtained by imposing a new mode of
achievement on two forces F_1 and F_2 are identical iff $F_1 = F_2$.

The following laws of identity for derived illocutionary forces are immediate consequences of the set-theoretical properties of the operations on the components of illocutionary force.

3.5 $[\Psi_1][\Psi_2]F = [\Psi_1 \cup \Psi_2]F = [\Psi_2][\Psi_1]F$ and similarly for $[\Sigma_1][\Sigma_2]F$.

The illocutionary force obtained by adding first sincerity conditions Ψ_2 and then sincerity conditions Ψ_1 to an illocutionary force F is identical with the force obtained by adding first sincerity conditions Ψ_1 and then sincerity conditions Ψ_2, and with the illocutionary force obtained by adding to F the union of those sincerity conditions.

3.6 $[\mu_1][\mu_2]F = [\mu_1 \& \mu_2]F = [\mu_2][\mu_1]F$.

The illocutionary force obtained by adding first mode of achievement μ_2 and then mode of achievement μ_1 to an illocutionary force F is identical with the force obtained by adding first mode of achievement μ_1 and then mode of achievement μ_2 to F, and is also identical with the illocutionary force obtained by adding to F the conjunction of these modes of achievement.

3.7 $[\theta_1][\theta_2]F = [\theta_1 \cap \theta_2]F = [\theta_2][\theta_1]F$.

The illocutionary force obtained by adding first propositional content conditions θ_2 and then propositional content conditions θ_1 to an illocutionary force F is identical with the force obtained by adding first θ_1 and then θ_2 to F and with the force obtained by adding to F the intersection of these propositional content conditions.

IV. SOME LAWS CONCERNING ILLOCUTIONARY COMMITMENT.

It follows from our axioms that the relation $\triangleright$ of illocutionary commitment is both reflexive and transitive. It is transitive by axiom I. The proof that it is reflexive follows easily from the following lemmas:

Lemma 1: A speaker who achieves an illocutionary point on a proposition with a certain degree of strength is committed to that point on that proposition with that degree.

If $i\Pi^k P$ then $i\hat{\Pi}^k P$.

Proof:
Use the definition of $\hat{\Pi}$ and the reflexivity of strict implication.

Lemma 2: A speaker who expresses a psychological state with a certain degree of strength is committed to having that state with that degree of strength.

Proof:
Use the definition of strong propositional attitude commitment.

4.1 The law of reflexivity of $\triangleright$.

The speaker is committed to all of the illocutionary acts that he performs. $\mathscr{A} \triangleright \mathscr{A}$ is proved by induction on the length of $\mathscr{A}$.
Basis: $\mathscr{A}$ is of the form $F(P)$.
Clearly, if $F(P)(i) = 1$ then by definition $\triangleright F(P)$ since $i\Pi_F^k P$ entails $i\hat{\Pi}^k P$ and a_i is committed to presupposing $\Sigma_F(i, P)$ and to having $\Psi_F(i, P)$ if he presupposes $\Sigma_F(i, P)$ and expresses with degree $\eta(F)$, $\Psi_F(i, P)$ by the preceding lemmas.

Case 1. $\mathscr{A}$ is of the form $\neg\mathscr{A}'$.
Suppose that it is not the case that $\triangleright \neg\mathscr{A}'$. Then by definition, for no $\mathscr{A}''$, $\mathscr{A}''(i) = 1$ and $\{\mathscr{A}', \mathscr{A}''\}$ is not simultaneously performable. Consequently, $\neg\mathscr{A}'(i) = 0$ since it is incompatible with $\mathscr{A}'$. Thus, by contraposition, if $\neg\mathscr{A}'(i) = 1$ then $\triangleright \neg\mathscr{A}'$ and $\neg\mathscr{A}' \triangleright \neg\mathscr{A}'$.

Case 2. $\mathscr{A}$ is of the form $(\mathscr{A}_1 \& \mathscr{A}_2)$.
Suppose that $(\mathscr{A}_1 \& \mathscr{A}_2)(i) = 1$. Then by definition $\mathscr{A}_1(i) = 1$ and $\mathscr{A}_2(i) = 1$. Now, by the induction hypothesis $\mathscr{A}_1 \triangleright \mathscr{A}_1$ and $\mathscr{A}_2 \triangleright \mathscr{A}_2$. Consequently, $(\mathscr{A}_1 \& \mathscr{A}_2) \triangleright (\mathscr{A}_1 \& \mathscr{A}_2)$ by definition.

Case 3. $\mathscr{A}$ is of the form $(P \Rightarrow \mathscr{A}')$.
Suppose that it is not the case that $\triangleright (P \Rightarrow \mathscr{A}')$. Then, by definition, for no $\mathscr{A}''$ both $\mathscr{A}''(i) = 1$ and for all j where $\mathscr{A}''(j) = 1$ and $P(w_j) = 1$, $\triangleright \mathscr{A}'$. Consequently, $(P \Rightarrow \mathscr{A}')(i) = 0$ for by the law of *modus ponens*, for all j where $(P \Rightarrow \mathscr{A}')(j) = P(w_j) = 1$, $\mathscr{A}'(j) = 1$ and, since $\mathscr{A}' \triangleright \mathscr{A}'$ by the induction hypothesis, for all such j, $\triangleright \mathscr{A}'$. Thus, by contraposition, if $(P \Rightarrow \mathscr{A}')(i) = 1$ then it is also the case that $\triangleright (P \Rightarrow \mathscr{A}')$. Consequently $(P \Rightarrow \mathscr{A}') \triangleright (P \Rightarrow \mathscr{A}')$.

4.2 ▷ *is not anti-symmetric.*

$\mathscr{A}_1 \triangleright \mathscr{A}_2$ and $\mathscr{A}_2 \triangleright \mathscr{A}_1$ does not entail $\mathscr{A}_1 = \mathscr{A}_2$.

Illocutionary congruence is weaker than identity. Thus, for example, if P is necessarily true, the conditional illocutionary act $(P \Rightarrow \mathscr{A})$ is congruent with illocutionary act $\mathscr{A}$ but is nevertheless not identical with it. Similarly if $F_1(P_1)$ and $F_2(P_2)$ are self-defeating then these illocutions are congruent but they are not necessarily identical. Actually, illocutionary congruence is weaker than strict equivalence since when P is necessarily true, illocutionary acts $\mathscr{A}$ and $(P \Rightarrow \mathscr{A})$ are congruent but have different conditions of success since P must be expressed in case of a successful performance of the conditional speech act and not in the other case.

4.3 ▷ *is neither universal nor empty.*

It is not the case that for no $\mathscr{A}$, $\mathscr{A}'$, $\mathscr{A} \triangleright \mathscr{A}'$ since ▷ is reflexive. It is also not the case that for any $\mathscr{A}$, $\mathscr{A}'$, $\mathscr{A} \triangleright \mathscr{A}'$. Otherwise all illocutionary acts would be self-defeating. There are performable illocutionary acts since all illocutionary forces are possible. This is proved by the following theorem:

4.3.1 *All illocutionary forces are possible illocutionary forces.*

For all illocutionary forces F, there exists at least one performable illocutionary act of the form $F(P)$.

Proof:

Suppose that a primitive illocutionary force F is not possible. In that case $\mathrm{Prop}_F(i) = \varnothing$. But this is false. Consequently, all primitive illocutionary forces are possible. Now, if F is a derived illocutionary force that is not primitive then it must also be possible since it is obtained by applying one or several operations to a primitive illocutionary force and the rules of closure of the set of all illocutionary forces do not change the illocutionary point and consequently preserve possibility.

The philosophical significance of the fact that all illocutionary forces are possible is best seen by contrasting illocutionary force with propositional content in this regard. There are impossible propositions, and indeed the negation of every necessary proposition is an impossible proposition. But there cannot analogously be any impossible illocutionary forces for such a force would fail to be an illocutionary force altogether. Because the notion of illocutionary force has to do with the "pragmatics" of language, with how language is used, an impossible illocutionary force would serve no purpose and so would not be a force at all. Analogously there cannot be any necessary illocutionary forces.

Corollary: All illocutionary points are non-empty.

For each Π, $\Pi^0 \neq \varnothing$.

Each illocutionary point can be achieved with the null degree of strength.

4.4 *A speaker is committed to an illocution iff he performs an illocutionary act that commits him to that illocution.*
Proof:
By definition, if some illocution $\mathcal{A}_2(i) = 1$ and $\mathcal{A}_2 \triangleright \mathcal{A}_1$, then $\triangleright \mathcal{A}_1$. Now suppose that for some $\mathcal{A}_1, \triangleright \mathcal{A}_1$. By the axiom of foundation, this entails that there exists a strong illocution $\mathcal{A}_2$ performed as i such that $\mathcal{A}_2 \triangleright \mathcal{A}_1$.

4.4.1 *An illocutionary act is performable iff it does not commit the speaker to all illocutionary acts.*
Proof:
By definition, if $\mathcal{A}$ is not performable then for all $\mathcal{A}'$, $\mathcal{A} \triangleright \mathcal{A}'$. Now, suppose that for all $\mathcal{A}'$, $\mathcal{A} \triangleright \mathcal{A}'$. Then for any illocutionary $\mathcal{A}'$ such that $\{i/\triangleright\mathcal{A}'\} = \varnothing$, $\mathcal{A} \triangleright \mathcal{A}'$. Consequently, for no $i \in I$, $\mathcal{A}(i) = 1$, i.e. $\mathcal{A}$ is not performable. An example of an illocution $\mathcal{A}$ such that, for no i, $\triangleright \mathcal{A}$ is any illocution $!(P)$ where, for no $i \in I$, $P \in \mathrm{Prop}_1(i)$. Two consequences of this theorem are:

4.4.2 *All and only the self-defeating illocutionary acts commit the speaker to all illocutionary acts.*

4.4.3 *A set Γ of illocutionary acts is simultaneously performable iff it is not the case that for all illocutions $\mathcal{A}$, $\Gamma \triangleright \mathcal{A}$.*

4.5 *Two illocutionary acts are congruent iff a speaker is committed to both under the same conditions.*

$$\mathcal{A}_1 \simeq \mathcal{A}_2 \text{ iff } \{i/\triangleright\mathcal{A}_1\} = \{i/\triangleright\mathcal{A}_2\}.$$

Proof:

Use the transitivity of $\triangleright$ and the axiom of foundation.

4.6 *Simultaneous performability is illocutionary consistency.*

A set of illocutionary acts is simultaneously performable iff it is consistent. Thus if it is not possible to perform simultaneously several illocutionary acts, then it is also not possible to be simultaneously committed to them in a possible context of utterance, and conversely.

Proof:

If Γ is simultaneously performable, it is illocutionarily consistent by the reflexivity of $\triangleright$. Suppose now that Γ is not simultaneously performable. Then, by definition, for any inconsistent illocutionary act $\mathscr{A}$ $\Gamma \triangleright \mathscr{A}$. Consequently, Γ is also inconsistent, for if for some $i \in I$, for all $\mathscr{A}' \in \Gamma, \triangleright \mathscr{A}'$, then it would also be the case that $\triangleright \mathscr{A}$ by the axiom of foundation and the transitivity of $\triangleright$.

4.7 *Each consistent set of illocutionary acts is dominated by a consistent illocution.*

If $\Gamma \subseteq$ Act is a consistent set of illocutionary acts, then for some illocution $\mathscr{A}^*$, for all $\mathscr{A} \in \Gamma$, $\mathscr{A}^* \triangleright \mathscr{A}$, and $\mathscr{A}^*$ is consistent.

Proof:

If Γ is consistent, then, for some $i \in I$, for all $\mathscr{A} \in \Gamma, \triangleright \mathscr{A}$. Take $\mathscr{A}^*$ to be a strong illocution performed at i. Such a strong illocutionary act exists by the axiom of foundation.

Of course any set of illocutions is dominated by a speech act since self-defeating illocutions commit the speaker to all speech acts. But *only* consistent sets of illocutions are dominated by a *consistent* speech act for only self-defeating illocutionary acts commit the speaker to self-defeating illocutionary acts. Notice that none of the speech acts that dominate a set of illocutionary acts may belong to it. Thus, for example, if neither $F_1(P_1) \triangleright F_2(P_2)$ nor $F_2(P_2) \triangleright F_1(P_1)$, then no member of $\{F_1(P_1), F_2(P_2)\}$ dominates it.

Some consistent sets of illocutionary acts contain one of the illocutions that dominate them. They have a greatest element that is unique modulo illocutionary congruence. These are: the sets containing all illocutionary acts that a speaker simultaneously performs in a context of utterance, i.e. $\{\Gamma /$ for some $i \in I$, $\Gamma = \{\mathscr{A} / \mathscr{A}$

$(i) = 1$}} and the sets containing all illocutionary acts to which a speaker is committed in a context of utterance i.e. $\{\Gamma /$ for some $i \in I$, $\Gamma = \{\mathscr{A}/\triangleright \mathscr{A}\}\}$.

4.8 *Failure of the compactness theorem.*

By the contraposition of theorem 4.6, sets of illocutionary acts which are not dominated by a consistent speech act are inconsistent. As a consequence of this, some infinite sets of illocutionary acts are inconsistent although all their finite subsets are consistent. This is the case, for example, for all infinite sets of illocutionary acts of the form $\{F(P), [+1]F(P_1), [+2]F(P_2), \ldots\}$ whose finite subsets are consistent, since in each context of utterance where a speaker achieves an illocutionary point, he achieves that illocutionary point with a greatest degree of strength k. Such infinite sets of illocutions exist since there are infinite sets of illocutionary forces of form $\{F, [+1]F, [+2]F, \ldots\}$. The theorem of compactness is then false in illocutionary logic. It is not true that a set of illocutionary acts is consistent iff all its finite subsets are consistent.

4.9 *The failure of the law of extensionality.*

It is not the case that for all P, Q, and F, if $P(w_i) = Q(w_i)$ then $F(P)(i) = F(Q)(i)$, and similarly for $\triangleright$.

The successful performance of (and commitment to) an elementary illocutionary act is not a function of the truth value of its propositional content.

4.10 *The failure of the law of compatibility of $\dashv$ with respect to $\triangleright$ and $\triangleright$.*

It is not the case unrestrictedly that if $P \dashv Q(w) = 1$ then $F(P) \triangleright F(Q)$.

Thus, for an illocutionary force F, the fact that a proposition P strictly implies another proposition Q does not entail that an illocutionary act of form $F(P)$ commits the speaker to an illocutionary act of form $F(Q)$. There are various reasons why the inference:

$$\frac{P \dashv Q(w) = 1}{F(P) \triangleright F(Q)}$$

is not valid unrestrictedly.

(1) The performance of $F(P)$ does not entail that the speaker is committed to Π_F on Q with the characteristic mode of achievement and degree of strength of F.

$F(P) \not\triangleright F(Q)$ because for some $i \in I$, $F(P)$ is performed in i and it is not the case that $i \hat{\Pi}_F Q$ or mode $(F)(i, Q) = 1$.

Thus, for example, to promise to do a future action represented by P does not commit the speaker to promising to do the future action represented by $(P \vee Q)$ even if P strictly implies $(P \vee Q)$, for the performance of an act of promising to do P does not achieve the illocutionary point or purpose of committing the speaker to a promise to do the disjunctive action represented by $(P \vee Q)$ for any arbitrary proposition Q.

(2) The performance of $F(P)$ does not entail that Q satisfies the propositional content conditions of F.

$F(P) \not\triangleright F(Q)$ because for some $i \in I$, $F(P)$ is performed in i but it is not the case that $Q \in \text{Prop}_F(i)$.

Thus, for example, any proposition P that is future with respect to a time t_i, strictly implies a proposition of the form $(P \vee Q)$. But Q is not necessarily future with respect to t_i. Consequently, for some P and Q, P strictly implies $(P \vee Q)$ but a prediction that P does not commit the speaker to a prediction that $(P \vee Q)$.

(3) The performance of $F(P)$ does not entail that the speaker is committed to presupposing all preparatory conditions nor to having all psychological states of $F(Q)$. $F(P) \not\triangleright F(Q)$ because for some $i \in I$, $F(P)$ is performed in i but it is not the case that a_i is committed either to presupposing all propositions $\Sigma_F(i, Q)$ or to having all psychological states $\Psi_F(i, Q)$ in i.

Thus, for example, any proposition P strictly implies the tautology $(P \to P)$. But any speaker who reminds a hearer that P does not necessarily presuppose that he might have forgotten the truth of $(P \to P)$. Consequently to remind a hearer that P does not commit the speaker to reminding him that $(P \to P)$.

Actually, not only strict implication but also strict equivalence is not compatible unrestrictedly with $\triangleright$.

4.10.1 *The failure of the law of compatibility of* $\dashv\vdash$ *with respect to* $\triangleright$.
It is not the case unrestrictedly that if $P \dashv\vdash Q(w) = 1$ then $F(P) \triangleright F(Q)$.

It follows from this that it is not the case that all necessarily equivalent propositions are identical in illocutionary logic. The law of substitutibility of strictly equivalent propositions fails since it is not the case unrestrictedly that for any propositions P, Q, if $(P \leftrightarrow Q)(w) = 1$ then $F(P) \simeq F(Q)$.

4.10.2 *Propositional identity.*

Illocutionary logic imposes stronger conditions than strict equivalence of truth conditions for propositional identity. By the law of propositional identity, two propositions P and Q are identical iff for all illocutionary forces F, illocutionary acts $F(P)$ and $F(Q)$ are strictly equivalent and have the same conditions of success. It is a consequence of this law that some laws of propositional identity of intensional logic fail in illocutionary logic. Thus, for example, it is not the case that any proposition P is identical with its conjunction with any tautology, e.g. that $P = P \mathbin{\&} (Q \vee \sim Q)$, for there are propositional content conditions (for example Prop2 and Prop3) such that for some P and Q for all i where $P \in \mathrm{Prop}_F(i)$, $Q \notin \mathrm{Prop}_F(i)$, and consequently $F(P) \not\simeq F(P \mathbin{\&} (Q \vee Q))$ when $F(P)$ is performable.

Since all illocutionary forces are obtained from the few primitive illocutionary forces by operations that preserve strict equivalence the law of propositional identity has the following corollary:

4.11 *Strict equivalence between all illocutionary acts of the form $F(P)$ and $F(Q)$ with a primitive illocutionary force is a necessary and sufficient condition for the propositional identity between P and Q.*
For all P, $Q \in \mathrm{Prop}$, $P = Q$ iff, for all *primitive* illocutionary forces F, $F(P) \equiv F(Q)$.

4.12 *Criteria of identity for illocutionary acts.*

In philosophical logic propositions are sometimes identified with their truth conditions. Can illocutions be similarly identified in illocutionary logic with their conditions of success, i.e. is it the case that $\mathscr{A}_1 = \mathscr{A}_2$ iff $\mathscr{A}_1 \equiv \mathscr{A}_2$? As we said in Chapter 4, this criterion of identity is not valid for illocutionary acts in general in our logic because not all self-defeating illocutions are identical. But it is valid for performable elementary illocutionary acts, because any difference of logical form between two performable illocutionary acts must be reflected in their conditions of success. Two different performable illocutionary acts must be performed under different conditions. A stronger and complete law of identity for illocutionary acts is the following:[1] Two illocutionary acts are identical iff they have both the same conditions of success and the same conditions of failure, i.e. if it is not possible to succeed or fail to perform one in a context of utterance without succeeding or failing to perform the other in the same context. As we have defined success and failure this law is language-dependent, in the sense that its application depends on the resources of specific languages. The notion of failing to perform an illocutionary act is defined in terms of *trying*, and trying is defined in terms of uttering a sentence that expresses that act in that language as used, whether literally or not literally, on that occasion.

4.13 *On the logical form of elementary illocutionary acts.*

In connection with this discussion of the criteria of identity of illocutionary acts, it is also worth pointing out that elementary illocutions of the form $F(P)$ are *not* ordered pairs of the form $\langle F, P \rangle$, i.e. that it is not the case that $F_1(P_1) = F_2(P_2)$ iff $F_1 = F_2$ and $P_1 = P_2$, as is sometimes assumed. In other words the set of all elementary illocutionary acts is not of the form $\Phi \times \text{Prop}$. Clearly in illocutionary logic if $F_1 = F_2$ and $P_1 = P_2$ then $F_1(P_1) = F_2(P_2)$. But the converse is not true. In the performance of an elementary illocution, an illocutionary force F is *applied* to a propositional content P. The applications of different forces to the same propositional content may constitute the performance of the same illocutionary act, just as in arithmetic the application of different functions to the same number may yield the same results.

Thus, for example, a report and an assertion that God created the world are identical speech acts although their illocutionary forces are different since $\|\text{report}\|$ has a particular propositional content condition. Similarly the question and the request respectively expressed by the sentences "Is he coming?", "Please tell me whether he is coming" are identical because they have the same

---

[1] D. Vanderveken, 'What is an illocutionary force?'

conditions of success although they have different illocutionary forces with different propositional content conditions.

V. RELATIVE INCOMPATIBILITY AND SELF-DEFEATING SPEECH ACTS.

5.1 *The five sorts of cases of relative incompatibility.*

It follows from the definitions of the conditions of success and of illocutionary commitment that two illocutionary acts $F_1(P_1)$, $F_2(P_2)$ are relatively incompatible if the successful performance of $F_1(P_1)$ is relatively inconsistent (1) with the achievement of the illocutionary point of F_2 on P_2, or (2) with the characteristic mode of achievement of illocutionary point of F_2, or (3) with the satisfaction by Q of the propositional content conditions of F_2, or (4) with the presupposition of the preparatory conditions of $F_2(P_2)$, or finally (5) with a commitment to the psychological state of $F_2(P_2)$. We will now consider each of these five sorts of cases of relative incompatibility and give examples of some of them.

5.1.1 *Relative inconsistency of a successful performance of $F_1(P_1)$ with the achievement of the illocutionary point of F_2 on P_2.*

If, for all $i \in I$, $F_1(P_1)$ is performed on i only if it is not the case that $i\Pi_{F_2}P_2$ then $F_1(P_1) > < F_2(P_2)$.

Two illocutionary acts with relatively inconsistent illocutionary points are for that reason relatively incompatible. This type of incompatibility exists, for example, between a promise to carry out a future action $Pr(P)$ and the assertion that one will not carry out that action $\vdash (\sim P)$ because of the existence of an assertive commitment in the achievement of the commissive illocutionary point. It exists also between a declaration that P and an assertion that $\sim P$; because of the existence of an assertive commitment in the achievement of the declarative illocutionary point.

5.1.2 *Relative inconsistency of a successful performance of $F_1(P_1)$ with the mode of achievement of illocutionary point of $F_2(P_2)$.*

If, for all $i \in I$, $F_1(P_1)$ is performed in i only if mode $(F_2)(i, P_2)$ = 0, then $F_1(P_1) > < F_2(P_2)$.

Thus, two illocutionary acts with relatively inconsistent modes of achievement of their illocutionary points are relatively incompatible. This type of incompatibility exists, for example, between cases of commanding and begging with the same propositional content. In a command, the speaker achieves the directive illocutionary point by invoking a position of authority over the hearer, and this excludes the humble mode of achievement of begging that leaves an option of refusal to the hearer.

5.1.3 *Relative inconsistency of a successful performance of* $F_1(P_1)$
with the satisfaction by P_2 *of the propositional content conditions of* F_2.
   If, for all $i \in I$, $F_1(P_1)$ is performed in i only if $P_2 \notin \mathrm{Prop}_{F_2}(i)$,
   then $F_1(P_1) > < F_2(P_2)$.
Thus, illocutionary acts with relatively inconsistent propositional content conditions are relatively incompatible. For example, a retrodiction that P and a prediction that $\sim P$ are relatively incompatible, for if P is a proposition about the past at time of utterance t, i.e. if P is admissible as the propositional content of a retrodiction in a context i, then its negation $\sim P$ cannot be a proposition about the future at that time, i.e. is not admissible as the propositional content of a prediction in that context.

5.1.4 *Relative inconsistency of a successful performance of* $F_1(P_1)$
with the presupposition of the preparatory conditions of $F_2(P_2)$.
   If, for all $i \in I$, $F_1(P_1)$ is performed in i only if a_i does not presuppose $\Sigma_{F_2}(i, P_2)$ in i, then $F_1(P_1) > < F_2(P_2)$.
Thus, illocutionary acts with preparatory conditions that cannot simultaneously be presupposed to obtain are relatively incompatible. For example, one cannot congratulate and condole a hearer for the same event under precisely the same aspects and for the same reasons, because congratulations presuppose that the event in question was good for the hearer and condolence presupposes that the event was bad for him. Also, an illocutionary act whose illocutionary point is relatively inconsistent with the presupposition of the preparatory conditions of another illocutionary act is relatively incompatible with that act. For example, an assertion that one is unable to do act A is relatively incompatible with a promise to do A, because a preparatory condition of a promise is

that the speaker is capable of doing what he commits himself to doing.

5.1.5 *Relative inconsistency of a successful performance of $F_1(P)$ with a commitment to the psychological state of $F_2(P_2)$.*

If, for all $i \in I$, $F_1(P_1)$ is performed in i only if a_i is not committed to $\Psi_{F_2}(i, P_2)$ in i then $F_1(P_1) > < F_2(P_2)$.

Thus, illocutionary acts with psychological states to which one cannot simultaneously be committed are relatively incompatible. This is why for example a speaker cannot succeed in both boasting and lamenting that P because the speaker cannot consistently be committed to being satisfied and dissatisfied about the same phenomena under the same aspects and for the same reasons. Since it must always be possible for the speaker to be sincere, illocutionary acts with relatively inconsistent sincerity conditions are also relatively incompatible. If no speaker can possess psychological states $\Psi_{F_1}(i, P_1) \cup \Psi_{F_2}(i, P_2)$ then $F_1(P_1) > < F_2(P_2)$. Thus, for example, one reason a speaker cannot simultaneously swear that P and testify that $\sim P$ is that he cannot rationally believe both that P and that $\sim P$. Also, an illocutionary act whose illocutionary point is relatively inconsistent with the expression of the psychological state of another illocutionary act is relatively incompatible with that act. Thus, for example, an assertion that one does not intend to carry out a future course of action is relatively incompatible with a promise to carry out that course of action; that is because a promise has the sincerity condition that the speaker intends to do what he commits himself to doing and an assertion that one does not have a certain psychological state is relatively inconsistent with the expression of that psychological state. Finally, an illocutionary act whose preparatory conditions cannot be presupposed simultaneously with the expression of the sincerity conditions of another illocutionary act is also relatively incompatible with that illocutionary act. For example, a speaker cannot both recommend that the hearer carry out a certain course of action and simultaneously complain under the same aspects that he will carry it out because one cannot consistently both presuppose that a course of action is good and express dissatisfaction about it under the same aspects and for the same reasons.

The previous theorems about relative incompatibility have the following natural corollaries concerning self-defeating illocutionary acts.

5.2 Self-defeating illocutionary acts.

By definition, an illocution $F(P)$ is *self-defeating* iff its conditions of success cannot possibly obtain. Thus, $> F(P) <$ iff $\{i \in I, F(P)(i) = 1\} = \varnothing$. Since a set of illocutionary acts is consistent iff it is performable, no self-defeating illocutionary act is consistent. $> F(P) <$ iff for no $i \in I, \triangleright F(P)$. As a consequence of this, an illocutionary act $F(P)$ is both *self-defeating* and inconsistent if any one or more of the following conditions obtains:

5.2.1 *The illocutionary point cannot be achieved on the propositional content.*

If, for no $i \in I$, $i\Pi_F P$ then $> F(P) <$.

Thus, for example, a promise of the form "I promise not to keep this promise" or an assertion of the form "All my assertions are false" are self-defeating because their illocutionary points are empty. For the same reason, all declarations with an inconsistent propositional content are self-defeating.

5.2.2 *The illocutionary point cannot be achieved with the required mode of achievement of F on the propositional content.*

If, for some $i \in I$, $i\Pi_F P$ but, for no $i \in I$, mode $(F)(i, P) = 1$ then $> F(P) <$.

Thus, for example, an order of the form: "I order you to disobey all orders" is self-defeating. A speaker can succeed in attempting to get a hearer to disobey all directives made to him by invoking a position of authority or power. But in such a case he cannot direct the hearer by invoking a position of authority or power, for his attempt would be inconsistent.

5.2.3 *The inadequacy of the propositional content.*

If, for all $i \in I$, $P \notin \mathrm{Prop}_F(i)$ then $> F(P) <$.

Thus, for example, a prediction made today of the form "I predict that John Paul the Second has been elected as Pope" or an apology of the form "I apologize for Peano's arithmetic" are self-defeating illocutionary acts, because a prediction has to be about the future and an apology has to be about something the speaker is, directly or indirectly, responsible for.

5.2.4 *The impossibility of presupposing the preparatory conditions of $F(P)$.*

If, for no $i \in I$, a_i presupposes $\Sigma_F(i, P)$ in i then $> F(P) <$.

Thus, for example, a speaker cannot succeed in promising by saying "I promise to do it, and I cannot keep this promise", because such a "promise" would deny its own presupposition, namely the capacity of the speaker to keep it.

5.2.5 *The impossibility of expressing the psychological state of $F(P)$.*

If, for no $i \in I$, a_i expresses $\Psi_F(i, P)$ in i then $> F(P) <$.

Thus, for example, it is paradoxical to say, without further explanation, "I apologize for that course of action which benefited you", because one cannot consistently express sorrow for something done for a hearer under an aspect while expressing belief that it benefits him under that aspect. Since a speaker cannot succeed in expressing a psychological state that he cannot possibly have, illocutionary acts with inconsistent sincerity conditions are self-defeating. Thus, for example, a promise of the form "I will and won't give you five dollars" is self-defeating because no speaker can possibly intend both to carry out and not to carry out the same future course of action under the same description.[2]

VI. ILLOCUTIONARY NEGATION.

In the next sections we will specify a few laws of inference for illocutionary denegations, conditional speech acts, and conjunctions of illocutionary acts. These laws are immediate consequences of the definitions of the conditions of success of and of the conditions of commitment to these complex illocutionary acts. An axiomatization of the set of all laws governing the illocutionary connectives is attempted by Daniel Vanderveken in a forthcoming paper along the lines of his 1981 proof of completeness of formal

---

2 For further discussion of self-defeating and paradoxical illocutionary acts, see D. Vanderveken, 'Illocutionary logic and self-defeating speech-acts'. Self-defeating illocutionary acts are often useful as indirect speech acts. For example, if I say sarcastically 'You are right and consequently 2 + 2 = 5', I am implying that the speaker is wrong.

pragmatics. This kind of proof can be used for the purpose of illocutionary logic, because illocutionary negation and the illocutionary conditional are in some sense modalities on illocutionary acts since the definition of their conditions of success requires a quantification over all possible contexts of utterance and not only a reference to the actual context of utterance, and makes use of a reflexive relation of illocutionary compatibility between contexts that is similar to the relation of accessibility between worlds.[3]

6.1 *The law of non-contradiction.*

All illocutionary acts are relatively incompatible with their illocutionary denegations.

Thus, for example, a speaker cannot simultaneously claim and disclaim a proposition P. As a consequence of this law a speaker cannot perform an act of illocutionary denegation of the form $\neg \mathscr{A}$ at a time when he performs an act that commits him to $\mathscr{A}$. Thus, for example, if an order commits the speaker to granting permission, a speaker cannot successfully say: "I order you to leave the room and I do not permit you to do it."

6.2 *All and only the self-defeating illocutionary acts commit the speaker to their illocutionary denegation.*

$\mathscr{A} \rhd \neg \mathscr{A}$ iff $> \mathscr{A} <$.

6.3 $\neg$ *is not success functional.*

It is not the case that $\neg \mathscr{A}$ is performed at i iff $\mathscr{A}$ is not performed at i. The non-performance of $\mathscr{A}$ at i does not entail that $\neg \mathscr{A}$ is performed at i.

Here are a few new laws governing illocutionary negation:

6.4 *Failures of the laws of excluded middle and of reduction.*

It is not the case that $\mathscr{A}$ is performed at i or $\neg \mathscr{A}$ is performed at i.

3 See D. Vanderveken, 'A strong completeness theorem for pragmatics', in the *Zeitschrift für Mathematische Logik und Grundlagen der Mathematik*, vol. 27 (1981). The completeness proof required for a logic of illocutionary denegation and the conditional illocutionary acts should resemble formally a Henkin's completeness proof for the Brouwer modal system, because illocutionary compatibility is reflexive and symmetric like accessibility in Brouwer's logic, and the definition of the conditions of success of complex acts of form $\neg \mathscr{A}$ and $(P \Rightarrow \mathscr{A})$ resembles the definition of the truth conditions of complex propositions of form $\Box \sim P$ and $P \dashv\mathbin{\subset} Q$ in that logic.

It is not the case that $\daleth \daleth \mathcal{A} \triangleright \mathcal{A}$.

Thus, for example, it is not the case that either a speaker accepts or refuses a directive to do act A at each moment. It is not the case that if he says "I do not refuse to come" he is *ipso facto* committed to accepting a directive to come. Illocutionary negation in this respect resembles intuitionistic negation since in intuitionist logic it is also not valid that $P \vee \sim P$ and that $(\sim \sim P \rightarrow P)$.

6.5 *Conditions of commitment to acts of illocutionary denegation.*

$\mathcal{A}_1 \triangleright \daleth \mathcal{A}_2$ iff the set $\{\mathcal{A}_1, \mathcal{A}_2\}$ is not simultaneously performable.

An illocutionary act $\mathcal{A}_1$ commits the speaker to the illocutionary denegation of an act $\mathcal{A}_2$ iff it is not possible for a speaker to perform both $\mathcal{A}_1$ and $\mathcal{A}_2$. As a consequence of this we have the following laws:

6.5.1 *The law of introduction of illocutionary negation.*

If $\mathcal{A}_1 > < \mathcal{A}_2$ then $\mathcal{A}_1 \triangleright \daleth \mathcal{A}_2$.

If two illocutionary acts are relatively incompatible, then a successful performance of the first commits the speaker to the illocutionary denegation of the second.

Thus, for example, since $\|\text{permit}\| (P) > < \|\text{forbid}\| (P)$, because $\|\text{permit}\| (P) = \daleth \|\text{forbid}\| (P)$, $\|\text{forbid}\| (P) \triangleright \daleth \|\text{permit}\| (P)$. A speaker who forbids a hearer to do something is committed to the act of illocutionary denegation of not granting him permission to do it. Since an illocutionary act is relatively incompatible with its illocutionary denegation, i.e. $\mathcal{A} > < \daleth \mathcal{A}$, the law of introduction of illocutionary negation has the following corollary regarding double illocutionary negation:

6.5.2 *Each illocution commits the speaker to the denegation of its illocutionary denegation.*

$\mathcal{A} \triangleright \daleth \daleth \mathcal{A}$.

Thus, for example, a speaker who accepts a proposal to do something is committed to the act of illocutionary denegation of not refusing to do it. Similarly a speaker who claims P is committed to not disclaiming P since $\|\text{disclaim}\| = \daleth \|\text{claim}\|$.

6.5.3 *The law of contraposition.*

If $\mathcal{A}_1 \triangleright \mathcal{A}_2$ then $\daleth \mathcal{A}_2 \triangleright \daleth \mathcal{A}_1$.

If an illocutionary act $\mathscr{A}_1$ commits the speaker to an illocutionary act $\mathscr{A}_2$ then the illocutionary denegation $\neg\mathscr{A}_2$ of illocutionary act $\mathscr{A}_2$ commits him to the illocutionary denegation $\neg\mathscr{A}_1$ of $\mathscr{A}_1$.

Thus, for example, if to refuse to do something commits the speaker to the denegation act of not agreeing to do it, then to agree to do something commits him to the denegation act of not refusing to do it. Similarly, if a prediction that P commits the speaker to an assertion that P then a denegation of an assertion that P commits the speaker to a denegation of a prediction that P. It follows from the law of contraposition for illocutionary negation that illocutionary negation preserves illocutionary congruence.

6.5.3.1 *The law of compatibility of $\neg$ with respect to $\simeq$.*

If $\mathscr{A}_1 \simeq \mathscr{A}_2$ then $\neg\mathscr{A}_1 \simeq \neg\mathscr{A}_2$.

If two illocutionary acts are congruent then so are their denegations. The same law holds for strict equivalence when $\mathscr{A}_1$ and $\mathscr{A}_2$ are not self-defeating.

Thus, for example, if $\mathscr{A}_1 \equiv \mathscr{A}_2$ and $\mathscr{A}_1$ is performable then $\neg\mathscr{A}_1 \equiv \neg\mathscr{A}_2$.

6.5.4 *A set* $\Gamma \cup \{\mathscr{A}\}$ *is simultaneously performable and consistent* iff $\Gamma \not\rhd \neg\mathscr{A}$.

Is it also the case in illocutionary logic that $\Gamma \rhd \mathscr{A}$ iff $\Gamma \cup \{\neg\mathscr{A}\}$ is not simultaneously performable? By definition if $\Gamma \rhd \mathscr{A}$ then $\Gamma \cup \{\neg\mathscr{A}\}$ is inconsistent, but is the converse true?

It is true if either one of the following laws holds:

(1) If $\{\mathscr{A}_1, \neg\mathscr{A}_2\}$ is not simultaneously performable then $\mathscr{A}_1 \rhd \mathscr{A}_2$.

(2) If $\neg\mathscr{A}_1 \rhd \neg\mathscr{A}_2$ then $\mathscr{A}_2 \rhd \mathscr{A}_1$.

VII. CONJUNCTIVE ILLOCUTIONARY ACTS.

By definition the operation of conjunction & is success-functional: $\mathscr{A}_1 \,\&\, \mathscr{A}_2$ is performed at i iff $\mathscr{A}_1$ is performed at i and $\mathscr{A}_2$ is performed at i, and similarly for illocutionary commitment. From these definitions one can derive the following laws about $\rhd$ and conjunction.

7.1 *The law of introduction of* &.

$\mathscr{A} \rhd (\mathscr{A}_1 \& \mathscr{A}_2)$ iff $\mathscr{A} \rhd \mathscr{A}_1$ and $\mathscr{A} \rhd \mathscr{A}_2$.

An illocutionary act commits the speaker to a conjunction of two illocutionary acts iff it commits the speaker to both conjuncts.

7.2 *The law of elimination of* &.

$(\mathscr{A}_1 \& \mathscr{A}_2)$ and $(\mathscr{A}_1 \& \mathscr{A}_2) \rhd \mathscr{A}_2$.

A conjunction of two illocutionary acts commits the speaker to both conjuncts.

7.3 *Compatibility of* & *with respect to* $\rhd$.

If $\mathscr{A}_1 \rhd \mathscr{A}_3$ and $\mathscr{A}_2 \rhd \mathscr{A}_4$ then $(\mathscr{A}_1 \& \mathscr{A}_2) \rhd (\mathscr{A}_3 \& \mathscr{A}_4)$.

Notice that there are illocutionary acts $F_1(P_1)$, $F_2(P_2)$ such that $F_1(P_1) \& F_2(P_2) \rhd F(P)$ for some $F(P)$ while $F_1(P_1) \not\rhd F(P)$ and $F_2(P_2) \not\rhd F(P)$.

Thus, for example, *Modus Ponens* is a theorem of propositional illocutionary logic, i.e. $\vdash (P) \& \vdash (P \to Q) \rhd \vdash (Q)$, but it is not a theorem that $\vdash (P) \rhd \vdash (Q)$ or that $\vdash (P \to Q) \rhd \vdash (Q)$. An assertion that P and an assertion that $(P \to Q)$ together commit the speaker to an assertion that Q but an assertion that P or an assertion that $(P \to Q)$ alone does not commit the speaker to an assertion that Q. The converse of 7.3 is therefore not a law of illocutionary logic.

It follows from the law of compatibility of $\rhd$ with respect to & that the operation of conjunction preserves illocutionary congruence.

7.3.1 *Compatibility of* & *with respect to* $\simeq$.

If $\mathscr{A}_1 \simeq \mathscr{A}_3$ and $\mathscr{A}_2 \simeq \mathscr{A}_4$ then $(\mathscr{A}_1 \& \mathscr{A}_2) \simeq (\mathscr{A}_3 \& \mathscr{A}_4)$.

Like truth-functional conjunction of propositions, the operation of conjunction of illocutionary acts obeys the following laws:

7.4 *The law of idempotence of* &.

$(\mathscr{A} \& \mathscr{A}) \simeq \mathscr{A}$.

7.5 *The law of commutativity.*

$(\mathscr{A}_1 \& \mathscr{A}_2) \equiv (\mathscr{A}_2 \& \mathscr{A}_1)$.

In ordinary language temporal ordering of speech acts often affects content. "Go outdoors and wipe the mud off your feet" is not equivalent to "Wipe the mud off your feet and go outdoors". In spite of their surface grammar such acts are not of the form $\mathscr{A}_1 \& \mathscr{A}_2$.

7.6 The *law of associativity*.
$$((\mathscr{A}_1 \& \mathscr{A}_2) \& \mathscr{A}_3) \equiv (\mathscr{A}_1 \& (\mathscr{A}_2 \& \mathscr{A}_3)).$$

7.7 $(\mathscr{A} \& \neg \mathscr{A})$ is self-defeating.

7.8 $(\mathscr{A} \& \mathscr{A}) \equiv \mathscr{A}$ where $\mathscr{A}$ is any self-defeating illocutionary act.

7.9 $(\mathscr{A} \& \neg \mathscr{A}) \simeq \mathscr{A}$ where $\mathscr{A}$ is any self-defeating illocutionary act.

7.10 $\mathscr{A}_1 \equiv (\mathscr{A}_1 \& \mathscr{A}_2)$ iff $\mathscr{A}_1 \vartriangleright \mathscr{A}_2$.

VIII. CONDITIONAL ILLOCUTIONARY ACTS.

A conditional illocutionary act of the form $(P \Rightarrow \mathscr{A})$ differs from the illocutionary act $\mathscr{A}$ that is its consequent in that when it is performed $\mathscr{A}$ is not performed categorically but only on the condition that the proposition P that is its antecedent is true. This has the following consequences:

8.1 *The illocutionary conditional is neither truth functional nor success functional.*
  It is not the case that $(P \Rightarrow \mathscr{A})$ is performed at i iff $P(w_i) = 0$ or $\mathscr{A}$ is performed at i.
The success of a conditional illocutionary act is not a function of the success of its consequent or of the truth of its antecedent.

8.2 *The law of Modus Ponens.*
  If $(P \Rightarrow \mathscr{A})$ is performed at i and $P(w_i) = 1$, then $\mathscr{A}$ is performed at i.
A conditional illocutionary act of the form $P \Rightarrow F(Q)$ strongly commits the speaker to $F(Q)$ when P is true in the world of utterance.
  This law, incidentally, is not valid for illocutionary acts of the

form $F(P \rightarrow Q)$ and therefore $(P \Rightarrow FQ) \neq F(P \rightarrow Q)$. Conditional illocutionary acts of the form $P \Rightarrow F(Q)$ do not have the logical form $F(P \rightarrow Q)$ of illocutionary acts with conditional propositional contents.

8.3 *The law of introduction of* $\Rightarrow$.
$\mathscr{A}_1 \rhd (P \Rightarrow \mathscr{A}_2)$ iff for all i where $\mathscr{A}_1(i) = 1$ and $P(w_i) = 1$, $\rhd \mathscr{A}_2$.

An illocutionary act commits the speaker to a conditional illocutionary act iff in all contexts of utterance where it is performed and where the antecedent of the conditional is true, the speaker is committed to the consequent of that conditional illocutionary act.

8.4 *Conditional illocutionary acts with necessarily true antecedents are congruent with their consequents.*
If $\square P(w) = 1$ then $(P \Rightarrow \mathscr{A}) \simeq \mathscr{A}$.

8.5 *Conditional illocutionary acts with impossible antecedents.*
If $\sim \lozenge P(w_i) = 1$ then $(P \Rightarrow \mathscr{A}) \not\rhd \mathscr{A}$.
A conditional illocutionary act with an impossible antecedent does not commit the speaker to its consequent.

8.6 *There are conditional illocutionary acts to which all illocutions commit the speaker.*
If $\sim \lozenge P(w_i) = 1$ or $\mathscr{A}_2$ is self-defeating then for any $\mathscr{A}_1$, $\mathscr{A}_1 \rhd (P \Rightarrow \neg \mathscr{A}_2)$.
Any illocutionary act commits the speaker to a conditional illocutionary act where the antecedent is impossible or where the consequent is the denegation of a self-defeating speech act. This law bears an obvious analogy to the so-called paradoxes of strict implication.

8.7 *Law of attenuation of the antecedent.*
If $(P \dashv Q)(w) = 1$ then $(Q \Rightarrow \mathscr{A}) \rhd (P \Rightarrow \mathscr{A})$.
A conditional illocution commits the speaker to all conditional acts with the same consequent whose antecedents strictly imply its antecedent.
A corollary of this law is:

8.7.1 *The substitutibility of strictly equivalent antecedents within conditional illocutions.*

If $(P \dashv\vdash Q)(w) = 1$ then $(P \Rightarrow \mathcal{A}) \simeq (Q \Rightarrow \mathcal{A})$.
Conditional illocutionary acts of the form $(P \Rightarrow \mathcal{A})$, $(Q \Rightarrow \mathcal{A})$ with strictly equivalent antecedents are congruent.

8.8 *The law of attenuation of the consequent.*

If $\mathcal{A}_1 \rhd \mathcal{A}_2$ then $(P \Rightarrow \mathcal{A}_1) \rhd (P \Rightarrow \mathcal{A}_2)$.
A conditional illocutionary act commits the speaker to all conditional illocutionary acts with the same antecedent whose consequents are acts to which the consequent of the original act commits the speaker.

A consequence of this law is:

8.8.1 *The operation of the conditional preserves illocutionary congruence.*

If $\mathcal{A}_1 \simeq \mathcal{A}_2$ then $(P \Rightarrow \mathcal{A}_1) \simeq (P \Rightarrow \mathcal{A}_2)$.

8.9 *Conditional illocutionary acts with true antecedents and incompatible consequents are incompatible.*

If $\mathcal{A}_1 > < \mathcal{A}_2$ and $P(w_i) = Q(w_i) = 1$ then it is not the case that $(P \Rightarrow \mathcal{A}_1)(i) = (Q \Rightarrow \mathcal{A}_2)(i)$.
The following are laws where the conditional $\Rightarrow$ has properties similar to material implication $\rightarrow$.

8.10 *Distributivity of $\Rightarrow$ with respect to &.*

$(P \Rightarrow (\mathcal{A}_1 \& \mathcal{A}_2)) \simeq ((P \Rightarrow \mathcal{A}_1) \& (P \Rightarrow \mathcal{A}_2))$.

8.11 $((P \Rightarrow \mathcal{A}) \& (\sim P \Rightarrow \mathcal{A})) \simeq \mathcal{A}$.

8.12 $(P_1 \Rightarrow \mathcal{A}) \& (P_2 \Rightarrow \mathcal{A}) \simeq ((P_1 \vee P_2) \Rightarrow \mathcal{A})$.

8.13 $(P_1 \Rightarrow (P_2 \Rightarrow \mathcal{A})) \simeq ((P_1 \& P_2) \Rightarrow \mathcal{A})$.

8.14 *Peirce's law.*

$\mathcal{A} \rhd (P \Rightarrow \mathcal{A})$.
Any illocutionary act performed categorically commits the speaker to performing it on any condition.

A more complete axiomatic study of the illocutionary connectives is beyond the scope of this book. It should be made along the lines of the recent developments of modal logic and attempt to answer questions such as these: Are there other possible and syntactically realized operations on illocutionary acts in English, and if so can they be defined in terms of our three primitive operations ⌐, &, and ⟹? For example, are the occurrences of "or" and "and" in such directives sentences as "Do that again and I'll hit you", "Come here or I'll hit you", "Come here and I'll give you five dollars!", analyzable as conditionals?

Chapter 8

LAWS FOR ILLOCUTIONARY
FORCES

The purpose of this chapter is to state the main laws that hold for the primitive and simple illocutionary forces. Most of these laws follow from the recursive definition of the set of all illocutionary forces, and the postulates concerning the components of illocutionary forces. In what follows, $\mathscr{A}$, $\mathscr{C}$, $\mathscr{D}$, $\mathscr{E}$, and $\mathscr{T}$ are variables respectively for assertive, commissive, directive, expressive, and declarative illocutionary forces.

I. LAWS FOR NON-EXPRESSIVE ILLOCUTIONARY FORCES.[1]

We will begin by stating some general laws of illocutionary consistency that hold for all non-expressive illocutionary forces.

I.I *The illocutionary consistency of the speaker.*

If $\Pi_{F_1} = \Pi_{F_2} \neq \Pi_5$ then $F_1(P) > < F_2(\sim P)$.

An elementary illocutionary act that is not expressive is relatively incompatible with any illocution with the same illocutionary point whose propositional content is the truth functional negation of its propositional content. Thus, for example, a speaker cannot successfully say: "I urge you to do this and I request that you do not do it", "I promise you to come and I vow not to come", "I assure you that she is here and she is not here."

If F_1 and F_2 are directive forces, $F_1(P)$ is incompatible with $F_2(\sim P)$ because the directive point cannot be achieved on a contradiction $(P \& \sim P)$, and $i\Pi_3 P$ and $i\Pi_3 \sim P$ entail $i\Pi_3(P \& \sim P)$ by the law of introduction of $\&$. If F_1 and F_2 are declarative forces then $F_1(P)$ and $F_2(\sim P)$ have relatively inconsistent conditions of achievement of their illocutionary point

---

1 These laws do not hold for expressive forces because the expressive point is the only point where variable sincerity conditions are part of the point.

since by the law of non-contradiction their propositional contents P and $\sim P$ cannot both be true in the world of utterance. Now if F_1 and F_2 are both assertive or commissive, their sincerity conditions are relatively inconsistent given our postulates governing belief and intention. Acts that have relatively inconsistent conditions of achievement of their illocutionary point or relatively inconsistent sincerity conditions are relatively incompatible.

Corollaries of the law of illocutionary consistency are:

1.1.1 *The relative incompatibility of an elementary illocutionary act with its propositional negation.*

For all $F \in \Phi$, $F(P) > < F(\sim P)$ when $\Pi_F \neq \Pi_5$.

Any elementary illocutionary act that is not expressive is relatively incompatible with its propositional negation. Thus, for example, a speaker cannot say: "I both order and forbid you to leave the room" or "I both assert and deny that she is here", for to forbid someone to do something is to order him not to do it, and to deny that something is the case is to assert that it is not the case. Thus $\|\text{forbid}\|\,(P) = \,!\,(\sim P)$ and $\|\text{deny}\|\,(P) = \vdash (\sim P)$.

1.1.2 *Propositional negation commits the speaker to illocutionary negation.*

For all $F \in \Phi$, $F(\sim P) \rhd \neg F(P)$ when $\Pi_F \neq \Pi_5$.

A speaker who performs the propositional negation of an illocution that is not expressive is committed to the illocutionary denegation of that illocution. Thus, for example, $\|\text{forbid}\|\,(P) \rhd \neg\,!\,(P)$. Forbidding someone to leave the room commits the speaker to the denegation of an order to him to leave the room since forbidding is the propositional negation of an order. Thus $\|\text{deny}\|\,(P) \rhd \neg \vdash (P)$. A denial that Cleopatra was Greek commits the speaker to the denegation of an assertion that Cleopatra was Greek. Similarly $\|\text{vow}\|\,(\sim P) \rhd \neg \|\text{vow}\|\,(P)$; $\|\text{insist}\|\,\sim P \rhd \neg \|\text{insist}\|\,(P)$.

1.1.3 For all $F \in \Phi$, $F(P) \rhd \neg F(\sim P)$ when $\Pi_F \neq \Pi_5$.

A speaker who performs an elementary illocution that is not expressive is committed to the illocutionary denegation of the propositional negation of that illocution. Thus, for example, since $\|\text{permit}\|\,(P) = \neg\,!\,(\sim P)$, $!\,(P) \rhd \|\text{permit}\|\,(P)$. An order commits the speaker to granting permission. Thus $\vdash (P) \rhd \neg \operatorname{deny}(P)$. An assertion commits the speaker to the denegation of a denial.

II. LAWS FOR SIMPLE ILLOCUTIONARY FORCES.

By definition a simple illocutionary force has no special mode of achievement of its illocutionary point and has only propositional content, preparatory, and sincerity conditions determined by that illocutionary point. Its degrees of strength of illocutionary point and of sincerity conditions are identical. Thus a simple illocution is either a primitive force such as $\vdash$ or $\perp$ or a derived force that differs from a primitive force only by its degree of strength, as for example $\|\operatorname{suggest}\| = [-1]\ !$ and $\|\operatorname{pledge}\| = [+1]\ \perp$. The distinctive feature of simple illocutionary forces is stated by the two following theorems that express the simplicity of such forces in terms of conditions of success and conditions of commitment.

2.1 *The performance of an illocutionary act with a simple illocutionary force amounts to the achievement of the illocutionary point on the propositional content and to the expression of the sincerity conditions with the required degree of strength.*

When F is simple, $F(P)$ is performed at i iff $i\Pi_F^{\text{degree}(F)}P$ and a_i expresses with degree $\eta(F)$ the psychological states $\Psi_F(i, P)$.
Proof:
By definition $F(P)(i) = 1$ only if $i\Pi_F^{\text{degree}(F)}P$ and a_i expresses $\Psi_F(i, P)$ with degree $\eta(F)$. Now by definition if F is a simple illocutionary force, it has no special mode of achievement of its illocutionary point and all its propositional content, preparatory, and sincerity conditions are determined by its illocutionary point Π_F. Consequently if $i\Pi_F P$ then $P \in \operatorname{Prop}_F(i)$, a_i presupposes $\Sigma_F(i, P)$ and expresses $\Psi_F(i, P)$ in i. Moreover if $i\Pi_F P$ then a_i presupposes $\sigma(P)$ in i. Therefore if both $i\Pi_F^{\text{degree}(F)}P$ and a_i expresses $\Psi_F(i, P)$ with degree $\eta(F)$ in i, then $F(P)(i) = 1$.

2.2 *A speaker is committed to an illocution with a simple force iff he is committed to the illocutionary point on the propositional content and to the psychological states determined by the sincerity conditions with the required degree of strength.*
Since in the simple cases the illocutionary point determines the

propositional content, sincerity, and preparatory conditions, and since by definition in these cases there are no other components not determined by illocutionary point, then any speech act which commits the speaker to an illocutionary point on a propositional content and to the psychological state determined by that point with a certain degree of strength automatically commits him to a speech act with a simple illocutionary force. This is true *only* for simple forces.

Theorems 2.1 and 2.2 are obvious consequences of the definitions of the conditions of success of and of the conditions of commitment to elementary illocutionary acts with a simple illocutionary force.

The following corollary of theorem 2.1 concerns illocutionary entailment.

2.1.1 *Illocutionary entailment is identical with the relation of having a greater or equal degree of strength for simple illocutionary forces with the same point.*

If Γ is a set of simple illocutionary forces, for any two illocutionary forces F_1, $F_2 \in \Gamma$ such that $\Pi_{F_1} = \Pi_{F_2}$, $F_1 \rhd F_2$ iff degree $(F_1) \geqslant$ degree (F_2).

Each set Γ of simple illocutionary forces with the same illocutionary point has therefore the same logical structure as the set of integers representing the degrees of strength of these forces. The two sets are isomorphic in the algebraic sense. Consequently illocutionary entailment is a well ordering on all finite sets of simple illocutionary forces with the same illocutionary point. If Γ is a finite set of simple illocutionary forces with the same illocutionary point then for all non-empty subsets Δ of Γ there exists a unique illocutionary force $F \in \Delta$ such that for all $F' \in \Delta$, $F' \rhd F$. Illocutionary entailment is also a total ordering on all sets of simple illocutionary forces with the same illocutionary point.

If Γ is a set of simple illocutionary forces with the same illocutionary point then for any two illocutionary forces F_1, $F_2 \in \Gamma$, either $F_1 \rhd F_2$ or $F_2 \rhd F_1$.

The next theorems concern strong and weak illocutionary commitments.

2.3 *The restricted compatibility of strict implication with respect to* $\triangleright$ *for simple illocutionary forces.*

For any pair of simple illocutionary forces F_1 and F_2 such that $\eta(F_1) \geqslant \eta(F_2)$, if $P_1 \dashv\!\!\!\!- P_2(w) = 1$ then $F_1(P_1) \triangleright F_2(P_2)$ iff 1) if $P_1 \in \text{Prop}_{F_1}(i)$ then $P_2 \in \text{Prop}_{F_2}(i)$ and 2) $\Psi_{F_1}(i, P_1) \triangleright \Psi_{F_2}(i, P_2)$.

If F_1 and F_2 are simple illocutionary forces and the degree of strength of F_1 is not weaker than the degree of strength of F_2, then if a proposition P_1 strictly implies another proposition P_2, the illocutionary act $F_1(P_1)$ strongly commits the speaker to the illocutionary act $F_2(P_2)$ iff P_2 satisfies the propositional content conditions of F_2 if P_1 satisfies those of F_1, and it is not possible to possess all psychological states expressed in the performance of $F_1(P_1)$ in a context of utterance without also possessing those of $F_2(P_2)$ with respect to the same context. Thus for example a declaration that P strongly commits the speaker to an assertion that P because if a speaker believes that he brings about a state of affairs that P, he also believes that P.

Proof:

Use the law of restricted compatibility of $\dashv\!\!\!\!-$ with respect to illocutionary point and the definition of $\triangleright$.

2.4 *The restricted compatibility of strict implication with respect to* $\triangleright$ *for simple illocutionary forces.*

For any pair of simple illocutionary forces F_1 and F_2 such that $\eta(F_1) \geqslant \eta(F_2)$, if $P_1 \dashv\!\!\!\!- P_2(w) = 1$ then $F_1(P_1) \triangleright F_2(P_2)$ iff 1) if $P_1 \in \text{Prop}_{F_1}(i)$ then $P_2 \in \text{Prop}_{F_2}(i)$ and 2) $\Psi_{F_1}(i, P_1) \triangleright \Psi_{F_2}(i, P_2)$.

If P strictly implies Q and F_1 and F_2 are simple forces satisfying the premises of this theorem, then the successful performance of an illocutionary act $F_1(P_1)$ with a simple illocutionary force commits the speaker to an illocutionary act of the form $F_2(P_2)$ iff (1) P_2 satisfies the propositional content conditions of F_2 if P_1 satisfies those of F_1 and (2) the psychological states expressed in the performance of $F_1(P_1)$ commit the speaker to having the psychological states expressed in the performance of $F_2(P_2)$. Thus, for example, a promise that P commits the speaker to an assertion that $\diamondsuit P$ because it is not possible to intend to carry out a future action without being committed to believing that it is possible to carry out that action.

The law of a restricted compatibility of $\dashv$ with respect to $\triangleright$ states when the strict implication $P \dashv Q(w) = 1$ entails the illocutionary commitment $F(P) \triangleright F(Q)$ for simple illocutionary forces. The truth of the strict implication $P \dashv Q$ is not a sufficient condition for the illocutionary commitment $F(P) \triangleright F(Q)$ for a simple F.

A question that naturally arises at this point is: Is strict implication a necessary condition for illocutionary commitment with regard to simple illocutionary forces? Is it the case that $F(P) \triangleright F(Q)$ only if $P \dashv Q$ is true for all simple illocutionary forces F? All the cases we consider satisfy this condition whenever $F(P)$ is performable. Intuitively it seems plausible, because illocutionary commitment is a restriction of the notion of strict implication for simple illocutionary forces.

The laws of restricted compatibility of strict implication with respect to strong and weak illocutionary commitment for simple illocutionary forces (theorems 2.3 and 2.4), together with the hypotheses concerning belief, intention, and desire, entail the following laws of elimination and of introduction of logical constants within simple illocutionary forces:

2.5 *Introduction of* &.

If F is a simple non-expressive illocutionary force, $F(P)$ & $F(Q) \triangleright F(P \& Q)$.

The performances of two illocutionary acts $F(P)$, $F(Q)$ with a simple non-expressive illocutionary force strongly commit the speaker to an illocutionary act of the same force whose propositional content $(P \& Q)$ is the conjunction of their propositional contents.

Thus, for example, two assertions that P and that Q strongly commit the speaker to an assertion that $(P \& Q)$: $\vdash (P)$ & $\vdash (Q) \triangleright \vdash (P \& Q)$.

2.6 *Elimination of* &.

If F is a simple non-expressive illocutionary force, $F(P \& Q) \triangleright F(P)$ & $F(Q)$.

The successful performance of an illocutionary act with a simple non-expressive illocutionary force F whose propositional content $(P \& Q)$ is the conjunction of two propositions P, Q strongly commits the speaker to both illocutionary acts $F(P)$ and $F(Q)$. Thus, for example, $!(P \& Q) \vartriangleright !(P) \& !(Q)$. A directive to do acts A and B strongly commits the speaker to a directive to do A and a directive to do B. It follows from the laws of introduction and of elimination of $\&$ that when F is a simple non-expressive illocutionary force, two acts of the form $F(P \& Q)$ and $F(P) \& F(Q)$ are strictly equivalent.

Thus, for example, $\vdash (P \& Q) \equiv \vdash (P) \& \vdash (Q)$; $\perp (P \& Q) \equiv \perp (P) \& \perp (Q)$; $!(P \& Q) \equiv !(P) \& !(Q)$ and similarly for the other primitive illocutionary forces.[2]

2.7 *Elimination of* $\vee$.

If F is a simple non-expressive illocutionary force, $P_1 \dashv\!\!\varepsilon\ Q(w) = P_2 \dashv Q(w) = 1$ and both $F(P_1) \vartriangleright F(Q)$ and $F(P_2) \vartriangleright F(Q)$, then $F(P_1 \vee P_2) \vartriangleright F(Q)$.

Thus, for example, if the truth of the disjunction $(P_1 \vee P_2)$ strictly implies the truth of Q, and if both an assertion that P_1 and an assertion that P_2 strongly commit the speaker to the assertion that Q then an assertion that $(P_1 \vee P_2)$ will also strongly commit the speaker to the assertion that Q. Notice that if, for simple illocutionary forces F, $F(P) \vartriangleright F(Q)$ only if $P \dashv\!\!\varepsilon\ Q(w) = 1$ whenever $F(P)$ is performable, the law of elimination of $\vee$ is equivalent to the simpler statement:

If F is a simple non-expressive illocutionary force, $F(P_1)$ and $F(P_2)$ are performable, and both $F(P_1) \vartriangleright F(Q)$ and $F(P_2) \vartriangleright F(Q)$ then $F(P_1 \vee P_2) \vartriangleright F(Q)$.

If both illocutionary acts $F(P_1)$ and $F(P_2)$ strongly commit the speaker to illocutionary act $F(Q)$ where F is a simple illocutionary force, then the illocutionary act $F(P_1 \vee P_2)$ whose propositional content is the disjunction of P_1 and P_2 also strongly commits the speaker to the illocutionary act $F(Q)$.

2.8 *Failure of the law of introduction of* $\vee$.

It is not the case for all simple illocutionary forces that $F(P) \vartriangleright F(P \vee Q)$.

---

2 The law of introduction of $\&$ for declaration requires a meaning postulate for action stating the distributivity of δ with respect to $\&$: $\delta ut(P \& Q) = (\delta ut P \& \delta ut Q)$.

The reasons for the failure of the law of introduction of disjunction are: First, the fact that P satisfies the propositional content conditions of F does not imply that $P \vee Q$ also satisfies these conditions. For the simple commissive and directive illocutionary forces F, in case $Q \notin \text{Prop}_F(i)$, $(P \vee Q) \notin \text{Prop}_F(i)$. If, for example, Q does not represent a future course of action then neither does $(P \vee Q)$. Secondly, it is sometimes possible for the speaker to express the psychological state of $F(P)$ without being committed to having the psychological state of $F(P \vee Q)$. For certain simple F, the psychological states $\Psi_F(i, P)$ do not commit the speaker to the states $\Psi_F(i, P \vee Q)$. If, for example, Q represents a future course of action of the hearer b_i that is very bad for the speaker a_i, a_i might want or desire P without wanting or desiring that $(P \vee Q)$.

2.9 *Elimination of* → (*A Generalized Modus Ponens*).
    If F is a simple non-expressive illocutionary force, $F(P)$ & $F(P \rightarrow Q) \triangleright F(Q)$.
The successful performance of two illocutionary acts with a simple non-expressive illocutionary force F whose propositional contents are respectively P and $P \rightarrow Q$ weakly commit the speaker to an illocutionary act with the same force and propositional content Q.
    Thus, for example, $! (P)$ & $! (P \rightarrow Q) \triangleright !(Q)$, $\vdash (P)$ & $\vdash (P \rightarrow Q) \triangleright Q$.

2.10 *Elimination of* ~ .
    If F is a simple non-expressive illocutionary force, $F(P)$ & $F(\sim P) \triangleright F(Q)$ for any Q.

The preceding laws of introduction and elimination of truth functions within primitive illocutionary forces can easily be generalized and proved to hold for *most* illocutionary forces syntactically realized or named by performatives in English because most modes of achievement, propositional content, preparatory, and sincerity conditions that are expressed in English preserve the illocutionary commitments stated by these laws. Thus, for example, since the preparatory condition of the illocutionary force of advice obeys the law of elimination of & (i.e. to presuppose that it is good that P & Q commits the speaker to presupposing that it is good that P), it is also the case that advising the hearer that $(P \& Q)$ commits the speaker to advising him that P. We will state the conditions under which the operations on illocutionary force preserve illocutionary commitment in the next section.

A general law of non-contradiction for all illocutionary forces follows from the preceding theorems.

2.11 *The law of non-contradiction.*

For all F, $> F(P \& \sim P) <$ when $\Pi_F \neq \Pi_5$.

All elementary non-expressive illocutionary acts of the form $F(P \& \sim P)$ are self-defeating.

Proof:

The proof of this corollary is based on the laws of elimination of $\&$ and on the fact that for each non-expressive illocutionary force F, there is a simple non-expressive force F^* such that $F(P \& \sim P) \rhd F^*(P \& \sim P)$.

Although there are performable illocutionary acts of the form $F(P \& \sim Q)$ where Q is strictly implied by P (when for example it is possible to believe both P and Q), there are no performable illocutionary acts with the self-contradictory propositional content $(P \& \sim P)$ because of the axiom of possible sincerity of the speaker, when F is not expressive.

2.12 *No distribution of F with respect to* $\vee$.

For a simple illocutionary force F, the successful performance of $F(P \vee Q)$ does not entail the successful performance of or a commitment to $F(P)$ or $F(Q)$.

The reason for this is that sometimes the psychological states $\Psi_F(i, P \vee Q)$ do not commit the speaker to having psychological states $\Psi_F(i, P)$ or $\Psi_F(i, Q)$. A speaker may believe a disjunction of the form $(P \vee Q)$ on the basis of the information that at least one of the two propositions P, Q is true without having been told which one is true. In such a case, he believes the disjunction $(P \vee Q)$ without believing either of the disjuncts P and Q. Similarly, a speaker may intend at a time t to carry out a future disjunctive course of action $P \vee Q$ without having made up his mind at that time as to which of the two courses of action represented by P and by Q he will carry out.

2.13 *A modified Modus Tollens.*

For a simple illocutionary force F, $F(P \to Q)$ & $\neg F(Q) \rhd$ $\neg F(P)$ when $\Pi_F \neq \Pi_5$.

Thus, for example, if a speaker both claims that $P \to Q$ and disclaims Q he is committed to disclaiming P. Consequently: For a simple non-expressive illocutionary force F, $F(P \to Q) F(\sim Q) \rhd$ $\neg F(P)$. Thus, for example, the simultaneous successful performances of an assertion that $(P \to Q)$ and of a denial that Q commit the speaker to the illocutionary denegation of an assertion that Q.

III. LAWS OF PRESERVATION OF ILLOCUTIONARY COMMITMENT.

As we said earlier, the laws of commitment for illocutionary acts with a simple force hold for most actual illocutionary forces named by English illocutionary verbs because most components of such illocutionary forces satisfy the conditions under which these illocutionary commitments are preserved. These conditions are stated in the following theorems.

3.1 *The operation of adding new propositional content conditions* θ *to an illocutionary force* F *preserves the strong illocutionary commitment* $F(P) \rhd F(Q)$ *when* P *satisfies the propositional content conditions* θ *only if* Q *does (and similarly for* $\rhd$*).*

Thus if $F(P) \rhd F(Q)$ and, for all i, $P \in \theta(i)$ only if $Q \in \theta(i)$, then $[\theta] F(P) \rhd [\theta] F(Q)$. Similarly, if $F(P) \rhd F(Q)$ and $P \in \theta(i)$ only if $Q \in \theta(i)$, then $[\theta] F(P) \rhd [\theta] F(Q)$.

For example, the operation of adding the propositional content condition that the propositional content is a past or present proposition with respect to the moment of utterance preserves the illocutionary commitment $\vdash (P \& Q) \rhd \vdash (P)$, because if a conjunction of two propositions is past or present with respect to a moment of time so are both conjuncts. As a consequence of this, a report that $P \& Q$ strongly commits the speaker to a report that P since $\|$report$\|$ is obtained from assertion by adding such a propositional content condition.

3.2 *The operation of adding new preparatory conditions* Σ *to an illocutionary force F preserves the illocutionary commitment* $F(P) \triangleright F(Q)$ *when it is not possible to presuppose the propositions* $\Sigma(i, P)$ *determined by the new preparatory conditions* Σ *without presupposing also propositions* $\Sigma(i, Q)$ *(and similarly for* $\triangleright$ *).*

Thus if $F(P) \triangleright F(Q)$ and, for all i, a_i presupposes $\Sigma(i, P)$ in i only if a_i presupposes $\Sigma(i, Q)$ in i, then $[\Sigma]F(P) \triangleright [\Sigma]F(Q)$. Similarly, if $F(P) \triangleright F(Q)$ and, for all i, a_i presupposes $\Sigma(i, P)$ in i only if a_i is committed to presupposing $\Sigma(i, Q)$ in i, then $[\Sigma]F(P) \triangleright [\Sigma]F(Q)$.

For example, the operation of adding the preparatory condition that the speaker has been requested to carry out the future course of action represented by the propositional content preserves the illocutionary commitment $\perp (P \& Q) \triangleright \perp (P)$, because a speaker who presupposes that he has been requested to carry out two actions presupposes that he has been requested to carry out each of them. As a consequence of this an acceptance of an offer that $P \& Q$ commits the speaker to an acceptance that P since $\|\text{accept}\|$ is obtained from the primitive commissive by adding that preparatory condition.

3.3 *The operation of adding new sincerity conditions* Ψ *to an illocutionary force F preserves the illocutionary commitment* $F(P) \triangleright F(Q)$ *when the psychological states* $\Psi(i, P)$ *that are determined by the new sincerity conditions strongly commit the speaker to the psychological states* $\Psi(i, Q)$ *(and similarly for* $\triangleright$ *).*

Thus if $F(P) \triangleright F(Q)$ and $\Psi(i, P) \triangleright \Psi(i, Q)$ then $[\Psi]F(P) \triangleright [\Psi]F(Q)$, and similarly if $F(P) \triangleright F(Q)$ and $\Psi(i, P) \triangleright \Psi(i, Q)$ then $[\Psi]F(P) \triangleright [\Psi]F(Q)$.

For example, the operation of adding the sincerity condition that the speaker is proud of the state of affairs represented by the propositional content preserves the illocutionary commitment $\vdash (P \& Q) \triangleright \vdash (P)$ because it is not possible to express pride in the existence of a state of affairs represented by a conjunction without being strongly committed to being proud of the states of affairs represented by each conjunct. Consequently boasting that $(P \& Q)$ commits the speaker to boasting that P since $\|\text{boast}\|$ is obtained from assertion by adding that sincerity condition.

3.4 *The operation of imposing the additional mode of achievement μ
to an illocutionary force F preserves the illocutionary commitment
$F(P) \rhd F(Q)$ when it is not possible to achieve the illocutionary
point of F on P in that mode without achieving that point with that
mode on Q (and similarly for $\rhd$).*

Thus if $F(P) \rhd F(Q)$ and, for all $i \in I$, $\{(i,P)/i\Pi_F P$ and
$\mu(i,P) = 1\} \subseteq \{(i,Q)/i\Pi_F Q$ and $\mu(i,P) = 1\}$, then $[\Psi]F(P) \rhd$
$[\Psi]F(Q)$. Similarly, if $F(P) \rhd F(Q)$ and $\mu(i,P) = 1$ only if
$\mu(i,Q) = 1$, then $[\mu]F(P) \rhd [\mu]F(Q)$.

For example, the operation of adding the mode of achievement
that the speaker intends to convince the hearer of the truth of the
propositional content preserves the illocutionary commitment
$\vdash (P \& Q) \rhd \vdash (P)$ because it is not possible to intend to convince
someone of the truth of a conjunction without intending to
convince him of the truth of each conjunct. As a consequence of
this assuring someone that $(P \& Q)$ commits the speaker to assuring him that P.

3.5 *The operations of increasing and decreasing the degrees of strength
preserve the illocutionary commitment $F(P) \rhd F(Q)$ when it is not
possible to achieve Π_F on P with degree $(F) + 1$ without achieving
Π_F on Q with the same degree and when the psychological states
$\Psi_F(i,P)$ strongly commit the speaker to the psychological states
$\Psi_F(i,Q)$.*

Thus if $F(P) \rhd F(Q)$, $i\Pi_F^{\text{degree}(F)+1}P$ only if $i\Pi_F^{\text{degree}(F)+1}Q$
and $\Psi_F(i,P) \rhd \Psi_F(i,Q)$, then $[+1]F(P) \rhd [+1]F(Q)$ and
similarly for $[-1]F$.

For example, the operation of increasing the degrees of strength
preserves the illocutionary commitment $\perp (P \& Q) \rhd \perp (Q)$, because a strong commitment to carrying out the course of action
represented by a conjunction is a strong commitment to carrying
out the course of action represented by each conjunct, and because
an intention to do $(P \& Q)$ is an intention to do each of P and Q.
As a consequence of this a pledge that $P \& Q$ commits the speaker
to a pledge that P.

Most modes of achievement and propositional content, preparatory, and sincerity conditions of illocutionary forces that are
syntactically realized or named by verbs in English preserve the
illocutionary commitments between illocutionary acts with the

same primitive force in the precise sense defined by the previous theorems. This can be easily checked by looking at the semantic definitions of English illocutionary verbs in Chapter 9. Consequently, the specification of the valid patterns of illocutionary commitment between elementary illocutionary acts with a primitive force constitutes most of the characterization of the relations of illocutionary commitment.

In the next sections we will state laws for illocutionary forces with a specific illocutionary point, e.g. for assertive, for commissive, directive, declarative, or expressive illocutionary forces.

IV. LAWS FOR ILLOCUTIONARY FORCES WITH A COMMON POINT.

4.1 *The illocutionary force of commitment is the primitive commissive illocutionary force.*

If $\eta(\mathscr{C}) \geqslant 0$, $\mathscr{C} \rhd \perp$.

All commissive illocutionary forces with degrees of strength equal to or greater than zero entail the illocutionary force of commitment to a future course of action. Thus, for example, $\|\text{vow}\| \rhd \perp$, $\|\text{promise}\| \rhd \perp$, $\|\text{swear}_2\| \rhd \perp$, $Pr \rhd \perp$.

4.2 *The illocutionary force ! is the primitive directive.*

If $\eta(\mathscr{D}) \geqslant 0$, $\mathscr{D} \rhd !$.

All directive illocutionary forces with degrees of strength equal to or greater than zero entail the illocutionary force !. Thus, for example, $\uparrow \rhd !$, $\downarrow \rhd !$, $\|\text{supplicate}\| \rhd !$, $\|\text{beg}\| \rhd !$.

4.3 *Any commissive illocution commits the speaker to an assertive illocution with the same propositional content.*

For all simple assertive illocutionary forces a with degree $(a) \leqslant$ degree $(\mathscr{C})$, $\mathscr{C}(P) \rhd a(P)$. In particular, $\perp(P) \rhd \vdash(P)$.
This law is a consequence of the following lemma about the commissive point:

Lemma 1. *The achievement of the commissive point commits the speaker to the assertive.*

If $i\Pi_2^k P$ then $i\Pi_1^k P$.

(Use the fact that a commitment to perform an act commits

the speaker to the truth of the proposition that it will be performed.) Thus, for example, a promise to carry out a certain future course of action commits the speaker to an assertion that he will carry out that future course of action. $\|\text{vow}\|(P) \triangleright \vdash (P)$. In English the close connection between the assertive and the commissive is lexically realized in the first person occurrence of "will", as in "I will do it." Historically this is the most primitive form of the commissive but it also carries an assertive commitment.

Two consequences of this law are:

4.3.1 *Non-deniability of the propositional content of a commissive illocution.*

For all P, $\mathscr{C}(P) > \, < a(\sim P)$.

Any commissive illocutionary act is relatively incompatible with a denial of its propositional content.

4.3.2 *The liar paradox for commissives.*

$> \mathscr{C}(P) \, \& \, a(\sim P) <$.

No speaker can succeed in asserting that he is performing a commissive illocutionary act that he will not keep. This is why, for example, a self-referential utterance of the form "I promise I will not keep this promise" is paradoxical.

4.4 *The illocutionary force of declaration is the primitive and the only simple declarative illocutionary force.*

For all declarative forces $\mathscr{T}$, $\mathscr{T} \triangleright T$.

This law is a consequence of the fact that the declarative point can be achieved only with the null degree of strength.

4.5 *The law of the truth of the propositional content of a successful declaration.*

If $\mathscr{T}(P)$ is performed in i then P is true in w_i.

Any successful declaration has a true propositional content since the achievement of the declarative illocutionary point brings about the state of affairs represented by the propositional content. Consequently, successful declarations always have a success of fit. In these cases, "saying makes it so".

This law has the following linguistically significant corollaries concerning performative sentences:

4.5.1 *Any illocution can be performed by way of performing a declaration.*

If Q is true in a world w iff $F(P)(i[w/w_i]) = 1$ and $T(Q)$ is performed in i, then $F(P)$ is also performed in i.

A speaker who declares that he is performing an illocutionary act is committed to performing that illocutionary act. This is why successful utterances of performative sentences, which express declarations of performance of illocutionary acts, constitute performances of those acts. Thus, for example, by uttering successfully performative sentences of the form "I ask you if it is raining" or "I assert that it is snowing", a speaker respectively asks a question or makes an assertion by way of declaring that he is asking or that he is asserting. He could have performed these speech acts more directly by saying "Is it raining?" and "It is snowing." On our analysis of performative sentences, there is a semantic relation somewhat analogous to entailment between performative sentences such as "I ask you whether it is raining" and the corresponding non-performative sentences, such as "Is it raining?" The performative sentence entails the corresponding non-performative in the sense that it is not possible to perform the illocutionary act literally expressed by the first in a context of utterance without also performing the illocutionary act literally expressed by the second in that context. The converse of course is not true because one can perform an illocutionary act without declaring that one is performing it. A speaker who says, for example, "Is it snowing?" asks a question but does not make a declaration. Our view runs counter to that of those linguists[3] who have defended the so-called performative analysis, the thesis that every sentence of English has a performative verb in its "deep structure". On our view, there is indeed a semantic relation between a sentence such as "It is raining" and the corresponding performative "I assert that it is raining", but they are not equivalent since the latter entails the former but not conversely.[4]

---

3 See J. R. Ross, 'On declarative sentences', in R. A. Jacobs and P. S. Rosenbaum (eds.), *Readings in English Transformational Grammar* (Waltham, Mass.: Ginn & Co., 1970).

4 In any case the arguments for the performative analysis were, in general, syntactical and not semantical. For a criticism of these arguments see J. R. Searle, 'Speech acts and recent linguistics', in *Expression and Meaning*.

4.6 *Any act of illocutionary denegation can be performed by way of a declaration.*

If Q is true in w iff $F(P)(i[w/w_i]) = 1$ and $T(\sim Q)$ is performed in i then $\neg F(P)$ is also performed in i.

A speaker who declares that he does not perform an illocution performs an illocutionary denegation of that illocution. Thus, for example, by uttering performative sentences of the form "I do not promise to come", "I do not assert that it is raining", a speaker performs respectively the denegations of a promise and of an assertion by way of declaring that he does not promise and that he does not assert.

A consequence of this law is the following:

4.6.1 *Relative incompatibility of an illocutionary act with a declaration of non-performance of that act.*

If Q is true in w iff $F(P)$ is performed in $i[w/w_i]$ then $T(\sim Q)$ and $F(P)$ are not simultaneously performed in i.

This theorem explains why utterances of the form "It is raining but I do not assert that it is raining" are self-defeating.

The following corollaries of the law of success of fit of declaratives concern modalities:

4.6.2 *The law of the possibility of truth of the propositional content of a non-defective illocution with the world-to-word direction of fit.*

If $\Pi_F = \Pi_2$, Π_3, or Π_4 then $F(P)$ is performed at i non-defectively only if $\diamondsuit P(w_i) = 1$.

The philosophical significance of this law derives from the fact that the aim of commissives, directives, and declaratives is not to describe the world but to change it. Unless such a change is physically possible, the speech act is defective. This law has the following consequences:

If $\Pi_F = \Pi_2$, Π_3, or Π_4 and $(P \dashv \sim Q)(w) = 1$ then, for no $i \in I$, both $F(P)$ and $F(Q)$ are performed non-defectively at i.

If F has the world-to-word direction of fit, two illocutions of force F with relatively inconsistent *propositional contents* cannot be performed simultaneously *without being defective* in the world of utterance. Thus, for example, simultaneous promises, requests, orders, and declarations with relatively inconsistent propositional contents are *defective*.

In the case of declarations the law is even stronger. Declarative illocutionary acts with relatively inconsistent propositional contents are relatively incompatible. No speaker (not even God) could bring about by declaration two relatively inconsistent states of affairs.

4.7 *The illocutionary force of declaration illocutionarily entails that of assertion.*
$$\mathcal{T} \rhd \vdash.$$
Any declarative illocution strongly commits the speaker to an assertion of its propositional content.

This law is a consequence of the fact that the achievement of the declarative point strongly commits to the assertive, which is stated in the following lemma:

Lemma 1. $\Pi_4 \subset \Pi_1^0.$

This inclusion follows from the law of a restricted compatibility of strict implication with respect to illocutionary point, and from the fact that the belief that one brings about a state of affairs contains the belief that this state of affairs obtains.

4.7.1 *Non-deniability of the propositional content of a declaration.*
$$\mathcal{T}(P) > < a(\sim P).$$
The conjunction of theorems 4.7, 4.3.1 and 4.7.1 is equivalent to the following general law about direction of fit:

4.7.2 *Non-deniability of the propositional content of an illocution with a non-empty direction of fit, whose success in achieving fit, depends on the speaker.*
If $\Pi_F = \Pi_1, \Pi_2,$ or Π_4 then $F(P) > < a(\sim P).$

4.8 *The preparatory conditions and propositional presuppositions of a declaration are satisfied.*
If $T(P)$ is performed in i then $\sigma(P) \cup \Sigma_T(i, P)/w_i/.$
Proof:
By definition if $T(P)(i) = 1$ then $P(w_i) = 1$ and consequently $\sigma(P)/w_i/.$ Moreover, if $T(P)(i) = 1$, $i\Pi_4 P.$ Consequently, for the proposition $\diamondsuit Q \in \Sigma_T(i, P)$ such that $Q(w) = 1$ iff $i[w/w_i]\Pi_4 P,$ $\diamondsuit Q(w_i) = 1$ since $w_i R w_i.$

Declarations are the strongest kind of illocutionary acts because their successful performance is sufficient to bring about success of fit of the propositional content by changing the world to match the propositional content. But it is a mistake to take them as paradigmatic for all speech acts and to take their verbal expressions as paradigmatic for all illocutions. Austin's correct general insight that any successful utterance whatever is the performance of an illocutionary act and thus any utterance brings about a new state of affairs, namely the state of affairs that that act has been performed, should not be confused with the special insight that for a restricted class of illocutionary acts the performance of the act brings about the state of affairs represented by its propositional content.

4.9 *Any illocutionary force entails an expressive force.*

$$F \triangleright [\eta(F)][\Psi_F] \dashv.$$

Any illocutionary act strongly commits the speaker to the expressive illocution which consists of expressing its sincerity conditions with the required degree of strength.

Thus, for example, $\vdash \triangleright [\Psi_{Bel}] \dashv$ where $\Psi_{Bel}(i, P) = \{Bel(P)\}$. The illocutionary force of assertion entails the illocutionary force of expressing belief. Similarly $! \triangleright [\Psi_{Des}] \dashv$ where $\Psi_{Des}(i, P) = \{Des(P)\}$. The primitive directive illocutionary force entails the primitive illocutionary force of expressing desire. In the sense in which declarations are the strongest type of speech act, expressives are the weakest. No other type of speech act commits a speaker to a declaration; every type commits the speaker to an expressive. The reason for this is that expressives are simply defined in terms of the expression of psychological states and every type of speech act of the form $F(P)$ is an expression of a psychological state whose propositional content is P. And just as it is a mistake to think of declarations as paradigmatic for all speech acts, so it is a corresponding mistake to think of expressives as paradigmatic for all speech acts, a mistake because there is more to making an assertion than expressing a belief, more to giving an order than expressing a desire. The expressive point is the weakest illocutionary point: it is not possible to achieve any illocutionary point without also achieving that point.

Chapter 9

SEMANTICAL ANALYSIS OF
ENGLISH ILLOCUTIONARY VERBS

In this chapter, we will use the formal apparatus of illocutionary logic to analyze over a hundred English illocutionary verbs. We will specify which illocutionary forces are named by these verbs.

Because there is no one-to-one correspondence between illocutionary verbs and illocutionary forces it is essential to make a clear distinction between them. Illocutionary forces are, so to speak, natural kinds of uses of language, but we can no more expect the vernacular expressions to correspond exactly to the natural illocutionary kinds than we can expect vernacular names of plants and animals to correspond exactly to the natural biological kinds. Many possible illocutionary forces do not have a corresponding verb in English nor even a corresponding illocutionary force indicating device, and frequently one and the same illocutionary force is named by several non-synonymous verbs. Many authors on the subject of illocutionary acts mistakenly assume that wherever there are two non-synonymous illocutionary verbs, they must name two different illocutionary forces. But several illocutionary verbs are not names of illocutionary forces at all, since they do not imply any particular illocutionary point, but, for example, refer only to the style or manner in which an illocutionary act is performed. The verb "announce" is a case in point: it does not name an illocutionary force since almost any illocutionary force can be announced. Announcing carries no restriction as to its illocutionary point. One can announce statements, promises, warnings, orders, apologies, etc. The same holds for the verbs "interject", "interpose", and "exclaim". Furthermore, different non-synonymous illocutionary verbs such as "assert" and "state" may be used to name the same illocutionary force. The difference in meaning between these two verbs has to do with the fact that there are features of conversations connected to the meaning of such verbs which go beyond their illocutionary components, as we will shortly explain in their definition. Also, many verbs that name speech acts are not illocutionary verbs because they refer only to features of the utterance act. Some examples are "hiss", "mutter", "grumble", "whine", and "shout".

In what follows, we will be concerned almost exclusively with those verbs that genuinely name illocutionary forces, that is to say those verbs that imply an illocutionary point as part of their meaning. Even confining ourselves to verbs which name illocutionary forces, we find that they are extremely various; and not all of them have the features of such paradigms as "state", "promise", "request", and "command". For example, some illocutionary verbs such as "boast" do not have a performative use. One cannot say, "I boast that I own a new car." The reason for this appears to be that boasting, like hinting and insinuating, is one of those illocutionary acts that are intrinsically concealed. To the extent that the speaker makes his intentions explicit, as the performative verb would serve to do, to that extent his speech act would be less a case of hinting, insinuating, or boasting.

One of the most pervasive distinctions among these verbs is between those that name an illocutionary force which is essentially hearer-directed, that is where the speech act must be aimed at a specific hearer, and those where the speech act can be addressed to anyone or no one. Promising, warning, notifying, informing, and ordering are in this sense essentially hearer-directed, while stating, conjecturing, vowing, and pledging are not. A promise is by definition always a promise *to* someone, even when the speaker makes a promise to himself. Statements need not in that sense be aimed at any specific hearer, but rather simply involve the speaker's adopting a certain stance to the propositional content. Connected to this basic distinction between essentially hearer-directed and not essentially hearer-directed acts are two other distinctions. First, we need to distinguish those acts that require an overt public performance from those that can be performed in silent soliloquy. Declaring war and resigning from office require a public performance, conjecturing and asserting do not. All hearer-directed acts where the hearer is not identical with the speaker require a public performance. Secondly, some verbs name events which can be illocutionary acts but which need not be – for example, warning and reminding. I can warn you that it is going to rain and remind you to take your umbrella by performing the appropriate speech acts. Indeed both verbs have performative occurrences. But you can also be literally reminded to take your umbrella by the sight of dark clouds and be warned that it is going to rain by the same sight. The reason that such verbs name events which can be but need not be illocutionary acts appears to be that since both are hearer-directed, the same effect on the hearer, which it is the aim of the illocutionary act to produce, can also be produced by something which is not a speech act at all. Reminding for example involves calling to mind something that the hearer might have forgotten, and this can be done by speech act or non-speech act means. Such verbs, which name events that can be but need not be illocutionary acts, we will call *hybrids*.

Some verbs which name speech acts are achievement verbs which express more than the successful performance of the speech act. The difference for example between arguing and proving is the difference between performing a speech act or speech acts and performing these acts in such a way as to satisfy certain criteria of proof: "argue" is an illocutionary verb in the strict sense, "prove" is a success verb which expresses something more than just illocutionary force. Finally, some illocutionary verbs are systematically ambiguous between different illocutionary points. For example, "advise" and "warn" are systematically ambiguous between the illocutionary point of a directive and that of an assertive. This is because a case of advising or warning can be *either* a case of telling the hearer what is the case, with a view to getting him to do something about it, *or* it can be one of telling him to do something *because* something is the case. And this systematic ambiguity is reflected in the syntax of English since both "advise" and "warn" take both "that" clauses (characteristic of assertives) as well as the infinitive (characteristic of directives), e.g. "I warn you that the train will be late" and "I warn you to stay away from my wife."

In cases of ambiguity of sense between different illocutionary points, we will indicate which sense is being defined by writing after the illocutionary verb the number of the illocutionary point that is associated with this sense. Thus, for example, in our symbolism "advise$_1$" and "advise$_3$" will name respectively the assertive and the directive illocutionary forces of acts of advising.

To summarize, even in this brief discussion we find at least the following distinctions to be made among illocutionary verbs:

1. The distinction between those that name illocutionary forces and those that do not, for example between "order" and "announce".
2. The distinction between those that name conversational features in addition to illocutionary force and those that do not, for example between "describe" and "pledge".
3. The distinction between those that take a performative use and those that do not, for example between "promise" and "boast".
4. The distinction between those that are essentially hearer-directed and those that are not, for example between "inform" and "state".
5. The distinction between those that name essentially public events and those that can be performed in soliloquy, for example between "resign" and "conjecture".
6. The distinction between hybrids and non-hybrids, between for example "warn" and "command".
7. The distinction between illocutionary success verbs and illocutionary verbs proper, between for example "prove" and "argue".
8. The distinction between verbs that are systematically ambiguous between different illocutionary points and those that imply only one illocutionary point, between for example, "advise" and "request".

It goes without saying at this point in our analysis that a fairly high degree of idealization is necessary to give a systematic account of these verbs. A look at any large dictionary will reveal that just about every one of the verbs we discuss has several different meanings. We will be concerned with the central or standard or paradigmatic illocutionary senses of these various verbs, and even those senses we will have to idealize to some degree in order to give a systematic account.

I. ENGLISH ASSERTIVES.

We will discuss the following English assertives: *assert, claim, affirm, state, deny, disclaim, assure, argue, rebut, inform, notify, remind, object*, *predict*, *report*, *retrodict*, *suggest*, *insist*, *conjecture*, *hypothesize*, *guess*, *swear*, *testify*, *admit*, *confess*, *accuse*, *blame*, *criticize*, *praise*, *complain*, *boast*, and *lament*.

(1) *assert*.

The primitive assertive is "assert", which names the illocutionary force of assertion: $\|\text{assert}\| = \vdash$.

(2) *claim*, (3) *affirm*, (4) *state*.

These three assertives have the same illocutionary point, mode of achievement, degree of strength, propositional content conditions, preparatory conditions, and sincerity conditions as "assert". They name the same illocutionary force. Though "state", "affirm", "claim", and "assert" are all subject to the same feature analysis in our system, there are none the less important differences between them. These differences are not relevant for our purposes because in general they come from relations between sequences of illocutionary acts in conversations and not from within the structure of each act. In ordinary speech, the notion of a statement has to do with giving a full account of something or taking an official position on something, as, for example, when a politician makes a statement to the press. Notice that in this sense making a statement is more than just making an assertion, remark, or affirmation. A statement in this sense would generally involve a series of assertive illocutionary acts. Claiming and asserting are more closely connected to the notion of the speaker's rights, as when in a non-assertive sense of "claim" and "assert" one can speak of someone's *laying claim* to something or asserting his rights. Affirming, in ordinary speech, is usually opposed to denying. Affirming carries the notion of making a positive assertion as opposed to a negative assertion. Stating something is connected to the notion of setting something forth or representing something normally for the benefit or edification of the hearer. Affirming and claiming on the other hand have to do more with *taking a stand*. "Assert", by the way, etymologically derives from the Latin *asserere*, meaning to put one's hand on the head of a slave, either to free him or to claim him.

(5) *deny*.

A denial that P is the propositional negation of an assertion that P. Thus, for all P, $\|\text{deny}\|(P) = \vdash(\sim P)$. To deny that P is simply to assert not P.

(6) *disclaim*.

$\|disclaim\| = \neg \|claim\|$. An act of disclaiming is the illocutionary denegation of a claim.

(7) *assure*$_1$.

When one assures one tries to make the hearer *feel sure*, normally because he already has some doubts. To assure is to assert with the perlocutionary intention of convincing the hearer of the truth of the propositional content in the world of the utterance. This perlocutionary intention increases the degree of strength of the illocutionary point and determines the preparatory condition that the hearer has some doubts about the truth of the propositional content. Thus $\|assure_1\| = [\mu]\|assert\|$ where μ is a special mode of achievement such that $\mu(i, P) = 1$ iff mode $(\|assert\|)(i, P) =$ Int $a_i t_i \delta a_i t_i$ Bel $b_i t_i P(w_i) = 1$ and $|\mu| = 1$. "Assure" also has a commissive sense.

(8) *argue*.

Arguing is always either for or against a certain thesis. When one argues that P one asserts that P and gives reasons which support the proposition that P, normally with the perlocutionary intention of convincing the hearer that P. Thus $\|argue\|$ differs from $\|assure_1\|$ only by the fact that mode $(\|argue\|)(i, P) = 1$ iff a_i in i gives supporting reasons for P and mode $(\|assure_1\|)(i, P) = 1$.

(9) *rebut*.

To rebut is to argue against an argument or view already put forward. In the standard case, one rebuts an argument by arguing against it. "Rebut" differs from "refute" and "disprove" in that it is a genuine illocutionary verb and not a success verb, in the sense that "refute" and "disprove" are: when one rebuts one attempts to refute or disprove, but one may rebut without succeeding in refuting or disproving. Thus to rebut P is to argue that not P, with the additional preparatory condition that it has already been previously argued (or at least asserted) that P. Consequently, $\|rebut\|(P)$ differs from $\|argue\|(\sim P)$ only by the fact that $\Sigma_{\|rebut\|}(i, P) = [\Sigma_{\|argue\|}(i, \sim P) \cup \{$the proposition Q such that $Q(w) = 1$ iff for some $j \in I$, $t_j < t_i$ and $\vdash (P)$ is performed in $j[w/w_j]\}]$.

(10) *inform*, (11) *notify*.

Both of these are essentially hearer-directed. To inform is to assert to a hearer with the additional preparatory condition that the hearer does not already know what he is being informed of. To notify is to assert to a hearer with the additional mode of achievement that the hearer be put on notice. The hearer may in fact know but it may be important legally or otherwise that he be "put on notice" by a person who has the duty to notify him. These facts perhaps explain why both verbs conveniently take the passive in the performative occurrence with expressions referring to the hearer as direct objects. Thus, for example, one says, "You are hereby notified" or "You are hereby informed." But one cannot, for example, say "You are hereby asserted" or "You are hereby stated." The speaker informs or notifies the hearer by making a statement or assertion to him, but the direct object of "inform" and "notify" is a personal noun or pronoun referring to the hearer, whereas the indirect object is a "that" clause; in the case of "state" and "assert" the direct object is a "that" clause. Thus, $\|\text{notify}\|$ differs from $\|\text{assert}\|$ only by the fact that mode $(\|\text{notify}\|)(i, P) = 1$ iff mode $(\|\text{assert}\|)(i, P) = 1$ and the speaker a_i in the context i puts the hearer b_i on notice that P. On the other hand, $\|\text{inform}\|$ differs from $\|\text{assert}\|$ only by the fact that $\Sigma_{\|\text{inform}\|}(i, P) = [\Sigma_{\|\text{assert}\|}(i, P) \cup \{\text{the proposition that the hearer } b_i \text{ does not know that } P \text{ before time } t_i\}]$.

(12) *remind*.

To remind is to assert to a hearer with the additional preparatory condition that the hearer once knew and might have forgotten the propositional content. Thus, $\|\text{remind}\|$ differs from $\|\text{assert}\|$ only by having more preparatory conditions attributing propositional attitudes to the speaker. "Remind" is a hybrid verb because reminding does not need to be a speech act at all. Proust, for example, was reminded of events in the past by eating a madeleine. But it can be used performatively because one can achieve the effect of reminding by saying "I remind you that". "Remind" has both an assertive and a directive sense, for I can remind you that such and such is the case as I can remind you *to* do something: the assertive sense appears to be primary because of the connection between reminding and memory.

(13) *object.*

To object that P is to assert with the additional preparatory condition that some proposition which is incompatible with or contrary to the propositional content has been previously asserted, suggested, or otherwise put forward. In a legal context, when one objects to testimony one need not deny it, but rather object to its admissibility. The propositional content being objected to is: that the testimony is admissible; and the content of the objection is: that it is not admissible. The special feature of objecting is that the speaker takes issue with a previously presented or implied propositional content with a view to rebutting it, etc. There is also an expressive use of "object" where objecting is simply expressing disapproval of someone else's behavior.

(14) *predict.*

To predict is to assert with the propositional content condition that the propositional content is future with respect to the time of the utterance and the additional preparatory condition that the speaker has evidence in support of the proposition. Evidence is a special kind of reason. Thus, $\|\text{predict}\|$ differs from $\|\text{assert}\|$ by the fact that $P \in \text{Prop}_{\|\text{predict}\|}$ (i) iff P is future with respect to the time of utterance t_i and $\Sigma_{\|\text{predict}\|}(i, P) = [\Sigma_\vdash (i, P) \cup \{\text{the proposition that } a_i \text{ at time } t_i \text{ has evidence for } P\}]$. "Predict" is close to but not the same as "forecast", "foretell", and "prophesy". Reports using these verbs vary in their implied truth claims, and the acts named by these verbs vary in the subject matter of the propositional content and in the role of evidence in the performance of the acts. Thus to characterize a speech act as a prediction or forecast carries no implication as to its truth or falsity; but to say that something was foretold or prophesied generally implies that the speech act was true. Furthermore foretelling and prophesying unlike predicting and forecasting are usually done in the absence of scientific evidence. Predicting and foretelling carry no restrictions on subject matter other than that it be about the future; forecasting on the other hand is generally about the weather or business, and prophesying carries a heavy theological weight. Most of what would be classified as prophesy is in the realm of the sacred, and false prophesy is more than just a mistake – it seems to carry an implication of insincerity and perhaps even sacrilege.

(15) *report.*

To report is to assert with the propositional content condition that the propositional content is about the past with respect to the time of the utterance, or, in some cases, it can be about the present, but it cannot in general be about the future. I report on what has happened and I predict what will happen. The man who gives the weather report, for example, reports on the state of the weather and the recent history of the weather and may also predict what the weather will be. Thus, $\|\text{report}\|$ differs from $\|\text{assert}\|$ only by the fact that $\text{Prop}_{\|\text{report}\|}(i)$ is the set of propositions that are past or present with respect to the moment t_i.

(16) *retrodict.*

"Retrodict" is not a word in standard English but is a semi-technical term introduced to serve as an opposite to "predict". To retrodict is simply to assert a past proposition with respect to the time of the utterance, on the basis of present evidence. "Retrodict" differs in this respect from "report". I can, for example, report what I remember but if I make a statement on the basis of my memory it is not a retrodiction. Thus, $\|\text{retrodict}\|$ differs from $\|\text{assert}\|$ by the fact that $\text{Prop}_{\|\text{retrodict}\|}(i) = \{P/P$ is past with respect to time $t_i\}$ and $\Sigma_{\|\text{retrodict}\|}(i,\ P) = [\Sigma_\vdash (i,\ P) \cup \{$the proposition that a_i at time t_i has evidence for $P\}]$.

(17) *suggest*$_1$, (18) *insist*$_1$.

"Suggest" and "insist" have both a directive and an assertive use. I can suggest both that you do something and that something is the case. Similarly, I can insist on your doing something and insist that something is the case. It seems likely that the directive use is historically primary, but the assertive use is a genuine use in contemporary English. Both "insist" and "suggest" are essentially hearer-directed, unlike "speculate", "conjecture", "guess", and "hypothesize". $\|\text{Suggest}_1\|$ and $\|\text{insist}_1\|$ differ from $\|\text{assert}\|$ in their degrees of strength: $\|\text{suggest}_1\| = [-1]\|\text{assert}\|$. $\|\text{Insist}_1\|$ differs from $[+1]\|\text{assert}\|$ only by the fact that it has a special mode of achievement of its illocutionary point, namely persistence: mode $(\|\text{insist}_1\|)(i,P) = 1$ iff $i\hat{\Pi}_1 P$ in a persistent way.

(19) *conjecture.*

To conjecture that P is to weakly assert that P while presupposing that one has at least some slight evidence for P. Thus $\|\text{conjecture}\|$ differs from $\|\text{suggest}_1\|$ by the fact that $\Sigma_{\|\text{conjecture}\|}(i, P) = [\Sigma_{\|\text{suggest}_1\|}(i, P) \cup \{\text{the proposition that } a_i \text{ at time } t_i \text{ has evidence for the truth of } P\}]$.

(20) *hypothesize,* (21) *guess.*

"Hypothesize" and "guess" are also weak assertive verbs, similar to "conjecture". Hypothesizing, like conjecturing, requires at least some evidence or other sort of reason, but guessing can just be an unfounded stab in the dark. None of the three types of act is essentially hearer-directed, and indeed one can hypothesize, guess, or conjecture without performing any overt speech act at all.

(22) *swear₁.*

"Swear" has both an assertive and a commissive use. I can swear both that something is the case and that I will do something. In each case, an element of solemnity and increased degree of strength is added to the assertion or the commitment. Normally when one swears one calls upon God or some other supernatural agent or some sacred person or object or revered institution as part of the mode of achievement of the illocutionary act of swearing. In both the assertive and the commissive cases, the degree of strength of the illocutionary point is increased by the invocation of the sacred or the revered.

An oddity of the verb "swear" in English is that it has a special internal accusative, the noun "oath": whenever one swears one swears an oath. Institutionally "swearing" and "oath" refer to ways of ensuring that the speaker is really telling the truth, as his utterance will be relied on and important actions may be taken in such reliance. For this reason penalties attach to perjury. Thus, $\|\text{swear}_1\|$ differs from $\|\text{assert}\|$ only by the facts that mode $(\|\text{swear}_1\|)(i, P) = 1$ iff in the context the speaker commits himself under an oath to the truth of P, and degree $(\|\text{swear}_1\|) = $ degree $(\|\text{assert}\|) + 1$. (There is another non-illocutionary sense of "swear", in which it means any use of foul language.)

(23) *testify.*

Testifying is a special case of swearing. To testify is to assert in the capacity of being a witness and under an oath. This mode of achievement increases the degree of strength of the assertion and requires the additional preparatory condition that the speaker has witnessed the events (or is personally acquainted with the facts) represented by his testimony. Thus $\|\text{testify}\|$ differs from $\|\text{swear}_1\|$ only by the fact that mode($\|\text{testify}\|$)$(i, P) = 1$ iff mode ($\|\text{swear}_1\|$) $(i, P) = 1$ and the speaker is committed in i to the truth of P in his capacity as a witness, and $\Sigma_{\|\text{testify}\|}(i, P) = [\Sigma_{\vdash}(i, P) \cup \{\text{that } a_i \text{ has}$ witnessed before time t_i the state of affairs represented by $P\}]$.

There is a large set of illocutionary verbs that have to do with what is good or bad for the speaker or the hearer or what is good or bad in general. Most of these verbs are assertives, but they shade off into some expressives, and several of them have both an assertive and an expressive use. The verbs we have in mind here are such verbs as "criticize", "praise", "accuse", "admit", "confess", and "complain". Two other verbs that are related to these but which unlike them do not require an overt speech act are "credit" and "blame". I can in my thoughts credit you with your achievements and blame you for your faults without performing any public speech act, whereas I cannot praise, criticize, or accuse you without performing a public speech act. These verbs naturally come in minimal pairs, where each member of the pair contains all of the same features except one contrasting feature.

(24) *admit*.
To admit is to assert with the additional preparatory conditions that the state of affairs represented by the propositional content is bad (e.g. admit an error) and is in some way connected to the speaker. Thus, $\|\text{admit}\|$ differs from $\|\text{assert}\|$ only by the fact that $\Sigma_{\|\text{admit}\|}(i, P) = [\Sigma_{\vdash}(i, P) \cup \{\text{that the state of affairs } P \text{ is}$ bad and is connected to the speaker $a_i\}]$.

(25) *confess*.
To confess is to admit with the additional propositional content condition that the propositional content predicates of the speaker responsibility for a certain state of affairs, and with the additional preparatory condition that the state of affairs is bad, usually *very* bad (e.g. confess to a crime). If a state of affairs is bad, it is also bad to be the person who is responsible for it. Thus, whenever one confesses one admits, but not all admissions are confessions. $\|\text{Confess}\|$

differs from ‖admit‖ only by the fact that $\text{Prop}_{\|\text{confess}\|}$ (i) is the set of all propositions that are true in a world w iff a_i is responsible at time t_i in w for a state of affairs that Q and $\Sigma_{\|\text{confess}\|}(i, P) = [\Sigma_{\|\text{admit}\|}(i, P) \cup \{\text{the state of affairs that } Q \text{ is bad}\}]$.

(26) *accuse.*
To accuse is to assert to someone with the propositional content condition that the propositional content predicates responsibility to some individual for the existence of a state of affairs and with the preparatory condition that this state of affairs is bad. Thus, ‖accuse‖ differs from ‖assert‖ only by the fact that $P \in \text{Prop}_{\|\text{accuse}\|}$ (i) iff for some individual u, P is true in w iff u in w is responsible for a state of affairs that Q and $\Sigma_{\|\text{accuse}\|}(i, P) = [\Sigma_{\vdash}(i, P) \cup \{\text{the state of affairs that } Q \text{ is bad}\}]$. Confession differs from accusation only in that, when one confesses, one assigns responsibility to oneself, and, when one accuses, one assigns responsibility to some other agent, who is usually, but need not be, the hearer. One can accuse a third party. A speaker who accuses himself confesses. Sincere confessions are more likely to be true than other sorts of accusations simply because the speaker has better knowledge of his own behavior than of the behavior of others.

(27) *blame.*
The main difference between blaming and accusing appears to be that whereas blaming can be done privately in one's thoughts, accusing requires a public speech performance (as in "J'accuse" in French). Thus, an accusation is a public assignment of blame. For this reason, in the public performative use of "blame", ‖blame‖ = ‖accuse‖.

There are, as far as we know, very few positive favorable illocutionary verbs for assigning responsibility in English, perhaps because one is more concerned to assign responsibility for what is bad than one is inclined to assign it for what is good. "Credit" is the most obvious example which comes to mind. It, like "blame", does not require an overt speech act.

(28) *criticize*, (29) *praise.*
"Criticize" and "praise" form another pair. To criticize someone or something is to assert that a certain state of affairs that has to

do with him or it is bad while expressing disapproval of him or it. On the other hand, to praise someone or something is to assert that a certain state of affairs that has to do with him or it is good while expressing approval of him or it. To express approval (or disapproval) of something always commits the speaker to presupposing that it is good (or bad). "Criticize" and "praise", in short, differ in that criticizing has to do with something bad and praising with something good. However, it is important to point out that the subject matter is not restricted to the speaker and hearer. The speaker can be criticizing a play or a rug or praising a book or a movie. However, criticism and praise seem to attach to human (or animal) agents and their products. Thus, for example, one does not *criticize* the weather, one *complains* about the weather. Thus, $\|$criticize$\|$ differs from $\|$assert$\|$ only by the fact that $P \in \text{Prop}_{\|\text{criticize}\|}(i)$ iff for some proposition Q that has something to do with an animal or human agent or a product of such agent that is referred to in the expression of P, $P(w) = 1$ iff Q is bad in w, $\Sigma_{\|\text{criticize}\|}(i,P) = [\Sigma_\vdash(i,P) \cup \{\text{that} Q \text{ is bad}\}]$, and $\Psi_{\|\text{criticize}\|}(i,P) = [\Psi_\vdash(i,P) \cup \{\text{disapproval}(Q)\}]$. Similarly for praise, except that the words "good" and "approval" have to be substituted respectively for "bad" and "disapproval".

(30) *complain*$_1$.

"Complain" has both an assertive and an expressive use. In the assertive sense to complain about P is to assert that P with the additional sincerity condition that one is dissatisfied with P and the additional preparatory condition that the state of affairs that P is bad. In the expressive sense, to complain that P is simply to express dissatisfaction that P. To express dissatisfaction for a state of affairs commits the speaker to presupposing both the existence of that state of affairs and that it is bad. Thus, $\|$complain$_1\|$ differs from $\|$assert$\|$ only by the fact that $\Sigma_{\|\text{complain}\|}(i, P) = [\Sigma_\vdash(i, P) \cup \{\text{the state of affairs that } P \text{ is bad}, P\}]$ and $\Psi_{\|\text{complain}\|}(i, P) = [\Psi_\vdash(i, P) \cup \{\text{dissatisfaction}(P)\}]$.

(31) *boast*$_1$, (32) *lament*$_1$.

"Boast" and "lament", like "complain", have both an assertive and an expressive use. In the assertive sense, to boast that P is to assert P while expressing pride that P; to lament that P is to assert P while expressing dissatisfaction and sadness that P. Because of the ego involvement in boasting, a feature lacking in lamenting, the two do not form a minimal pair. Since to express pride is to express satisfaction for something that is related to oneself, the propositional content P of an act of boasting must have something to do with the speaker and the speaker must presuppose both that P is true and that the state of affairs that P is good for the speaker. Thus, $\|\text{boast}_1\| = [\Psi] \|\text{assert}\|$ where $\Psi(i, P) = \{\text{pride}(P)\}$.

On the other hand, $\|\text{lament}\|$ differs from $\|\text{complain}\|$ only by the fact that $\Psi_{\|\text{lament}\|}(i, P) = [\Psi_{\|\text{complain}\|}(i, P) \cup \{\text{sadness}(P)\}]$. "Boast", as we said, has no performative use.

II. ENGLISH COMMISSIVES.

We will discuss the following English commissives: *commit, promise, threaten, vow, pledge, swear, accept, consent, refuse, offer, bid, assure, guarantee, warrant, contract, covenant,* and *bet.*

Most of these verbs name acts that are essentially hearer-directed and all but three ("commit", "vow", and "pledge") require an overt public act.

(1) *commit.*
The primitive English commissive is "committ", which names the primitive commissive illocutionary force. Thus $\|\text{commit}\| = \bot$.

(2) *promise.*
The paradigm commissive verb is "promise", but as it has some rather special features which are not common to many other members of the set of commissive verbs, we are following Austin in using the verb "commit", to provide the name of this set generally. The special features of "promise" that distinguish it from other commissive verbs are, first, a promise is always made to a hearer to do something for his benefit, and, secondly, promises involve a rather special kind of commitment, namely an obligation. This undertaking of an obligation increases the degree of strength of the commitment. Thus $\|\text{promise}\|$ differs from $\|\text{commit}\|$ only by the fact that mode $(\|\text{promise}\|)(i, P) = 1$ iff a_i in i puts himself under an obligation to carry out the future course of action represented by P, degree $(\|\text{promise}\|)$ = degree $(\|\text{commit}\|) + 1$ and $\Sigma_{\|\text{promise}\|}(i, P) = [\Sigma_{\|\text{commit}\|}(i, P) \cup \{\text{the state of affairs that } P \text{ is good for } b_i\}]$.

(3) *threaten.*

Speech acts of threatening differ from promising, first, in that the undertaking is not to do something for the benefit of the hearer but rather to his detriment and, secondly, in that no obligation is involved in threatening. Because of the absence of obligation, threatening is not as institutionally dependent as promising. "Threaten" is a hybrid verb, since one can threaten without performing a speech act at all, as for example when one simply makes menacing gestures at someone. Because a threat need not be a speech act, non-human agents can literally threaten, e.g. dogs can make threatening noises and clouds can threaten bad weather. In this respect promises differ from threats because a promise must be a speech act, even if it is not performed in a language, but promises are similar to threats in that a promise, like a speech act threat, is essentially hearer-directed and must involve a public performance when the hearer is not identical with the speaker. As a speech act $\|\text{threaten}\|$ differs from $\|\text{commit}\|$ only by the fact $\Sigma_{\|\text{threaten}\|}(i, P) = [\{\text{the state of affairs that } P \text{ is bad for } b_i\} \cup \Sigma_{\vdash}(i, P)]$.

(4) *vow.*

Vows, unlike promises and threats, need not be directed at a hearer. In vowing to do something, I undertake to do it. But I need not undertake to do it either for or against my hearers. I may simply vow to perform better in the future or vow to get revenge on my absent enemies. Vowing furthermore has an additional element of solemnity which is not necessarily present in promising and threatening. Because of this solemnity, the degree of strength of a vow is greater than the degree of strength of a commitment. Thus, $\|\text{vow}\|$ differs from $\|\text{commit}\|$ only by the fact that mode $(\|\text{vow}\|)(i, P) = 1$ iff the speaker commits himself in a solemn way in i to doing the future course of action represented by P and degree $(\|\text{vow}\|) = \text{degree } (\|\text{commit}\|) + 1$. "Vow" is used not only as a commissive but as an assertive verb, as when one vows that something is the case. In such a use, one makes an extremely solemn assertion. Etymologically, "vow" comes from "avow", which is an assertive verb.

(5) *pledge.*

Pledging is much like vowing, only it does not necessarily have the solemnity of vowing. My pledges are undertakings but they need not be undertakings for or against my hearer. When, for example, I pledge allegiance to the flag, I do not in any sense address the flag. The syntax of "pledge" allows it to take both "that" clauses, and, unlike "vow", it also allows it to take nominal direct objects, as in, for example, the sentence "We pledge our lives, our fortunes, and our sacred honor." A pledge is a strong commitment to a future course of action. Thus, $\|\text{pledge}\| = [+1]\|\text{commit}\|$.

(6) *swear₂*.

The commissive sense of "swear" is obtained from the primitive commissive in the same way the assertive sense of "swear" is obtained from the primitive assertive. $\|\text{swear}\|$ differs from $\|\text{commit}\|$ only by the fact that mode $(\|\text{swear}\|)(i, P) = 1$ iff the speaker a_i commits himself to carrying out the future course of action in a solemn way by invoking some sacred object or revered institution and degree $(\|\text{swear}\|) = $ degree $(\|\text{commit}\|) + 1$. Thus mode $(\|\text{swear}_2\|)$ is a restriction of mode $(\|\text{vow}\|)$. As a consequence of this, a speaker who swears to do P is committed to a vow to do it.

(7) *accept*.

In one of the many senses of "accept", the most natural way to treat acceptances is as commissives which are responses to certain very restricted classes of directives and commissives, and where the propositional content of the acceptance is determined by the speech act to which it is a response. Thus if one receives an offer, invitation, or application one can accept or reject it, and in each case the acceptance commits the speaker in certain ways. For example, if you offer to sell me your house for $100,000 and I accept, I am committed to buying your house for $100,000. And even if you simply offer to wash my car and I accept, I am committed to letting you wash my car. Perhaps because the basic non-speech act concept of accepting is that of *receiving* something that is *given*, it is bad English to speak of "accepting" a request: rather one *grants* a request. But invitations and offers, like gifts, can be accepted. What is accepted, however, need not be good for the speaker, since one can accept responsibilities and obligations. When one accepts a directive the propositional content of the directive and its acceptance are identical. When one accepts a commissive the content of the acceptance is simply that the acceptor lets the original speaker do what he commits himself to doing. Thus ‖accept‖ differs from ‖commit‖ only by the fact that $\Sigma_{\|\text{accept}\|}(i, P) = [\Sigma_{\|\text{commit}\|}(i, P) \cup \{$the proposition that in some context j such that $a_j = b_i$, $t_j < t_i$ and $w_j = w$, a directive illocutionary act of form $[\pm n]\!\downarrow\!(P)$ is performed in $j\}$ or $\{$the proposition that an offer that R, where P is the proposition that a_i lets b_i do the course of action represented by R, is performed in $j\}]$.

(8) *consent.*

To consent to do something is to accept a directive to do it with the additional preparatory condition that one has reasons for not doing it and therefore one would probably not do it if one had not been requested. Thus, ‖consent‖ differs from ‖accept‖ only by the fact that $\Sigma_{\|\text{consent}\|}(i, P) = [\Sigma_{\|\text{accept}\|}(i, P) \cup \{\rho a_i t_i \sim P\}]$. "Consent", like "accept", has both a commissive and a directive sense. When I consent to your proposal that you do something I give you permission to do it (directive). "Permit" is the illocutionary denegation of "forbid" and thus permission is directive.

(9) *refuse.*

The negative counterparts to acceptances and consentings are rejections and refusals. Just as one can accept offers, applications, and invitations, so each of these can be refused or rejected. A refusal is the illocutionary denegation of an acceptance. And like ‖accept‖ in all of these cases, ‖refuse‖ has the additional preparatory condition that one has been given the option of acceptance or refusal. Strictly speaking one can only accept or refuse a speech act that allows for the option of acceptance or refusal. And that is why when one refuses to obey an order or command, one cannot say that one refuses the order or command but rather that one refuses to *obey* it, but with, for example, offers and invitations, one can say literally "I refused the offer" or "I refused the invitation." Thus ‖refuse‖ (P) is an illocutionary denegation which is performed in a context of utterance i iff $\neg$ ‖accept‖ (P) is performed in that context and the speaker a_i presupposes in i $\Sigma_{\|\text{accept}\|}(i, P)$.

(10) *offer.*

"Offer" is peculiar among commissive verbs in that it names a conditional commissive illocution. An offer is a promise that is conditional on the hearer's acceptance. An offer becomes binding only on acceptance. Roughly speaking the logical form of an offer is: this speech act commits me to perform a certain course of action if it is accepted by the hearer. Consequently, offer and accept are reciprocal verbs. One's offer becomes binding only if it is accepted, and one can accept an offer only if it has been made and has not been withdrawn. These features, by the way, are reflected exactly in the English and American law of contract. Thus an offer that P is performed in a context of utterance i iff a conditional illocutionary act of form $Q \Rightarrow Pr(P)$ is performed in i where Q is the proposition that is true in a world w iff $\|\text{accept}\| (P)$ is performed at $i[w/w_i]$.

(11) *bid*.

A bid, as for example when one bids at an auction, is a highly specialized and structured form of an offer. An object has been presented for sale, with the understanding that the purchaser will be the person who makes the highest offer. Offers are then invited; in this context the offers are called "bids". When one bids one offers to buy the object at such and such a price. When the auctioneer says "sold!", he is accepting the highest offer. In this sense $\|\text{bid}\|$ is derived from $\|\text{offer}\|$ by the addition of preparatory conditions.

(12) *assure₂*.

To assure (in the commissive sense) is to commit oneself to a future course of action with the perlocutionary intention of convincing the hearer that one will do it while presupposing that the hearer has doubts. As in the assertive sense this perlocutionary intention increases the degree of strength of the illocutionary point.

Thus $\|\text{assure}_2\| = [\mu] \|\text{commit}\|$ where $\mu(i, P) = 1$ iff $i\hat{\Pi}_2 P$ and Int $a_i t_i \delta a_i t_i$ Bel $b_i t_i P(w_i) = 1$, $|\mu| = 1$ and μ determines the preparatory condition Σ such that $\Sigma(i, P) = \{$that the hearer b_i has some doubts about P at time $t_i\}$.

It is interesting to notice that both the assertive and the commissive senses of $\|\text{assure}\|$ are obtained respectively from the primitive assertive and the primitive commissive by means of identical applications of the same operations. This shared form of derivation seems to be a general feature of illocutionary verbs in English that are ambiguous between two illocutionary points.

(13) *guarantee*, (14) *warrant*.
To guarantee something is to perform a complex speech act which is both assertive and commissive. A speaker who guarantees a certain object or state of affairs both asserts that this object or state of affairs will continue in a certain condition and promises the hearer a certain compensation (for example exchange or repair) if this turns out not to be the case. Thus $\|\text{guarantee}\|(P)$ is a complex illocutionary act which is performed in a context i iff for some $Q \in \text{Prop}_2(i)$ such that Q represents a future course of action of a_i that is a compensation for the non-existence of the state of affairs represented by P, both $\vdash (P)$ and $\sim P \Rightarrow \|Pr\|(Q)$ are performed in i.

Warrant is a guarantee usually within a legal context, concerned with properties and commercial products. $\|\text{Warrant}\|$ is $\|\text{guarantee}\|$ with additional propositional content conditions. What is guaranteed in case of warranty is either a certain commercial product or service or that the title to a certain property is secure.

(15) *contract*, (16) *covenant*, (17) *bet*.
There is a set of commissives that name joint commitments by both a speaker and a hearer, a hearer who then also becomes a speaker for the purpose of making his contribution to the joint commissive illocution. Two examples are "contract" and "bet". A contract is a mutual pair of commitments made by two contracting parties. Party A promises to do something for party B in return for which party B promises to do something for party A. The two commitments are not independent; in a genuine contract one is made in return for the making of the other. And this gives rise to the doctrine of the *quid pro quo* element of contracts. In the standard case of betting where one party makes a wager with another party, we have a similar mutuality. In betting on the outcome of a sporting event, the first party promises to pay the second party a sum of money if his team loses; the second party agrees to pay the first party a sum of money if that team wins. As we said earlier, it is essential to distinguish between a bet on the outcome of a conditional and a conditional bet.

Thus the special feature which distinguishes bets from other sorts of contracts is that bets are joint conditional promises where the antecedent of one participant's promise is the negation or opposite of the other's. For example, "I bet $5.00 the Giants will win" is of the form: "If the Giants win I promise to pay you $5.00 and in return if the Giants lose you promise to pay me $5.00." Since all bets are conditional promises, a conditional bet is a double conditional; and bets, like offers, require acceptance to come into effect. Thus the conditional bet "If the Giants win the Pennant I bet $5.00 they will win the World Series" is of the form: "If the Giants win the Pennant then if they lose the World Series I promise to pay you $5.00 and in return if they win you promise to pay me $5.00." To be a successfully performed speech act a bet has to be accepted. It is not enough for me to simply say "I bet you $5.00 that *P*."

Contracts are joint promises. "Covenant" in English has the same sense as "contract", but "covenant" is more solemn, archaic, and dignified, and hence is favored in law and in religion.

III. ENGLISH DIRECTIVES.

The directives we will analyze are: *direct, request, ask, urge, tell, require, demand, command, order, forbid, prohibit, enjoin, permit, suggest, insist, warn, advise, recommend, beg, supplicate, entreat, beseech, implore,* and *pray.*

(1) *direct.*
The primitive English directive verb is "direct", which we use as a name for the whole set of directives. "Direct" in English is generally used in the passive form: "You are hereby directed to ..." "Direct" names the primitive directive illocutionary force; $\|\text{direct}\| = !$.

Most directives in English have a special mode of achievement of their illocutionary point. The attempt to get the hearer to do something is made in a mode which allows the hearer the option of refusal or in a mode where refusal is precluded. Thus, for example, if I ask you to do something, I allow you the possibility of refusal as part of my speech act. On the other hand, if I order you to do it I am more peremptory and I give you no other option in my speech act. We will use "direct" in a sense that is neutral as regards the mode of achievement of allowing or not allowing the hearer the option of refusing. Thus the primitive directive does not have any special mode of achievement.

(2) *request* (⌇).

A request is a directive illocution that allows for the possibility of refusal. A request can be granted or refused by the hearer. Thus ‖request‖ differs from ‖direct‖ only by the fact that mode (‖ request ‖)$(i, P) = 1$ iff $i\hat{\Pi}_! P$ and the speaker in i allows the hearer the possibility of refusing to carry out the future course of action represented by P. "Request" is the paradigmatic directive verb, but since it is special in having a rather polite mode of achievement of its illocutionary point, it cannot be taken as the primitive directive.

(3) *ask*.

"Ask" has two quite distinct uses. One is in the notion of asking a question and the second is in the notion of asking someone to do something. Questions are always directives, for they are attempts to get the hearer to perform a speech act. In the simple directive sense, "ask" names the same illocutionary force as "request". In the sense of "ask a question" it means request that the hearer perform a speech act to the speaker, the form of which is already determined by the propositional content of the question. Thus if the question is a yes–no question requesting an assertive, the speaker expresses the propositional content of the answer in asking the question; and all that the hearer is asked to do is affirm or deny that propositional content. For example, to ask someone whether it is raining is to request him to perform a true assertion with the propositional content that it is or that it is not raining.

The illocutionary force of the illocutionary act that is requested to be performed in case of asking a question is not necessarily assertive. When the minister in the wedding chapel asks "Do you take this woman to be your lawful wedded wife?", he is asking for a response ("Yes I do", or "No I do not") that is a declaration and not an assertion. Thus ‖ask‖ (in the simple directive sense) = ‖request‖ and ‖ask?‖ in the sense of yes–no question differs from ‖direct‖ only by the fact that $P\in\text{Prop}_{\|\text{ask}\|}(i)$ iff, for some illocution $\mathscr{A}$, $P(w) = 1$ iff for some $t > t_i$, $\mathscr{A}$ is performed in $\langle b_i, a_i, t, l, w \rangle$.

In wh-questions the form of the question contains a propositional function, and the hearer is requested to fill in a value of the free variable in the propositional function in such a way as to produce a true complete proposition. Thus, for example, the question "How many people went to the party?" is of the form: "I request you, you tell me the correct value of x in 'x number of people went to the party'." A full characterization of the logical form of wh-questions cannot be made in this study because it would require the definition of the notions of a property, a relation and an elementary proposition, all of which are part of first order illocutionary logic.

(4) *urge*.

"Urge" has an assertive use, but it is primarily a directive and as such to urge is simply to advocate a course of action. It carries a greater degree of strength than "request", though it has neither the authority nor the power of "command" and "order", nor does it have the humility of "beg", "plead", "pray", etc. Urging has the additional preparatory condition that the speaker has reasons for the course of action urged. For example, if I urge you to leave the country immediately I would normally be required to provide some reason for your leaving the country. In that respect urging consists of something more than simply strongly requesting you to do something. Thus $\|\text{urge}\|$ differs from $[+1]\|\text{request}\|$ only by the fact that $\Sigma_{\|\text{urge}\|}(i, P) = [\Sigma_{\|\text{request}\|}(i, P) \cup \{\rho a_i t_i P\}]$.

(5) *tell₃*.

"Tell" is both assertive and directive. I can tell you that the train is late and tell you to get off my foot. To tell a hearer to do something is to direct him in a manner (or mode) which does not give him the option of refusal. Thus $\|\text{tell (to)}\| = [\mu]\|\text{direct}\|$ where $\mu(i, P) = 1$ iff the speaker does not allow the hearer in i the possibility of refusing to do the future action represented by P.

$\|\text{Tell (to)}\|$ differs from $\|\text{request}\|$ and $\|\text{ask}\|$ in that it is more peremptory and less polite, and this difference derives from the fact that $\|\text{request}\|$ and $\|\text{ask}\|$ allow the possibility of refusal while $\|\text{tell (to)}\|$ does not allow such a possibility.

(6) *require*, (7) *demand*.

Requiring or demanding of someone that he do something is telling him to do it with a greater degree of strength than simply telling or requesting. Requiring, but not demanding, also has an additional preparatory condition of need that it be done. Normally there must be a specific reason for requiring the act. Thus $\|demand\| = [+1]\|tell \ (to)\|$ and $\|require\| = [\Sigma]\|demand\|$ where $\Sigma(i, P) = \{\rho a_i t_i P\}$.

(8) *command*, (9) *order*.

The difference between telling someone to do something on the one hand and commanding or ordering him to do it on the other hand is that commanding and ordering have a greater degree of strength than telling, and this greater degree of strength derives from the fact that when one issues a command or an order one invokes a position of power or authority over the hearer. The main difference between commands and orders is that orders do not require an institutional structure of authority. One can order somebody to do something simply in virtue of one's position of power whether or not that power is institutionally sanctioned. The issuance of a command, however, requires that the speaker be in a position of *authority* over the hearer. Without too much idealization, one can say that orders require that the speaker be in a position of power, and one form of this power may be institutional authority; whereas commands require that the speaker be in a position of authority and not simply one of power. To direct someone by invoking a position of authority or power commits the speaker to not giving him the option of refusal (the "not" here is an illocutionary negation). Thus $\|command\|$ and $\|order\|$ differ from $\|demand\|$ only by the fact that mode ($\|command\|$)$(i, P) = 1$ iff mode ($\|demand\|$)$(i, P) = 1$ and a_i invokes a position of authority over b_i in his attempt to get him to do P and mode ($\|order\|$)$(i, P) = 1$ iff mode ($\|demand\|$)$(i, P) = 1$ and a_i invokes a position of power or authority over b_i; $\Sigma_{\|order\|}(i, P) = [\Sigma_1(i, P) \cup \{$the proposition that a_i at time t_i is in a position of power or authority over b_1 as regards $P\}]$; $\Sigma_{\|command\|}(i, P) = [\{$the proposition that a_i at time t_i is in a position of authority over b_i as regards $P\} \cup \Sigma_1(i, P)]$.

(10) *forbid*, (11) *prohibit*.

"Forbid" just means "order not". Forbidding is the propositional negation of ordering. Thus $\|\text{forbid}\|(P) = \|\text{order}\|(\sim P)$. "Forbid" and "prohibit" differ only in that prohibitions are more likely to be standing orders. They forbid something over a long period of time (as in "prohibition"). Thus $\|\text{prohibit}\|$ is $\|\text{forbid}\|$ with an additional propositional content condition concerning time. $\text{Prop}_{\|\text{prohibit}\|}(i) \subset \text{Prop}_{\|\text{forbid}\|}(i)$.

(12) *enjoin*.

To enjoin is to prohibit or forbid by some formal or official means; hence the notion of an injunction, which is a legal prohibition. An injunction is a prohibition or forbidding that is issued by a court of law or delivered in some other authoritative formal or official manner. An injunction can be either temporary or permanent. Thus, $\|\text{enjoin}\|$ differs from $\|\text{forbid}\|$ only by the fact that mode $(\|\text{enjoin}\|)(i, P) = 1$ iff $i\hat{\Pi}_1 \sim P$ in a formal or official manner.

(13) *permit*.

To grant permission to someone to do something is to perform the act of illocutionary denegation of forbidding him to do it.

The verbs "order", "forbid" and "permit" form a trio as follows: $\|\text{order}\|(P) = \hat{1}(P)$, $\|\text{forbid}\|(P) = \hat{1}(\sim P)$, $\|\text{permit}\|(P) = \daleth(\hat{1}\sim P)$.

(14) *suggest₃*, (15) *insist₃*.

Suggesting and insisting are respectively weak and strong directives. $\|\text{suggest}_3\| = [-1]\|\text{direct}\|$. $\|\text{insist}_3\|$ differs from $[+1]\|\text{direct}\|$ only by the fact that it has a special mode of achievement of its illocutionary point, namely persistence. Mode $(\|\text{insist}_3\|)(i, P) = 1$ iff $i\hat{\Pi}_1 P$ in a persistent way. As remarked earlier they each have an assertive sense.

(16) *warn*, (17) *advise*.

Warning and advising P can be either directives or assertives about the state of affairs represented by P. Both "warn" and "advise" take both "that" clauses and the infinitive. I can warn or advise you that such and such is the case or I can warn or advise you to do something. But the two uses are not independent. When I warn you that something is the case I am normally warning you that it is the case with a view to getting you to do something about it. Thus if I warn you (assertive) that the bull is about to charge, the aim of issuing a warning would normally be to get you to take some evasive action (directive). Similarly if I advise you (assertive) that the train will be late the aim of issuing the advice would normally be to get you to take some appropriate action (directive). On the other hand, when I warn you to do something, I would normally be asking you to do it (directive) while implying that if you do not do it, it would be bad for you (assertive), e.g. "I warn you to stay away from my wife!" Similarly, when I advise you to do something, I would normally be suggesting that you do it (directive) while implying that it would be good for you (assertive). The difference between warning and advising is that when I warn you, I warn you about a state of affairs which I presuppose is not in your interest; when I advise you, I advise you to do something which I presuppose is in your interest. This is why "advise" has a close affinity with "recommend". And this difference between "warn" and "advise" also explains why one and the same speech act sequence can be both a case of warning in the assertive sense and advising in the directive sense.

Thus I might say "I warn you that the bull is about to charge, and I advise you to get out of this field immediately." Thus $\|\text{warn}_1\|$ and $\|\text{warn}_3\|$ differ respectively from $\|\text{assert}\|$ and $\|\text{suggest}_3\|$ by the fact that $\Sigma_{\|\text{warn}_1\|}(i, P) = [\Sigma_{\vdash}(i, P) \cup \{\text{the state of affairs that } P \text{ is bad for } b_i\}]$ and $\Sigma_{\|\text{warn}_3\|}(i, P) = [\Sigma_{\|\text{suggest}_3\|}(i, P) \cup \{\text{the state of affairs that } P \text{ is bad for } b_i\}]$. On the other hand $\|\text{advise}_1\|$ and $\|\text{advise}_3\|$ differ respectively from $\|\text{assert}\|$ and $\|\text{suggest}_3\|$ by the fact that $\Sigma_{\|\text{advise}_1\|}(i, P) = [\Sigma_{\vdash}(i, P) \cup \{\text{the state of affairs that } P \text{ is good for } b_i\}]$ and $\Sigma_{\|\text{advise}_3\|}(i, P) = [\Sigma_{\|\text{suggest}_3\|}(i, P) \cup \{\text{the state of affairs that } P \text{ is good for } b_i\}]$.

(18) *recommend.*

To recommend is to advise with the additional preparatory condition that the state of affairs represented by the proposition is good in general and not merely good for the hearer. When one recommends, one always recommends a course of action or one recommends some person or thing to the hearer with a view to the hearer's then doing the act recommended and favoring the recommended person or thing. Thus $\|\text{recommend}\|$ differs from $\|\text{advise}_3\|$ only by the fact that $\Sigma_{\|\text{recommend}\|}(i, P) = [\Sigma_{\|\text{advise}_3\|}(i, P) \cup \{\text{the state of affairs that } P \text{ is good in general}\}]$.

(19) *beg*, (20) *supplicate*, (21) *entreat*, (22) *beseech*, (23) *implore*, (24) *pray*.

There are several verbs that mark a degree of strength of the speech act greater than "request", but where the degree of strength does not derive from any power or authority. Each of these verbs names a directive illocutionary force with a greater intensity of desire than simply asking or requesting, and in each case the act is performed in a more humble manner than is the case with requests. Thus these verbs differ from "request" in at least three respects: first, they express a greater intensity of desire; secondly, for that reason they have a greater degree of strength of illocutionary point; and thirdly, the illocutionary acts they express are performed in a more humble manner.

(19) *beg*.

To beg is to request humbly while expressing a strong desire, usually because of a strong need. Thus $\|\text{beg}\|$ differs from $\|\text{request}\|$ only by the fact that mode $(\|\text{beg}\|)(i, P) = 1$ iff mode $(\|\text{request}\|)(i, P) = 1$ and $i\hat{\Pi}_{\|\text{request}\|}P$ in a humble way and degree $(\|\text{beg}\|) = \eta(\|\text{beg}\|) = $ degree $(\|\text{request}\|) + 1$.

To beg as a directive has also another sense, which is to request very politely as in "I beg your pardon". In that sense, $\|\text{beg}\|$ differs from $\|\text{request}\|$ only by the fact that mode $(\|\text{beg}\|)(i, P) = 1$ iff mode $(\|\text{request}\|)(i, P) = 1$ and $i\hat{\Pi}_{\|\text{request}\|}P$ in a very polite way, and degree $(\|\text{beg}\|) = \eta(\|\text{beg}\|) = $ degree $(\|\text{request}\|) + 1$.

There is also another sense of "beg" which confines the humble request to the special situation of the "beggar", a professedly destitute person asking for gifts from supposedly more affluent strangers.

(20) *supplicate*.

To supplicate is to beg humbly. Thus it is to request very humbly: $\|\text{supplicate}\| = [\mu]\|\text{beg}\|$ where μ is a mode of achievement such that $\mu(i, P) = 1$ iff $i\hat{\Pi}_{\|\text{beg}\|}P$ in a very humble way.

(21) *entreat*, (22) *beseech*, (23) *implore*.

To entreat or to beseech or to implore is to beg earnestly. Thus it is to request both humbly and earnestly while expressing a strong desire: $\|\text{entreat}\| = \|\text{beseech}\| = \|\text{implore}\| = [\mu]\|\text{beg}\|$ where μ is the mode of achievement such that $\mu(i, P) = 1$ iff $i\hat{\Pi}_{\|\text{beg}\|}P$ earnestly.

(24) *pray.*

To pray is to entreat God (or some other sacred person or entity). Thus $\|\text{pray}\|$ differs from $\|\text{entreat}\|$ only by the fact that $P \in \text{Prop}_{\|\text{pray}\|}(i)$ iff $P \in \text{Prop}_{\|\text{entreat}\|}(i)$ and b_i is God or some other sacred person or entity (so that P represents a future course of action of God's with respect to the time of utterance t_i).

There is also an obsolete use of "pray" familiar from Shakespeare and still used in the law which just means "request", usually from a superior.

IV. ENGLISH DECLARATIVES.

Our list of declaratives contains: *declare, resign, adjourn, appoint, nominate, approve, confirm, disapprove, endorse, renounce, disclaim, denounce, repudiate, bless, curse, excommunicate, consecrate, christen, abbreviate, name,* and *call.*

In general declarations require an extralinguistic institution and a special position of the speaker and sometimes also of the hearer in that institution. In such cases the mode of achievement involves the speaker's invocation of his institutional powers. Thus for example if a speaker adjourns a meeting by declaring it adjourned there must be some institution of meetings and special roles empowering certain people to adjourn by declaration. These sorts of preparatory conditions and modes of achievement are typical of declarations. The only exceptions to these institutional requirements are, first, that some declarations invoke supernatural rather than merely institutional powers, as when someone is blessed or cursed, and, secondly, that some declarations such as "name" or "call" concern only language and therefore do not require an extralinguistic institution.

(1) *declare.*

The primitive declarative is "declare", which we use to give a name to the whole set: $\|\text{declare}\| = T$.

"Declare" names the primitive declarative illocutionary force.

"Declare" in English has also an assertive use. Etymologically the assertive use seems to be primary, because it comes from the Latin *clarare* meaning to make clear. We choose "declare" as the primitive declarative verb because it is a characteristic feature of all declarations that the speaker makes something the case by declaring it to be the case. All other English declaratives of the list can be obtained from the primitive "declare" by adding propositional content and preparatory conditions. For the most part it appears to be a matter of historical accident which of these propositional contents produces a new lexicalization in the form of an illocutionary verb, but in general they are not new illocutionary forces. This is because the propositional content and preparatory conditions are solely of non-linguistic (e.g. religious or political) significance rather than of linguistic significance.

(2) *resign.*
To resign is to perform a declaration to the effect that one hereby terminates one's tenure of a position. The preparatory conditions require that one holds the job and is empowered to relinquish it.

Thus if θ is the propositional content condition such that $P \in \theta(i)$ iff P is the proposition that a position X of the speaker a_i is terminated at time t_i, and if Σ is the preparatory condition such that $\Sigma(i, P) = \{$the proposition that the speaker a_i holds position X and is empowered to relinquish it at time $t_i\}$, then $\|\text{resign}\| = [\theta][\Sigma]\|\text{declare}\| = [\theta]\|\text{declare}\|$ because θ determines Σ.

(3) *adjourn.*
To adjourn is to perform a declaration by which a meeting is terminated. The preparatory conditions require the existence of an appropriate institutional context and the appropriate position of the speaker in that institution.

Thus if θ is the propositional content condition that $P \in \theta(i)$ iff P is the proposition that a meeting X to which a_i participates is terminated at time t_i, $\|\text{adjourn}\| = [\theta]\|\text{declare}\|$.

(4) *appoint.*
When one appoints by declaration, as for example in the sentence "I hereby appoint you chairman", one declares that somebody occupies a certain position or status. The usual preparatory conditions are required.

Thus if $P \in \theta(i)$ iff P is the proposition that the speaker b_i at time t_i occupies a certain position (or status) X, then $\|\text{appoint}\| = [\theta]\|\text{declare}\|$.

(5) *nominate*.

A closely related but not synonymous illocutionary verb is "nominate". In appointing the speaker declares someone to hold an office. In nominating, the speaker declares someone to be a candidate for an office. The preparatory conditions are similar to those for "appoint".

Thus if $P \in \theta(i)$ iff P is the proposition that someone is candidate for an office X at time t_i, $\|\text{nominate}\| = [\theta]\|\text{declare}\|$.

(6) *approve*.

To approve something in the declarative sense is to declare that it is valid or good. The appropriate preparatory conditions are required. Thus if $P \in \theta(i)$ iff P is the proposition that some state of affairs X is valid or good at time t_i, then $\|\text{approve}\| = [\theta]\|\text{declare}\|$. "Approve" also names a psychological state and can be used in making expressives.

(7) *confirm*.

In their declarative uses "confirm" and "approve" are closely related. Both approving and confirming alter the status of something by making it good or valid by declaration. Both require special authority. The main difference appears to be that confirm is normally a validation of some prior speech act, as for example when the US Senate confirms a presidential appointment. A good example of this point is "confirmation" in the Christian church, where a higher ecclesiastical authority confirms the original baptism. Approval may be of a prior speech act but need not be, as for example when a government agency approves a drug for medical use. To confirm is to approve with the additional preparatory condition that some declaration with the same propositional content has been performed within an institution by some speaker in a lesser position of authority than the speaker. Thus $\|\text{confirm}\| = [\Sigma]\|\text{approve}\|$ where $\Sigma(i, P) = \{\text{that some individual } u \text{ in a lesser position of authority than } a_i \text{ at time } t_i \text{ in a context of utterance } j \text{ at a time } t_j < t_i \text{ has performed a declaration that } P\}$.

(8) *disapprove*.

Oddly enough, "disapprove" as a declaration does not have a use fully corresponding to "approve". When one refuses or withholds approval from an application, for example, one does not normally describe the speech act as disapproving it (i.e. declaring it not to be valid) but rather as, for example, *withholding* or *denying approval*. Such cases are illocutionary denegations of approval. "Disapproval" is only rarely used as the name of a speech act but is rather the name of a psychological state, corresponding to the use of "approval" as the name of a psychological state.

(9) *endorse*₄.

"Endorse" has several meanings. In what is perhaps its most common use it can mark either an assertive or an expressive, normally an expressive – where one simply expresses one's approval or support for someone, for example, when one endorses a political candidate. In this sense one can also endorse by making an assertive act, such as "He is the best man for the job!" But "endorse" also has a related declarative use where it means to alter the status of something, normally when a document is altered by writing on the back of it (as is suggested by the etymology). Thus when one endorses a check by signing one's name on the back of it or when a driver's license is endorsed by the authorities, in each case the condition or status of the document is altered by declaration. Thus if $\theta(i) = \{P/\text{for some document } X, \text{ whose status}$ can be changed in a certain manner Y, P is the proposition that the status of X is changed in manner Y at time $t_i\}$, $\|\text{endorse}_4\| = [\theta]\|\text{declare}\|$.

(10) *renounce*, (11) *disclaim*₄.

When a speaker renounces something he makes it the case by declaration that he gives up or abandons it. This is related to "resign". In the law when one disclaims something one renounces any legal claim to it, thus making it the case by declaration that one has no longer legal rights to it. Thus if $\theta(i) = \{P/P \text{ is the}$ proposition that a_i gives up or abandons at time t_i ownership of something X or a commitment to $X\}$, $\|\text{renounce}\| = [\theta]\|\text{declare}\|$. If $\theta(i) = \{P/P \text{ is the proposition that } a_i \text{ gives up}$ or abandons at time t_i any legal claim to something $X\}$, $\|\text{disclaim}\| = [\theta]\|\text{declare}\|$. "Renounce" also has a use which is not declarative, as when one renounces one's previous beliefs. "Disclaim" also has an assertive use.

(12) *denounce$_4$*.
In its most common usage "denounce" is an assertive verb somewhat similar in meaning to "accuse". However, it also has a use as a declarative, as for example when a country denounces a treaty. In this sense to denounce is to make it the case that something is terminated by declaration.

Thus, if $\theta(i) = \{P/P$ is the proposition that some commitment X is terminated at time $t_i\}$, then $\|\text{denounce}\| = [\theta]\|\text{declare}\|$.

(13) *repudiate*.
Like "renounce", "repudiate" has a meaning in which it is not a declarative verb, but it is also used as a declarative. In its declarative sense, when a speaker repudiates something, he makes it the case that he is terminating an earlier commitment or obligation. Thus, if $\theta(i) = \{P/P$ for some claim X on a_i existing before t_i, P is the proposition that a_i is not committed or obligated any more by X at time $t_i\}$, $\|\text{repudiate}\| = [\theta]\|\text{declare}\|$.

We will now consider some declarations which are performed in a religious or supernatural context. These include "bless", "curse", "christen", "consecrate", and "excommunicate".

(14) *bless*.
To bless is to place the hearer in a state of God's grace by declaring him to be in that state. In such a case, the utterance act confers divine favor. Thus if θ is that propositional content condition such that $\theta(i)$ is $\{P/P(w) = 1$ iff b_i is in a state of God's grace at time t_i in $w\}$, $\|\text{bless}\| = [\theta]\|\text{declare}\|$.

(15) *curse*.
"Curse" is the opposite of "bless". In cursing, the speaker consigns the hearer to the evil of God's malediction by declaring him to be so consigned. Thus if $P \in \theta(i)$ iff P is the proposition that the hearer b_i is in a state of God's malediction at time t_i then $\|\text{curse}\| = [\theta]\|\text{declare}\|$.

(16) *excommunicate*.
When one excommunicates one excludes the hearer from the

community of Christians. As its morphology suggests, the idea of excommunication comes from the idea of excluding from communion. All excommunications exclude from the community by declaration.

Thus, if $P \in \theta(i)$ iff P is the proposition that b_i at time t_i is excluded from the community of Christians, $\|$excommunicate$\| = [\theta]\|$declare$\|$.

(17) *consecrate.*
When something is consecrated, it is given a sacred status by declaration. It is usually assigned to some sacred or religious purpose.

Thus, if $P \in \theta(i)$ iff P is a proposition that something or someone has some sacred status X at time t_i, $\|$consecrate$\| = [\theta]\|$declare$\|$.

(18) *christen.*
To christen is to declare that someone will have a particular name, to free him of original sin and to admit him in the Christian community. Thus to christen is to perform a declaration by which a name and a status are given to a person at baptism.

If $P \in \theta(i)$ iff P is the proposition that the hearer b_i has some name and status X at baptism and is admitted in the Christian community at time t_i and $\Sigma(i, P) = \{$the proposition that a_i in i is empowered to give the name X to b_i at baptism$\}$, then $\|$christen$\| = [\Sigma][\theta]\|$declare$\|$.

(19) *abbreviate,* (20) *name,* (21) *call.*
We now consider three declarations that do not require either institutional or supernatural power, because they concern only language itself.

To abbreviate is to shorten some linguistic expression by declaration. Thus if I say "I'll abbreviate 'free on board' as 'FOB'", I have then made it the case that "FOB" does duty for "free on board". If I name something by declaration I make it the case that the thing has the name I give it. Similar considerations apply to the declarative use of "call".

Thus, if $P \in \theta(i)$ iff for some pairs of expressions X and Y such that Y is shorter than X, P is the proposition that Y from time

t_i on does duty for X, $\|\text{abbreviate}\| = [\theta]\|\text{declare}\|$. If $P \in \theta(i)$ iff P is the proposition that some entity X is named by some expression Y at time t_i then $\|\text{name}\| = \|\text{call}\| = [\theta]\|\text{declare}\|$.

V. ENGLISH EXPRESSIVES.

Our list of expressives contains: *apologize, thank, condole, congratulate, complain, lament, protest, deplore, boast, compliment, praise, welcome,* and *greet.*

Expressive verbs name illocutionary forces whose point is to express the speaker's attitudes about the state of affairs represented by the propositional content. There is no illocutionary verb or performative in English that names the primitive expressive force $\dashv$. All English expressives name derived expressive illocutionary forces.

It is an odd fact about those verbs in English that name expressive illocutionary forces that almost without exception they indicate that there is something good or bad about the state of affairs represented by the propositional content of the expressive. Apparently we find it worthwhile to have a name for expressive illocutionary forces only if there is something good or bad involved, even though the concept of expressing a psychological state carries no such presupposition. In what follows many of the psychological states already carry the belief that the object of the state is good or bad, e.g. pleasure and sorrow. Furthermore most of the expressive speech acts that have acquired special verbs naming them are essentially hearer-directed.

(1) *apologize.*

The point of apologizing is to express sorrow or regret for some state of affairs that the speaker is responsible for. The preparatory condition is thus that the speaker must be responsible for the thing about which the sorrow is expressed. For this reason most of the things one apologizes for are one's actions, but they need not be actions provided that the speaker assumes responsibility for them. And the second preparatory condition is that the proposition is true and the state of affairs represented by the propositional content is bad for the hearer. Thus $\|\text{apologize}\|$ is an expressive illocutionary force of the form $[\Psi][\Sigma]\dashv$ where $\Psi(i, P) = \{\text{regret or remorse that } P\}$, and $\Sigma(i, P) = \{P, \text{the state of affairs that}$

P is bad for b_i, a_i at time t_i assumes responsibility for P}.

(2) *thank.*

The point of thanking is to express gratitude. The preparatory conditions are that the thing in question benefits or is good for the speaker and that the hearer is responsible for it. As with apologies, one normally thanks for actions, but the propositional content need not necessarily represent an action provided that the hearer is responsible. Thus, ‖thank‖ is an expressive illocutionary force of the form $[\Psi][\Sigma]\dashv$ where $\Psi(i, P) = \{$gratitude $(P)\}$, and $\Sigma(i, P) = \{P$, the proposition that b_i is responsible for the state of affairs that P at time t_i, that state of affairs is good for the speaker $a_i\}$. It is important to note that one apologizes to the hearer and one thanks the hearer in each case for something about him and his relation to the state of affairs specified in the propositional content.

(3) *condole.*

The verb "condole" is obsolete and has been replaced by the use of the noun "condolence". Thus one "sends one's condolences". When one condoles one expresses sympathy, and the preparatory condition is that the thing in question is bad for the hearer – usually some great misfortune. Thus ‖condole‖ is an expressive illocutionary force of the form $[\Psi][\Sigma][\theta]\dashv$ where $\Psi(i,P) = \{$sympathy $(P)\}$, $\theta(i) = \{P/P$ represents a state of affairs that has something to do with the hearer $b_i\}$, and $\Sigma(i, P) = \{P$, the state of affairs that P is (very) bad for the hearer $b_i\}$.

(4) *congratulate.*

The opposite of "condole" is "congratulate". In congratulating one expresses pleasure with the preparatory condition that the thing in question is beneficial or good for the hearer. Unlike thanking, and like condoling, congratulating need not involve an act or anything the hearer is responsible for. It may be simply some item of good fortune. Thus, ‖congratulate‖ is an expressive force of the form $[\Psi][\Sigma][\theta]\dashv$ where $\Psi(i,P) = \{$pleasure $(P)\}$ $\theta = \text{Prop}_{\|\text{condole}\|}$ and $\Sigma(i,P) = \{P$, the state of affairs that P is good for the hearer $b_i\}$. The symmetry between condole and congratulate is reflected in the fact that condoling is expressing sympathy for the misfortune of others; congratulating is expressing pleasure at the good fortune of others. In each case one condoles or congratulates only the person or persons whose fortune or misfortune is involved.

There is a whole series of verbs that concern bewailing, expressing sorrow, discontent, disapproval, and generally grumbling, grouching, and bitching. Among these are complain, lament, protest, and deplore. We will consider these in order.

(5) *complain.*

When one complains, one expresses discontent. The preparatory condition is that what one is expressing discontent about is bad, though this need not strictly be a presupposition since one can complain simply by saying that it is bad. There is no preparatory condition that the hearer must be in any way responsible for what one is complaining about. One can complain about the weather, inflation, or Gödel's theorem. This is why complaining can be either an assertive or an expressive. One can complain by asserting that something is bad or one can simply express one's discontent. One can say, for example, "That was a terrible thing to do" (assertive), or one can complain by saying "How awful!" (expressive). Thus, $\|complain\|$ is an expressive force of the form $[\Psi][\Sigma] \dashv$ where $\Psi(i,P) = \{\text{dissatisfaction } (P)\}$ and $\Sigma(i,P) = \{P, \text{the state of affairs that } P \text{ is bad}\}$.

(6) *lament.*

Lamenting, unlike complaining, need not be a speech act. One can simply feel sorrow for something and therefore be said to be lamenting it. There is, however, a use of the verb "to lament" in which it denotes strong public or overt expressions of sorrow. Again, as with complaining, one need not be assigning any responsibility to the hearer for the thing lamented. Thus $\|lament\|$ is an expressive force that differs from $\|complain\|$ only by the fact that $\Psi_{\|lament\|}(i,P) = \{\text{sorrow } (P), \text{dissatisfaction } (P)\}$. Lamenting is closely related to mourning for and grieving over, though mourning and grieving have closer connections with death and loss than does mere lamenting. One might reasonably be said to lament the passing of the glass milk bottle, but it would at best be ironic to say that one mourned for it or grieved over it.

(7) *protest.*

Protesting, like complaining and lamenting, presupposes that what is represented by the propositional context is bad. However, protesting has some special features of its own. First, the psychological state expressed is not mere sorrow or discontent, but rather disapproval, and protesting is a formal expression of disapproval. Secondly, though the hearer may not be directly responsible for the bad state of affairs, he must be able to change it and be responsible for it at least in the sense that he could change it and has not so far done so. For example, one may protest to higher authorities about the behavior of their subordinates. Thirdly, protesting is a demand for change.

Thus, for example, one protests to the authorities about some political or economic situation, but it would make no sense to protest about the weather; one would not know whom to protest to, though one can certainly complain about the weather. Thus, $\| \text{protest} \|$ is an expressive force such that $\Psi_{\| \text{protest} \|} (i, P) = [\{\text{disapproval} (P)\}]$, mode $(\| \text{protest} \|)(i, P) = 1$ iff a_i expresses disapproval for P in a formal way, $\eta(\| \text{protest} \|) = 0$, and $\Sigma_{\| \text{protest} \|} (i, P) = [\{P, \text{the state of affairs that } P \text{ is bad, the hearer } b_i \text{ has the authority to change that state of affairs}\}]$.

(8) *deplore.*

Deploring, like lamenting, need not be an overt speech act. One can simply bewail, bemoan, weep for, or feel outraged about something and thereby deplore it. However, "deplore" also has a use where it marks an overt speech act, strong expression of sorrow, or discontent, and, unlike lamenting, it seems to carry with it the implication that someone is responsible for the thing deplored. If I lament someone's death, I merely express feelings of sorrow about it. If I deplore his death, I am holding someone responsible for it, even though the person addressed in my deploring may not be the person I hold responsible. I might deplore the death of prisoners in South African jails, but it would make no sense for me to deplore the weather or the pattern of the tides. Thus, $\| \text{deplore} \|$ is an expressive force such that $\Psi_{\| \text{deplore} \|}(i, P) = [\{\text{sorrow or discontent for } P\}]$, $\eta(\| \text{deplore} \|) = +1$, and $\Sigma_{\| \text{deplore} \|}(i, P) = [\{P, \text{the state of affairs that } P \text{ is bad, someone is responsible for it}\}]$.

(9) *boast₅.*

Boasting is expressing pride with the presupposition that the thing one boasts about is good for the speaker (and therefore will be admired or envied by the hearer). Boasting, like complaining, can be either assertive or expressive. One can for example boast by saying that one did something good or that something good happened to one. As was remarked earlier boast does not and could not have a performative use. This is because "boast" carries with it the suggestion that the speaker is trying to conceal the fact that he is boasting. Similar remarks apply to brag. Thus, $\|\text{boast}_5\|$ is an expressive force of the form $[\Psi][\Sigma][\theta]\dashv$ where $\Psi(i,P) = \{\text{pride } (P)\}$, $\theta(i) = \{P/P$ represents a state of affairs that has something to do with the speaker $a_i\}$, and $\Sigma(i,P) = \{P$, the state of affairs that P is good for the speaker $a_i\}$.

(10) *compliment.*

To compliment is to express approval of the hearer for something. Complimenting presupposes that the thing the hearer is complimented for is good, though it need not necessarily be good for him. One might, for example, compliment him on his heroic and self-sacrificing behavior. Thus $\|\text{compliment}\|$ is an expressive force of the form $[\Psi][\Sigma][\theta]\dashv$ where $\Psi(i,P) = \{\text{approval } (P)\}$, $\theta(i) = \{P/P$ represents a state of affairs that has something to do with the hearer$\}$, and $\Sigma(i, P) = \{P$, the state of affairs that P is good$\}$. Compliment, like boast, can be either assertive or expressive. Other verbs in the class of expressive verbs that mark favorable expressions of attitude are "praise", "laud", and "extol". Unlike complimenting, praising, lauding, and extolling carry no suggestion that the hearer is necessarily related to the thing being praised, lauded, or extolled.

(11) *praise.*

To praise is to express approbation. It therefore presupposes that the thing praised is good. $\|\text{Praise}\|$ is an expressive force of the form $[\Psi][\Sigma][\theta]\dashv$ where $\Psi(i,P) = \{\text{approbation } (P)\}$, $\theta = \text{Prop}_{\|\text{compliment}\|}$, and $\Sigma = \Sigma_{\|\text{compliment}\|}$.

(12) *welcome,* **(13)** *greet.*

"Greet" is only marginally an illocutionary act since it has no propositional content. When one greets someone, for example, by saying "Hello", one indicates recognition in a courteous fashion. So we might define greeting as a courteous indication of recognition, with the presupposition that the speaker has just encountered the hearer. To welcome somebody is to receive him hospitably, and thus welcoming might be defined as an expression of pleasure or good feeling about the presence or arrival of someone. Welcoming, like greeting, is essentially hearer-directed.

APPENDIX 1

Semantic tableaux for illocutionary entailment

The semantic definitions of illocutionary verbs of Chapter 9 generate relations of illocutionary entailment between illocutionary forces with the same point. Indeed when the illocutionary force named by an illocutionary verb f_2 is obtained in the semantic definition of f_2 from the illocutionary force named by an illocutionary verb f_1 by successive applications of the operations on illocutionary forces of restricting the mode of achievement, increasing the degrees of strength and adding propositional content, preparatory, and sincerity conditions, the illocutionary force $\| f_2 \|$ illocutionarily entails the illocutionary force $\| f_1 \|$. In these cases there is a strong illocutionary entailment of $\| f_1 \|$ by $\| f_2 \|$ since any successful performance of an illocutionary act of form $\| f_2 \|(P)$ strongly commits the speaker to an illocutionary act of form $\| f_1 \|(P)$. In this appendix, we shall construct semantic tableaux representing various illocutionary entailments generated by our semantic definitions of illocutionary verbs. These semantic tableaux are useful devices for checking the accuracy of our definitions since adequate semantical definitions of illocutionary verbs must preserve the illocutionary entailments between the illocutionary forces named by those verbs, and must not introduce any new questionable illocutionary entailment.

Abbreviation:
We shall hereafter use $f_1 \rhd f_2$ as short for: $\| f_1 \|$ is derived from $\| f_2 \|$ by applying one or more of the operations named above.

SEMANTIC TABLEAUX.

A semantic tableau V for illocutionary entailment is a collection of the following items:

(1) a set $\mathcal{H}$ of illocutionary verbs;

    (2) a function λ that assigns to each illocutionary verb f a positive integer $\lambda(f)$ called the level of f;

    (3) a relation $\mapsto$ on $\mathcal{H}$.

$\mapsto$ is defined as follows:

For any two f and $f' \in \mathcal{H}$, $f' \mapsto f$ iff $f' \rhd f$ and for no $f'' \in \mathcal{H}$, both $f' \rhd f''$ and $f'' \rhd f$. "$f' \mapsto f$" is read: "f' is an immediate linguistic successor of f in $\mathcal{H}$".

The relation $\mapsto$ in V obeys the following clauses:

    C1. There is a unique illocutionary verb $f \in \mathcal{H}$ of level 1. This illocutionary verb is called the *origin* of the tableau.

    C2. For any illocutionary verbs f and $f' \in \mathcal{H}$, if $f' \mapsto f$ then $\lambda(f') = \lambda(f) + 1$.

A tableau is constructed by placing the origin of V at the bottom and the immediate successor(s) of each illocutionary verb f belonging to V above f from left to right (see fig. 1). And we shall draw a line segment from f to f' to indicate that f' is an immediate successor of f. At the left of this line segment, we shall usually mention the name(s) of the rule(s) by the application of which the illocutionary force named by the successor is obtained from the illocutionary force named by the predecessor.

We will call an illocutionary verb f belonging to a tableau V an *end point* of V if it has no successor. By a path in a tableau V we mean any finite sequence of illocutionary verbs which is such that

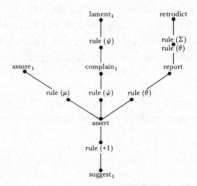

Fig. 1 Example of a semantic tableau of illocutionary logic. We will often write in our semantic tableaux μ, $+$, θ, Σ, Ψ as short rule (μ), rule $(+)$, rule (θ), rule (Σ), and rule (Ψ).

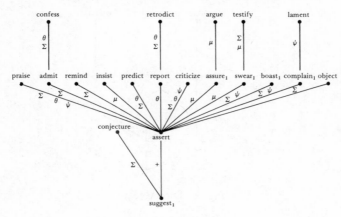

Fig. 2 Assertives

each term of the sequence (except the last) is the predecessor of the next.

Clearly if there is a path in a tableau where the first and last terms are respectively f_1 and f_2, then by definition $\| f_2 \| \rhd \| f_1 \|$. Thus, for example, since there is a path in fig. 1 beginning with assert and finishing with retrodict, $\| \text{retrodict} \| \rhd \| \text{assert} \|$. The illocutionary force of retrodiction illocutionarily entails the illocutionary force of assertion. Since there is in all tableaux V a path from the origin to all other illocutionary verbs, if $\lambda(f) = 1$ then for all $f' \in V$, $\| f' \| \rhd \| f \|$.

We will now present three semantic tableaux representing the illocutionary entailments existing respectively between the English assertives, commissives, and directives considered in Chapter 9 (see figs. 2, 3, 4).

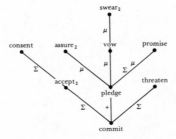

Fig. 3 Commissives

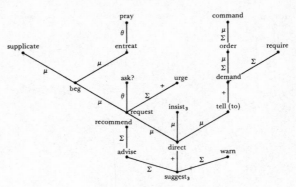

Fig. 4. Directives

A completeness theorem for semantic tableaux.

Our method of semantic tableaux for illocutionary entailment is complete in the following sense:

If $\mathcal{H}$ is a set of illocutionary verbs with the same point that are explicitly defined in Chapter 9, for any two verbs $f_1, f_2 \in \mathcal{H}$, $f_1 \triangleright f_2$ iff there is a semantic tableau V with a path from f_2 to f_1.

Proof:

By definition, if there is a path from f_2 to f_1, $f_1 \triangleright f_2$. Now if $f_1 \triangleright f_2$ then by theorem 2.3 of Chapter 7, $\| f_1 \|$ is obtained from $\| f_2 \|$ by applying one or more of the operations which consist in restricting the mode of achievement, increasing the degrees of strength, and adding new propositional content, preparatory, and sincerity conditions. Consequently (if our semantic definitions are sound), there is a path in a semantic tableau from f_2 to f_1.

APPENDIX 2

List of Symbols

Chapter numbers in parenthesis indicate where the symbol is introduced.

$a, a', a'', \ldots$ are variables for speakers; a_i names the speaker of context of utterance i (Ch. 2)

$b, b', b'', \ldots$ are variables for hearers (Ch. 2)

b_i names the hearer of context of utterance i (Ch. 2)

degree (F) names the degree of strength of illocutionary point of illocutionary force F (Ch. 2)

$f, f', f'', \ldots$ are variables for illocutionary force indicating devices (Ch. 1)

$f(p)$ names the elementary sentence which is composed by combining the illocutionary force indicating device f with the clause p (Ch. 1)

$i, i', i'', \ldots, i_1, i_2, \ldots$ and $j, j', j'', \ldots, j_1, j_2, \ldots$ are variables for possible contexts of utterance (Ch. 2)

$i[w/w_i]$ names the context of utterance that differs at most from context i by taking place in world w (Ch. 2)

k is a variable for integers (Ch. 2)

$l, l', l'', \ldots$ are variables for places of utterance. l_i names the place of utterance of context i

$m, m', m'', \ldots$ are variables for types of psychological states (Ch. 2)

$m(P)$ names the psychological state of type m with propositional content P (Ch. 2)

mode (F) names the mode of achievement of illocutionary force F (Ch. 2)

n is a variable for integers (Ch. 2)

$p, p', p'', \ldots$ are variables for clauses expressing propositions (Ch. 1)

$t, t', t'', \ldots, t_1, t_2, \ldots$ are variables for moments of time (Ch. 2)

t_i names the moment of time of utterance of the context i (Ch. 2)

$u, u', u'', \ldots, u_1, u_2, \ldots$ are variables for individual objects or entities (Ch. 1)

$w, w', w'', \ldots, w_1, w_2, \ldots$ are variables for possible worlds (Ch. 2);
"$\hat{w}$" names the set of all elementary propositions that are true in w (Ch. 2)

A, A', A'' are variables for acts in general

$\mathscr{A}, \mathscr{A}', \mathscr{A}'', \ldots, \mathscr{A}_1, \mathscr{A}_2, \ldots$ are variables for illocutionary acts (Ch. 4)

$\mathscr{A}$ is a variable for assertive illocutionary forces (Ch. 8)

$\mathscr{C}$ is a variable for commissive illocutionary forces (Ch. 8)

$\mathscr{D}$ is a variable for directive illocutionary forces (Ch. 8)

$\mathscr{E}$ is a variable for expressive illocutionary forces (Ch. 8)

$\mathscr{T}$ is a variable for declarative illocutionary forces (Ch. 8)

$F, F', F'', \ldots, F_1, F_2, \ldots$ are variables for illocutionary forces (Ch. 1)

$F(P)$ names the illocutionary act with force F and propositional content P (Ch. 1)

I names the set of all possible contexts of utterance (Ch. 2)

I_1, I_2, I_3 and I_4 names respectively the sets of all speakers, hearers, moments of time, and possible places of utterance (Ch. 2)

M names the set of all types of psychological states with propositions as content (Ch. 2)

$P, P', P'', \ldots, P_1, P_2, \ldots$ and $Q, Q', Q'', \ldots, Q_1, Q_2, \ldots$ are variables for propositions (Ch. 1)

$P(w)$ names the truth value of proposition P in possible world w (Ch. 6)

Pr names the illocutionary force of promise (Ch. 3)

Prop names the set of all propositions (Ch. 2)

Prop_F names the propositional content conditions of F

Prop_2 and Prop_3 name respectively the propositional content conditions determined by the commissive and the directive illocutionary points (Ch. 3)

R names the relation of accessibility between possible worlds (Ch. 2)

$\hat{U}$ names the set of all individual objects (Ch. 2)

$U(w)$ names the set of all individual objects that exist in world w

$U_t(w)$ names the set of all individual objects that exist at time t in world w (Ch. 2)

V is a variable for semantic tableaux (Appendix 1)

W names the set of all possible worlds (Ch. 2)

Z names the set of all integers (Ch. 2)

δutP names the proposition that is true in a world iff u at time t in that world brings about the state of affairs represented by proposition P (Ch. 2)

$\eta(F)$ names the degree of strength of the sincerity conditions of illocutionary force F (Ch. 2)

$\theta, \theta', \theta'', \ldots$ are variables for propositional content conditions (Ch. 2)

$[\theta]F$ names the illocutionary force that differs from force F only by the fact that it has additional propositional content conditions θ (Ch. 3)

$\bigcap \theta_\Pi$ and $\bigcup \theta_\Pi$ name respectively the intersection and the union of all propositional content conditions determined by point Π

φ^* names a function that associates with each possible context of utterance i, the set of all illocutionary acts that the speaker a_i expresses in that context with the intention of performing them (Ch. 4)

Φ names the set of all illocutionary forces (Ch. 2)

$\mu, \mu_1, \mu_2, \ldots$ are variables for modes of achievement (Ch. 2)

$\mu(\Pi)$ is a variable for a mode of achievement of illocutionary point Π (Ch. 2)

$\wedge \mu$ names a conjunction of modes of achievement satisfying a certain condition (Ch. 7)

$|\mu|$ names the greatest integer indicating the minimal degree of must be achieved if it has to be achieved with that mode (Ch. 2)

$[\mu]F$ names the illocutionary force that differs only from illocutionary force F by having additional mode of achievement μ (Ch. 3)

ρutP names the proposition that is true in a world w iff u at time t in that world has theoretical reasons to suppose that P is true in w or practical reasons for making it the case that P is true in w

$\sigma(P)$ names the set of all propositional presuppositions of proposition P

Γ and Δ are variables for sets of sentences, of propositions, of psychological states, of illocutionary forces, or of illocutionary acts

$[\Gamma]$ is the set of all psychological states to which the psychological states Γ strongly commit the speaker when $\Gamma \subseteq M \times \text{Prop}$ (Ch. 2)

[Γ] is the set of all propositions that are necessarily presupposed by a speaker who presupposes all propositions Γ when Γ ⊆ Prop (Ch. 2)

Π, Π′, Π″, ... are variables for illocutionary points (Ch. 2)

Π_F names the illocutionary point of force F (Ch. 1)

$\Pi_1, \Pi_2, \Pi_3, \Pi_4$, and Π_5 name respectively the assertive, the commissive, the directive, the declarative, and the expressive illocutionary points (Ch. 2)

$i\Pi P$ means that illocutionary point Π is achieved on proposition P in the context of utterance i (Ch. 2)

$i\Pi^k P$ means that illocutionary point Π is achieved with the degree of strength k on the proposition P in the context of utterance i (Ch. 2)

$\hat{\Pi}$ names a relation between contexts of utterance and propositions that determines the conditions of commitment to illocutionary point Π (Ch. 5)

Σ, Σ′, Σ″, ... are variables for preparatory conditions (Ch. 5)

Σ_F names the preparatory conditions of F (Ch. 2)

[Σ] F names the illocutionary force that differs from illocutionary force F only by the fact that it has additional preparatory conditions Σ (Ch. 3)

Ψ, Ψ′, Ψ″, ... are variables for sincerity conditions (Ch. 2)

Ψ_F names the sincerity conditions of force F (Ch. 2)

[Ψ] F names the illocutionary force that differs from F only by the fact that it has additional sincerity conditions Ψ (Ch. 3)

MATHEMATICAL SYMBOLS.

$=$ is the sign of equality

$\neq$ is the sign of inequality

$k \geqslant n$ means that k is equal to or greater than n

$k > n$ means that k is greater than n

$>$ also names the temporal relation of posteriority (Ch. 2)

$k \leqslant n$ means that k is equal to or smaller than n

$\leqslant$ also names the temporal relation of being anterior to or simultaneously with (Ch. 2)

$k < n$ means that k is smaller than n

$<$ also names the temporal relation of anteriority (Ch. 2)

List of symbols

1 names the integer one or the truth value: truth, or the success value: success

0 names the integer zero or the truth value: falsehood, or the success value: lack of success

$\emptyset$ names the empty set

$\in$ is the sign of membership

$\subseteq$ is the sign of inclusion

$\subset$ is the sign of proper inclusion

$\{x, y, \ldots, z\}$ names the set which contains $x, y \ldots$, and z

$\langle x, y, \ldots, z \rangle$ names the sequence whose first, second, ..., and last elements are respectively $x, y, \ldots$, and z

$\cap$ is the sign of intersection

$\cup$ is the sign of union

$X \times Y$ names the Cartesian Product of sets X and Y

LOGICAL SYMBOLS.

$\sim$ is the sign of truth functional negation (Ch. 2)

$\rightarrow$ is the sign of material implication (Ch. 2)

$\leftrightarrow$ is the sign of material equivalence (Ch. 2)

$\dashv$ is the sign of strict implication (Ch. 2)

$\Vdash$ is the sign of strict equivalence (Ch. 2)

& is the sign of conjunction between propositions (Ch. 2), between illocutionary acts (1–4), and between modes of achievement (Ch. 6)

$\vee$ is the sign of disjunction (Ch. 2)

$\Diamond$ is the sign of universal possibility (Ch. 2)

$\diamondsuit$ is the sign of physical possibility (Ch. 2)

$\square$ is the sign of universal necessity (Ch. 2)

$\boxdot$ is the sign of physical necessity (Ch. 2)

$\neg$ is the sign for illocutionary negation (Ch. 1)

$\Rightarrow$ is the sign of illocutionary conditional (Ch. 1)

$\rhd$ names the relation of strong illocutionary commitment between illocutionary acts (Ch. 4), or between psychological states (Ch. 2), or the relation of illocutionary entailment between illocutionary forces (Ch. 6)

$\triangleright$ names the relation of illocutionary commitment between illocutionary acts (Ch. 4), or between psychological states (Ch. 2)

Appendix 2

▷𝒜 means that the speaker is committed to illocutionary act 𝒜 in the context *i*

𝒜 ▷ means that 𝒜 is a strong illocutionary act performed in the context of utterance *i*

≡ names the relation of strict equivalence between illocutionary acts (Ch. 4)

≃ names the relation of illocutionary congruence (Ch. 4)

△ means that *i* is a non-empty context of utterance (Ch. 4)

> < names the relation of illocutionary incompatibility between illocutionary acts (Ch. 4)

≽ is the relation of compatibility between possible contexts of utterance (Ch. 2)

⊢ names the illocutionary force of assertion (Ch. 3)

⊥ names the primitive commissive illocutionary force (Ch. 3)

! names the primitive directive illocutionary force (Ch. 3)

↓ names the illocutionary force of requests (Ch. 3)

↑ names the illocutionary force of orders (Ch. 3)

? names the illocutionary force of questions (Ch. 3)

T names the illocutionary force of declarations (Ch. 3)

⊣ names the primitive expressive illocutionary force (Ch. 3)

‖ ‖ is the function that assigns to each illocutionary verb the force or type of speech act that it names (Ch. 2)

BIBLIOGRAPHY

Anscombe, G. E. M. *Intention*. Oxford: Blackwell, 1957
Austin, J. L. *How to do Things with Words*. Oxford: Clarendon Press, 1962
   Philosophical Papers. Oxford: Clarendon Press, 1961
Carnap, R. *Meaning and Necessity*. University of Chicago Press, 1947
Frege, G. *Foundations of Arithmetic*. Oxford: Blackwell, 1950
Montague, R. 'Universal grammar', *Theoria*, vol. 36, part 3 (1970), pp. 373–98
Ross, J. R. 'On declarative sentences', in R. A. Jacobs and P. S. Rosen-baum (eds.), *Readings in English Transformational Grammar*. Waltham, Mass.: Ginn & Co., 1970
Russell, B. 'On denoting', *Mind*, no. 56 (Oct. 1905), pp. 479–93
Searle, J. R. *Speech Acts*. Cambridge University Press, 1969
   Expression and Meaning. Cambridge University Press, 1979
   'Austin on locutionary and illocutionary acts', *Philosophical Review*, vol. 77, no. 4 (1968), pp. 405–24
   'Indirect speech acts' in P. Cole and J. L. Morgan (eds.), *Syntax and Semantics*, vol. 3, *Speech Acts*. New York: Academic Press, 1975 [Reprinted in Searle, *Expression and Meaning*, pp. 30–57]
   'A taxonomy of illocutionary acts', in K. Gunderson (ed.), *Language, Mind, and Knowledge, Minnesota Studies in the Philosophy of Science*, vol. 7. Minneapolis: University of Minnesota Press, 1975 [Reprinted in Searle, *Expression and Meaning*, pp. 1–29]
Vanderveken, D. 'Illocutionary logic and self-defeating speech acts', in J. R. Searle, F. Kiefer and W. Bierwisch (eds.), *Speech-Act Theory and Pragmatics*. Dordrecht, Netherlands: Reidel, 1980, pp. 247–72
   'Pragmatique, sémantique, et force illocutoire', *Philosophica*, vol. 27, no. 1 (1981), pp. 107–26
   'A strong completeness theorem for pragmatics', in *Zeitschrift für mathematische Logik und Grundlagen der Mathematik*, vol. 27 (1981), pp. 151–60
   'Some philosophical remarks on the theory of types in intensional logic', *Erkenntnis*, vol. 17, no. 1 (1982), pp. 85–112
   'What is an illocutionary force?', in M. Dascal (ed.), *Dialogue: An Interdisciplinary Study*. Amsterdam: Benjamins (forthcoming)
   'A model-theoretical semantics for illocutionary forces', *Logique et Analyse*, 103–4 (1983), pp. 359–94